JN413187

국병철/이병호
GMAT Focus Program

국병철/이병호

한국 GMATter들을 위한 최적의 개념필독서

GMAT Focus Program

GMAT 기초개념에서 685+까지

저자 **국병철 / 이병호**

Nothing is beyond **YOUR KEN**

EDUKEN®

Contents

GMAT 시험의 구성과 본서 활용 방법

Quantitative Reasoning (QR) PART I

Data Insights (DI) PART II

PART III   Critical Reasoning (CR)

PART IV   Reading Comprehension (RC)

PART V   Voca from official Guide

*GMAT 시험의 구성과 본서 활용

GMAT Focus edition시험 구성

	GMAT Focus edition
Section 1	Data Insights(20Q/45Min) – Data Sufficiency – Integrated Reasoning
Section 2	Quantitative Reasoning(21Q/45Min) – Problem Solving
Section 3	Verbal Reasoning(23Q/45Min) – Critical Reasoning – Reading Comprehension

본서는 QR, DI, VERBAL 전 영역의 접근방법과 그에 해당하는 Exercise, Question 및 Official Guide Sample Question 해설을 수록, 정리하였다.

본서는 GMAT공부를 시작하는 사람으로부터 시험을 앞둔 최종 정리 단계에 있는 모든 사람들에 게 활용될 수 있다.

처음 시작 단계에 있는 사람은 일단 첫 페이지부터 끝 페이지까지 한번 읽고(이해가 힘들더라도 일단 한번 읽고 시작하기 바란다) 다시 첫 페이지부터 보면서, 교재의 개념과 연관된 Official Guide 표시 문제를 같이 풀어보면서 하나하나 개념을 익힌다.

최종 정리 단계의 수험생은 한 페이지씩 읽고 이해하고 완전히 끝낸다는 기분으로 내용을 음미 하면서 기존의 학습 내용과 비교 정리하면 효과적이다. 이 때에도 교재의 개념정리와 더불어 표 시된 Official Guide 문제 중 2-3문제를 추려서 정리하길 바란다.

PART I
Quantitative Reasoning(QR)

Quantitative Reasoning (QR)

Chapter I.

Quantitative Reasoning introduction

1. What does QR cover?

	Quantitative Reasoning
QR Section	▪ QR section measures your algebraic and arithmetic foundational knowledge and how you apply this knowledge to solve problems.
Time & Questions	▪ 45 minutes & 21 multiple-choice questions
Type of Question	▪ Problem Solving
계산기	▪ No calculator (시험의 일부가 연산 능력 측정)
1등급 문제 핵심	▪ Answering these questions correctly relies on logic and analytical skills, not the underlying math skills. ▪ 1등급: 만점~1개

2. Sample QR Questions

Directions:

Solve the problem and indicate the best of the answer choices given.

Question:

If a certain wheel turns at a constant rate of x revolutions per minute, how many revolutions will the wheel make in k seconds?

(A) $60kx$

(B) kx

(C) $x \div k$

(D) $x \div (60k)$

(E) $kx \div 60$

Answer: (E)

3. QR 출제 범위

Sets	집합 개념, three sets
Counting methods	경우의 수, 순열, 조합
Probability	확률 & 통계
Algebra	대수학, 방정식, 부등식,
Word Problems	식 만들기, work rates, interests rates, speed, mixture, data interpretation
Arithmetic	정수 개념, factors, divisors, prime numbers
Real numbers	실수 (real numbers) 개념, percent, power and roots of numbers

4. QR 공략법

1	기출 문제 이론 및 공식 학습
2	기출 문제 풀이 (official guide questions 추천)
3	Official Practice Tests 를 통한 self-assessment 및 최신 문제 스타일 경험 **- 현재 Prep 강좌 제공 (최신 모의고사 8 회 해설 제공)**
4	최종 목표는 만점

Chapter II.
Sets (집합)

	집합(sets) 문제 출제 포인트
1	▪ 기본 & 응용 공식 확실히 개념 파악 및 암기 ▪ 영어 표현 친숙 하기
2	▪ **Three sets 기본 공식 & 변형 공식**
3	▪ **Double matrix 이해 & 실전 문제 응용**
4	집합의 다양한 확장 분야 ▪ **Probability** ▪ **Statistics** ▪ **Data insights logic (집합과 명제)**

1. Sets (집합)

1) sets 기본 개념

> **Definition**: In mathematics, a set is a collection of numbers or other objects. The objects are called the elements of the set. The list's order doesn't matter.

2) Sets (집합) 용어

Universal set (U)	a set which has elements of all the related sets
Union (합집합)	The **union** of two sets *A* and *B* is the set of all elements that are each in *A* or in *B* or both. The union is written as *A* ∪ *B*.
Intersection (교집합) (A ∩ B)	The **intersection** of two sets *A* and *B* is the set of all elements that are each in **both** *A* and *B*. The intersection is written as *A* ∩ *B*.
여집합 (A ∪ B)^c	Neither A nor B; Not A and Not B
cardinality	• The **cardinality** of a set is a measure of the **"number of elements"** of the set. • For example, the set A = {1, 2, 4 } contains 3 elements, and therefore has a **cardinality** of 3.

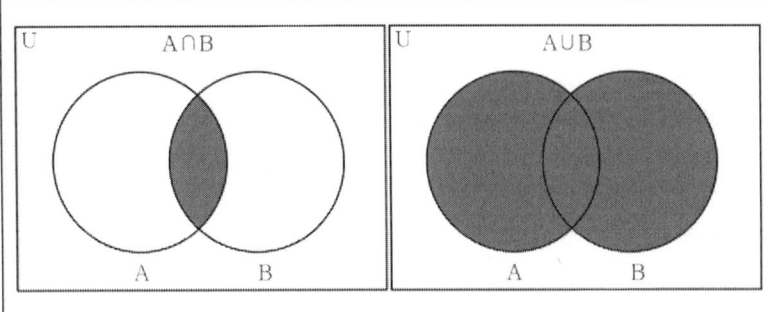
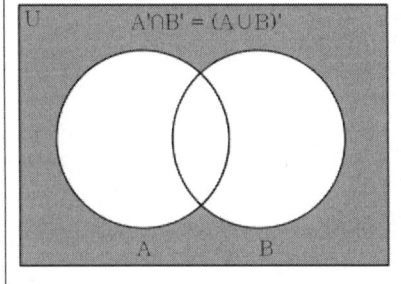

3) 부분 집합 (subsets) 정의

- 어느 집단에 속하는 항목 중에서 특정 조건을 만족하는 것으로 간주되는 것들의 집단.
- 두 집합 A와 B에 대해서 집합 A의 모든 원소가 집합 B의 원소일 때 '집합 A는 집합 B의 부분 집합'이라고 하며 A⊂B 또는 B⊃A 로 표현

4) 부분 집합 (subsets) 공식

- **공식**: n(A) = n 일 때, 집합 A의 부분집합의 개수 = 2^n

A = { 가, 나, 다 } 라고 할 때, A의 the number of subsets (부분집합)은 2^3 = 8 개이다.
곧, {   }, { 가 }, { 나 }, { 다 }, { 가, 나 }, { 가, 다 }, { 나, 다 }, { 가, 나, 다 }

Exercise 1

Suppose that **S** = {*A, B, C, D, E*}. The number of 2-element subsets of *S* may be calculated as:

Answer:

Question 1

Let S represents the set of integers from 1 to 9, what is the number of the subsets of S that contain the integer 9?

Answer:

5) 합집합 공식

- 합집합 정의: the set of all elements that are in A or in B or in both.
- 합집합 공식: The number of elements in the union of two finite sets S and T is the number of elements in S, plus the number of elements in T, minus the number of elements in the intersection of S and T.

합집합 공식 (general addition rule for two sets)	
교집합 존재 (intersection of A and B)	NO 교집합 (Mutually Exclusive Sets)
▪ $n(A \cup B) = n(A) + n(B) - n(A \cap B)$	▪ $n(A \cup B) = n(A) + n(B)$

Exercise 2

Each of 25 people is enrolled in history, mathematics, or both. If 20 of them are enrolled in history and 18 are enrolled in mathematics, how many are enrolled in both history and mathematics.

Answer:

2. 차집합 (difference of sets)

1) 차집합 개념 및 표현

If set A and set B are two sets, then set A difference set B is a set which has elements of A but no elements of B. It is denoted as **A – B**.

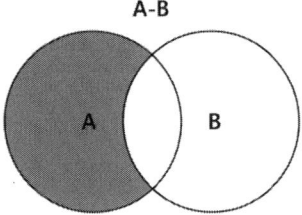

Example:

A = {1,2,3} and B = {2,3,4} ⇒ A – B = {1}

2) 차집합 영어 표현

n(A – B)	• only A
n(B – A)	• only B

3) 차집합 활용 응용 공식

n(A ∩ B)	**Typical: n(A ∩ B) = n(A) + n(B) - n(A ∪ B)**
n(A ∩ B)	차집합을 활용해서 n(A ∩ B) 구하기 • n(A ∩ B) = n(A) - n(A - B) • n(A ∩ B) = n(B) - n(B–A)
n (A ∪ B)	**Typical: n (A ∪ B) = n(A) + n(B) – n (A ∩ B)**
n (A ∪ B)	차집합을 활용해서 n(A ∪ B) 구하기 • n(A∪B) = n(A) + n(B – A) • n(A∪B) = n(B) + n(A – B)

3. Three Sets 공식

1) 기본 공식

■ **For three sets A, B and C 기본 rule**

$$n(A \cup B \cup C) = n(A) + n(B) + n(C) - n(A \cap B) - n(B \cap C) - n(C \cap A) + n(A \cap B \cap C)$$

2) 변형 공식

■ **변형 공식 (고난이도 문제):**

$$n(A \cup B \cup C) = n(A) + n(B) + n(C) - only (A \cap B) - only (B \cap C) - only(C \cap A)) - 2 n(A \cap B \cap C)$$

문제의 조건에서 data for n(A∩B)가 아니라 data for only (A∩B) 주어질 때는 변형 공식으로 문제를 접근해야 함.

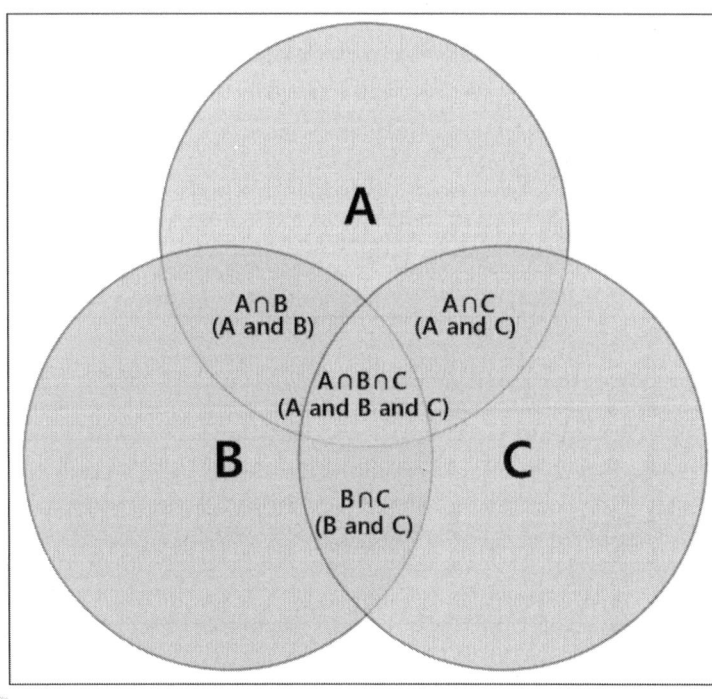

Only A = ?

n(A ∪ B ∪ C)ᶜ =주어질 때?

- **U = n(A ∪ B ∪ C) + n(A ∪ B ∪ C)ᶜ**

4. Double matrix 개념 및 활용 집합 문제

1) 개념

Double matrix is a tool for solving set problems
- 시험에서 주어지는 tool 이 아님, 문제를 풀기 위해서 스스로 만들어야 하는 것)
- **언제 사용**: when a certain population has two characteristics associated with it.

For example: employees at a company

1) Employees by gender (male & female)
2) Employees by education (college only & advanced degree)

- **How to Use:** missing data 찾기, or 특정 data 의 value 판단

	Male	Female	Totals
College only			
Advanced degree			
Totals			

Question 2:

In a shipment of 40 toys, each toy is either blue or green, and each toy is either small or large. In total, there are 30 small toys, and there are 14 blue toys. If the shipment contains 22 toys that are both small and green, how many toys are both large and blue?

	blue	green	Totals
Small			
Large			
Totals			

Answer:

Chapter 2 Answer Sheet

Exercise 1	10
Exercise 2	13

Question 1	2^8 = 256 개
Question 2	6
● 각 문제의 해설은 동영상 강좌에서 확인하시기 바랍니다.	

Chapter III.
Counting Methods (경우의 수)

경우의 수 문제를 풀 때 가장 중요한 팩트?	
"각 문제에 규칙이나 공식을 어떻게 사용할지 결정하는 것"	
1	▪ 경우의 수 ⇒ 합의 법칙 or 곱의 법칙?
2	▪ Permutation, combination rule, or two rules 동시에?
3	▪ 공식 없이 주어진 조건의 패턴을 찾아서 푸는 문제?

1. 경우의 수

GMAT 경우의 수 문제
문제의 주어진 set ⇒ 1) too large, or 2) the objects are related in a patterned way

경우의 수 문제 접근 (counting methods)	
Case 1: events 가 동시에 일어나지 않을 때 ⬇	Case 2: events 가 동시에 일어날 때 ⬇
합의 법칙 사용 • chapter 2 에서 공부한 sets or double matrix 사용 • 두 사건의 교집합이 존재?	곱의 법칙 • 순열 • 조합

2. 합의 법칙 (addition rule)

■ **합의 법칙: 함께 일어나지 않아 분류가 가능한 사건** 두 사건 A, B 가 동시에 일어나지 않을 때, 사건 A 가 일어나는 경우의 수가 m, 사건 B 가 일어나는 경우의 수가 n 이면, 사건 A 또는 사건 B 가 일어나는 경우의 수는 m + n 이다.
Exercise 1 There are two restaurants in our neighborhood, Pizza Shop and Soup Kitchen. Pizza Shop has 10 different pizzas on its menu, and Soup Kitchen has 7 soups on its menu.   **Answer :**

Exercise 2:

서로 다른 두 개의 주사위를 던질 때, 두 눈의 수의 합이 5 가 되는 경우와 두 눈의 수의 합이 7 이 되는 경우는 각각 다음과 같다.

Answer:

두 사건 교집합 존재?

Question 1:

서로 다른 두 개의 주사위를 던질 때, 두 눈의 수의 합이 3 또는 2 의 배수 (multiple) 되는 경우의 수는?

Answer:

3. 곱의 법칙 (the multiplication principle)

1) 개념

■ **곱의 법칙 (두 사건이 동시에 일어날 경우)**

When there are *m* ways to do one thing, and *n* ways to do another, then there are *m×n* ways of doing both.

Event 1 (m ways)	×	Event 2 (n ways)

For example, Example: 주사위 1 개와 동전 1 개를 <u>동시에</u> 던질 때 나오는 경우의 수

(1, head), (1 tail), (2, head), (2 tail), (3, head), (3 tail), (4, head), (4 tail), (5, head), (5 tail), (6, head), (6 tail),

곱의 법칙 사용: (6)(2) = 12 different ways

Exercise **3***:*

Suppose that a computer password consists of four characters such that the first character is one of the 10 digits from 0 to 9 and each of the next 3 characters is any one of the uppercase letters from the 26 letters of the English alphabet. How many different passwords are possible?

Answer.

Exercise **4***:*

Each time a coin is tossed, there are 2 possible outcomes—either it lands heads up or it lands tails up. Using this fact and the multiplication principle, you can conclude that if a coin is tossed 8 times, possible outcomes are?

Answer.

---

2) 순열 (permutation) 정의 및 구분

■ **정의: 서로 다른 n 개에서 r 개를 택하여 일렬로 배열하는 것**

A **permutation** (순열) can be thought of as a selection in which objects are selected one by one in a certain order.

순열 문제 접근 (permutation)	
Case 1: 전체 줄 세우기	**Case 2: 일부 줄 세우기**
⬇	⬇
5 명 중에서 5 명을 줄을 세우는 경우의 수 = 5! = 5×4×3×2×1 n!(n factorial) = n(n - 1)(n - 2)(2)(1)	**5 명 중에서 3 명을 줄을 세우는 경우의 수** = $_5P_3$ = 5×4×3 • $_nP_r = \frac{n!}{(n-r)!}$

Exercise **5**:

Suppose that 10 students are going on a bus trip, and each of the students will be assigned to one of the 10 available seats. Then the number of possible different seating arrangements of the students on the bus is

Answer.

Exercise **6**:

How many different 3-digit integers can be made from the numbers of 1, 2, 3, 4, 5?

Answer.

3) 중복집합 순열 (multi-set permutation)

■ Definition: 일반 순열에서 중복되는 것 (Item 순서)만큼 나누어 준다.

For example, {a, a, a, b, c} 배열 = $\frac{5!}{3!}$

■ 문제 유형 1: Letter Arrangement:

Exercise 7:
How many different words (including nonsense words) can you make by rearranging the letters of the word [**EFFERVESCENCE**]

Answer:

■ 문제 유형 2: Shortest path:

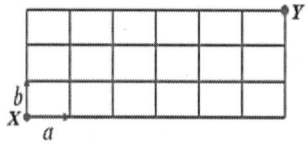

Exercise 8.
X 에서 Y 까지 가는 최소 거리 종류의 수

Answer:

Question 2:

If you want to move from point A to point B while staying on the lines, passing through point C, and going the shortest possible distance, how many different paths on this grid can you choose from?

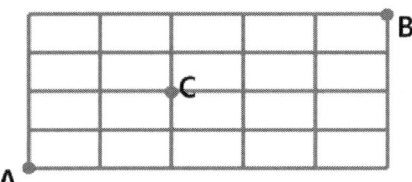

Answer:

4) 조합 (combination) 정의

- **정의:** 서로 다른 n 개에서 순서를 고려하지 않고 r 개를 택할 때, 이 r 개로 이루어진 각각의 집합을 n 개에서 r 개를 택한 조합(combination)이라 한다.

(1) 순열 & 조합 차이점

순열 (number of ways to select with order)	조합 (number of ways to select without order)
$_nP_r$ (number of ways to select with order) = $_nC_r \times$(number of ways to order) $\Rightarrow {_nC_r} = \dfrac{nPr}{(r)!}$	
⬇	⬇
5 명 중에서 3 명을 뽑아 줄을 세우는 경우의 수 = $_5P_3$ = 5×4×3	5 명 중에서 3 명을 뽑는 경우의 수 = $_5C_3$ $\Rightarrow {_5C_3} = \dfrac{5P3}{(3)!}$

(2) 조합 특징

$_nC_r$ 계산법 $= \dfrac{nPr}{(r)!} = \dfrac{n!}{r!(n-r)!}$	
$_nC_r = {_n}C_{n-r,}$	$_{10}C_9 = {_{10}}C_1 = 10$
$_nC_0$	1
$_nC_1 = n$	$_{1000}C_1 = 1{,}000$

(3) Combination (조합) 유형 Practice

Exercise 9

10 명의 Member (James, John 포함) 중에 3 명을 뽑아 committee member 를 구성하는 경우의 수

Answer:

Exercise 10

10 명의 Member (James, John 포함) 중에 3 명을 뽑아 committee member 를 구성할 때, 3 명의 Committee member 중에 반드시 James 와 John 포함

Answer:

Exercise 11

10 명의 Member (James, John 포함) 중에 3 명을 뽑아 committee member 를 구성할 때, 3 명의 Committee member 에 James 와 John 미포함

Answer:

Exercise 12

10 명의 Member (James, John 포함) 중에 3 명을 뽑아 committee member 를 구성할 때,
3 명의 Committee member 중에 James 와 John 중 적어도 1 명 포함한 경우의 수?

Answer:

5) 순열 & 조합 연습문제

Question	Answer
Question 3 Clarissa will create her summer reading list by randomly choosing 4 books from the 10 books approved for summer reading. She will list the books in the order in which they are chosen. How many different lists are possible?	
Question 4 Ben and Ann are among 7 contestants from which 4 semifinalists are to be selected. Of the different possible selection, how many contain neither Ben nor Ann?	
Question 5 Darrell has a collection of 40 DVDs, each of which contains one movie. There are 17 comedy movies, 14 fantasy movies, and 9 historical movies, where each historical movie takes place in a separate time period. The movies will be ordered on a shelf from left to right so that the movies of each type comedy, fantasy and historical are in a single group of consecutive movies. In addition, the historical movies will be ordered from earliest time period to latest time period. How many possible orderings of the movies are there?	

Question 6

For 7 soccer ball teams, each of them has to play with all the other teams. However, to decide which team wins, every two teams have to play 3 rounds and the team that win for the most times will ultimately win. How many rounds of game do all teams have to play in total?

Question 7

Consider all the permutations of the letters in the word **MISSISSIPPI**, where **I** is a vowel and the other letters are consonants. What is the number of permutations in which all the vowels are next to each other?

Exercise 1	17
Exercise 2	10
Exercise 3	$(10)(26)(26)(26) = 175,760$
Exercise 4	$(2)(2)(2)(2)(2)(2)(2)(2) = 2^8 = 256$
Exercise 5	$10! = (10)(9)(8)(7)(6)(5)(4)(3)(2)(1) = 3,628,800$
Exercise 6	$_5P_3 = 5 \times 4 \times 3 = 60$ 개
Exercise 7	$\dfrac{13!}{5!\,2!\,2!}$
Exercise 8	$\dfrac{9!}{6!\,3!}$
Exercise 9	$_{10}C_3$
Exercise 10	$_8C_1$
Exercise 11	$_8C_3$
Exercise 12	$_{10}C_3 - {}_8C_3 = 64$

Question 1	**24**
Question 2	$\dfrac{4!}{2!2!} \times \dfrac{5!}{3!2!} = \mathbf{60}$
Question 3	$_{10}P_4$
Question 4	$_5C_4$
Question 5	**(17!)(14!)(3!)**
Question 6	**21 games** $\times$ **3 = 63**
Question 7	$\dfrac{7!}{4!\times2!} \times \mathbf{8 = 840}$

Chapter IV.
Probability (확률)

확률 문제를 풀 때 가장 중요한 것?	
"중요 개념과 공식의 이해를 바탕으로 문제에 적용하는 것"	
1	▪ Probability ⇒ 합의 법칙 or 곱의 법칙?
2	▪ Probability 문제를 여사건으로 접근 가능?
3	▪ 독립시행 개념 & 공식 사용 가능?
4	▪ 조건부 확률 문제 등장!

1. 확률 (probability) Overview

1)개념

■ **Definition**

For any event E, the probability that E occurs is often denoted by $P(E)$.

$$P(E) = \frac{The\ number\ of\ outcomes\ in\ E}{The\ total\ number\ of\ possible\ outcomes}$$

Exercise 1:

Rolling a 6-sided die, the probability that the outcome is an odd number?

Answer:

---

2) 확률 특징

반드시 발생	• If an event E is certain to occur, then P(E) = 1.
절대로 NO 발생	• If an event E is certain not to occur, then P(E) = 0.
확률 범위	• If an event E is possible but not certain to occur, then 0 < P(E) < 1.
확률 sum	• The sum of the probabilities of all possible outcomes of an experiment is 1.
여사건	• The probability that an event E will not occur is equal to 1 - P(E). • **P(not A) = 1 – P(A)**

Question 1

If a person purchases 15 of the 3,000 tickets sold in a raffle that awards one prize, what is the probability that this person will <u>not</u> win?

Answer:

3) 확률 (probability) 분류

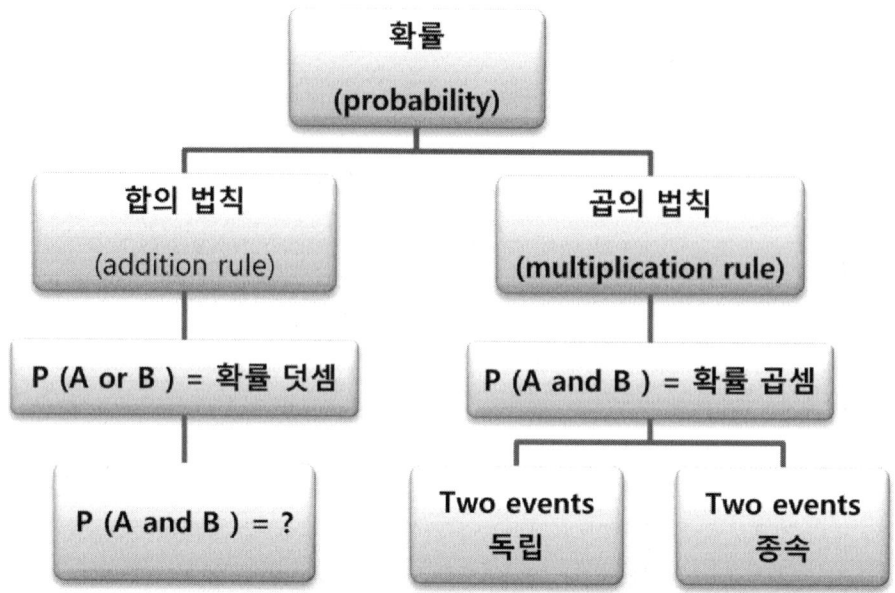

2. 확률 (probability) 덧셈정리

1) 덧셈정리 분류

확률 (probability) 덧셈공식 사용은 P (A and B) = 유무로 판단	
Case 1: P (A and B) = 존재	Case 2: P (A and B) = NO (exclusive events)
⬇	⬇
• P(A or B) = P(A) + P(B) – P(A and B)	• P(A or B) = P(A) + P(B)

2) 덧셈정리 연습

Exercise 2:

Consider the example in which a 6-sided die is rolled once. Let E be the event {1, 3, 5} that the outcome is an odd number. Let F be the event {2, 3, 5} that the outcome is a prime number. Then P(E∪ F)= ?

Answer:

Question 2

Consider an experiment with events A, B, and C for which P(A) = 0.23, P(B) = 0.40, and P(C) = 0.85. Suppose that events A and B are mutually exclusive and events B and C are independent. What are the probabilities P(A or B) and P(B or C) ?

Answer:

3. 확률 (probability) 곱셈정리

1) 곱셈정리 분류

확률 (probability) 곱셈법칙 사용은 독립 or 종속으로 판단	
Case 1: Two events 가 독립 (independent)	**Case 2: Two events 가 종속 (dependent)**
⬇	⬇
• 한 사건이 일어날 확률이 다른 사건이 일어날 확률에 영향을 미치지 않음	• 한 사건이 일어날 확률이 다른 사건이 일어날 확률에 영향을 미침 (조건부 확률)
• P(A and B) = $P(A) \times P(B)$	• P(A and B) = $P(A) \times P(B\|A)$ • P(A and B) = $P(B) \times P(A\|B)$

2) 곱셈정리 연습

Exercise 3

There are 7 green marbles and 3 blue marbles in a box. If we randomly select two marbles from this box, what is the probability of drawing a green marble and then a blue marble without replacement?

Answer:

Question 3

Bag A contains 6 white balls and 4 black balls and bag B contains 3 white balls and 2 black balls. A white ball is picked from bag A and put into bag B. Then, three balls are picked from bag B and put into bag A. Find the probability that a ball picked now from bag A is black.

Answer:

3) 조건부 확률 (conditional probability) 개념

어떤 사건이 일어난다는 전제 하에, 다른 사건이 일어날 확률

- Event A 가 일어났을 때, event B 가 일어날 확률:

$$P(B|A) = \frac{P(A \text{ and } B)}{P(A)}$$

영어 표현:

- If A and B are two events, then the conditional probability of B given A is defined as $P(B|A)$

Question *4*

I roll a fair die. Let A be the event that the outcome is an odd number, i.e., $A=\{1,3,5\}$. Also let B be the event that the outcome is less than or equal to 3, i.e., $B=\{1,2,3\}$. What is the probability of A given B, $P(A|B)$?

Answer:

4. 독립 시행 개념 및 공식

1) 개념

독립시행이란, 매번 같은 조건에서 어떤 시행을 반복할 때, 각 시행의 결과가 다른 시행의 결과에 영향을 주지 않는 시행.

독립 시행 문제의 조건:
- Each trial results in one of the two outcomes
- the outcome of any trial does not affect that of the others.
- 즉 독립인 시행을 여러 번 반복함.

Exercise 4

어느 양궁 선수는 10점 과녁을 맞힐 확률이 $\frac{1}{3}$ 이라 한다. 이 양궁 선수가 화살을 4번 쏘아 10점 과녁을 2번 맞힐 확률을 구하여 보자.

First Solution:

○	○	×	×	$= \left(\frac{1}{3}\right)^2\left(\frac{2}{3}\right)^2$

Second Solution: 4번 시도에서 2번 맞힐 사건이 언제 발생하는가?

Solution: $_4C_2$

Answer:

2) 독립시행 공식

이항 분포 공식 (Binomial distribution formula): $_nC_rP^rQ^{n-r}$		
어떤 일이 일어날 확률이 p	일어나지 않을 확률이 q	n 회의 상호 독립적인 시행으로 이 일이 r 회 일어날 확률
P^r	Q^{n-r}	$_nC_r$

Question 5:

What is the probability of getting 3 heads while tossing a coin 8 times?

Answer:

Question 6:

If the probability of raining on any given day in Atlanta is 50 percent, what is the probability of raining on exactly 3 days in a 5-day period?

Answer:

Exercise 1	$P(E) = \dfrac{\{1,3,5\}}{6} = \dfrac{3}{6} = \dfrac{1}{2}$
Exercise 2	$\dfrac{3}{6} + \dfrac{3}{6} - \dfrac{2}{6} = \dfrac{2}{3}$
Exercise 3	P(A and B)$= \dfrac{7}{10} \times \dfrac{3}{9} = \dfrac{7}{30}$
Exercise 4	$_4C_2 \left(\dfrac{1}{3}\right)^2\left(\dfrac{2}{3}\right)^2$

Question 1	$1- \dfrac{1}{200} = \dfrac{199}{200}$
Question 2	P (A or B) = 0.63 P (B or C) = 0.91
Question 3	$\dfrac{1}{15} + \dfrac{1}{4} + \dfrac{1}{10} = \dfrac{4+15+6}{60} = \dfrac{25}{60} = \dfrac{5}{12}$
Question 4	$P(A|B) = \dfrac{2}{3}$
Question 5	$_8C_3 \times \left(\dfrac{1}{2}\right)^3\left(\dfrac{1}{2}\right)^5$
Question 6	$_5C_3 \times \left(\dfrac{1}{2}\right)^3\left(\dfrac{1}{2}\right)^2$

Chapter V.
Statistics (통계)

통계 문제를 풀 때 가장 중요한 것?	
"문제에서 주어진 통계 data 를 보고 Interpret or Infer 할 수 있는 능력"	
1	• **Mean, median, mode ⇒ central tendency**
2	• **Range 와 표준편차 ⇒ measures of dispersion**
3	• **통계 문제는 statistical measures 구한 다음이 더 중요하다!**

1. 통계 분류

Data can be described numerically by various **statistics**, or **statistical measures**.

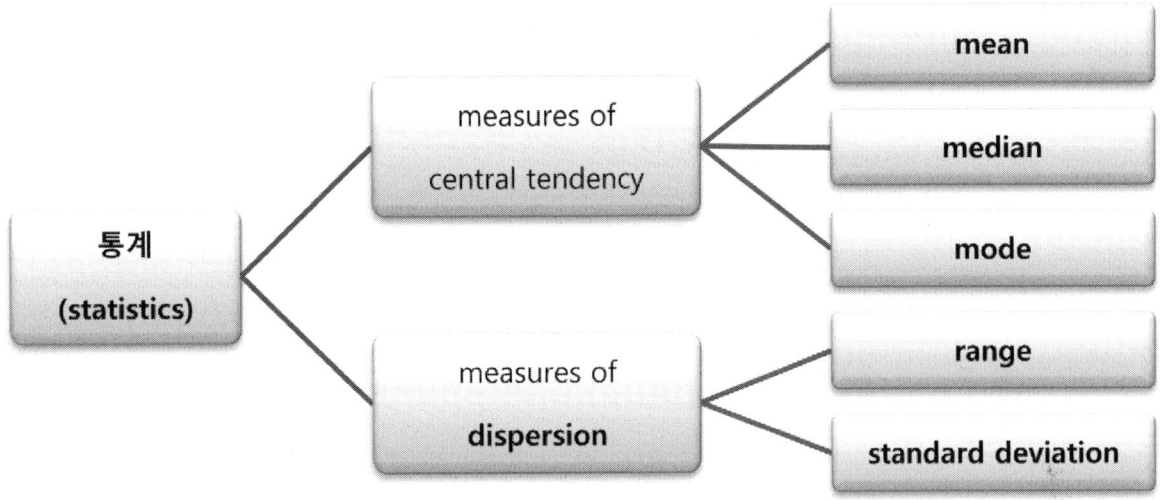

measures of central tendency	• the "center" of the data along the number line
measures of dispersion	• the degree of "spread" of the data

2. Measures of Central Tendency

1) 평균 (mean) 개념 및 포인트

$$\text{Mean (average)} = \frac{Sum\ of\ elements}{The\ number\ of\ elements}$$

2) Combined Mean

문제의 핵심: Combining two groups of different sizes and different group averages

	Group A	Group B
Number	a	b
Average	x	y

	Group A	Group B
Number	10 boys	20 girls
Average	17 years	20 years

- **Combined Average (m)** $= \dfrac{ax+by}{a+b}$

$$\frac{17 \times 10 + 20 \times 20}{10 + 20} = 19$$

변경식: $\dfrac{a}{b} = \dfrac{y-m}{m-x}$ $(y > m > x)$

- **언제 사용**: a or b 값을 구할 때

Question 1:

John pays 30% tax and Ingrid pays 40% tax. Their combined tax rate is 37%. If John's gross salary is $54000, what is Ingrid's gross salary?

Answer:

3) 중앙값 (median) 개념 및 포인트

중앙값은 데이터를 작은 수부터 큰 수 순서대로 정렬한 중간점입니다. 데이터의 반은 중앙값보다 작고, 나머지 반은 중앙값보다 큽니다.

중앙값 (median) 구하기	
Case 1: 집합의 numbers = odd (홀수)	Case 2: 집합의 numbers = even (짝수)
{1, 2, 3, 4, 5}	{1, 2, 3, 4, 5, 6}
⬇	⬇
• median = middle number	• median = the average of the two middle numbers
• median: 3	• median: $\frac{3+4}{2}$ = 3.5

Q 1	문제에서 a data set number 가 odd or even 인지 주어지지 않을 때?
A	1) Even case , 2) Odd case 각각 검증 필요.

Q 2	문제 조건: If median = one of the data values
A	집합의 numbers = odd (홀수) or even 가능

Q 3	문제 조건: If median ≠ one of the data values
A	집합의 numbers = even

Question 2:

Consider the data set {24,61,27,57,34,37,63,50, N} where N is a positive integer. What are the possible values of the median of the set?

Answer.

4) Mode (최빈값) 개념 및 포인트

Mode = 최빈값 (a higher frequency in a given set)

- 최빈값은 데이터 집합에서 가장 많이 등장한 데이터입니다.
- 최빈값이 없거나, 하나거나, 여러 개의 최빈값이 있을 수 있습니다.

For example, {2, 4, 5, 5, 6, 6, 7}

  - the mode of the data set: $\Rightarrow$ 5 and 6

Exercise 2:

{2, 4, 5, 5, 6, 6, 7}, what is the **mode number** of the list?

Answer:

3. Measures of Dispersion

1)Range 개념 및 포인트

The **range** of the numbers in a group of data is the difference between the greatest number G in the data and the least number L in the data; that is, $G - L$.

Range = Maximum – Minimum

Exercise 3:

The range of the five numbers 11, 10, 5, 13, 21 is

Answer:

Question 3

After taking a quiz, 25 students each received a score on the quiz that was an integer from 1 to 10, inclusive. The average (arithmetic mean) of the 25 scores was 8.8. Only 1 student received the lowest score, and the sum of the 24 scores greater than the lowest score was 217. What was the range of the 25 scores?

Answer:

2) Interquartile Range 개념

Interquartile range. It is defined as the difference between **the third quartile** and the **first quartile**, that is, $Q3 - Q1$. Thus, the interquartile range measures the spread of the middle half of the data.

Exercise 4: 16 numbers = {2, 4, 4, 5, 7, 7, 7, 7, 7, 7, 8, 8, 9, 9, 9, 9}, interquartile range = ?

First group ={2, 4, 4, 5, 7, 7, 7, 7}		Second group = {7, 7, 8, 8, 9, 9, 9, 9}	
Q1: first group 의 median	Q2 = median	Q3 = second group 의 median	
Q1 =	**Q2 =**	**Q 3 =**	

Answer: Interquartile range =

3) 표준편차 (standard deviation) 개념 및 포인트

- Standard Deviation: A measure of how dispersed the data is in relation to mean.
- 표준편차는 자료의 산포도를 나타내는 값입니다. 자료들이 넓게 흩어져 분포하면 그만큼 표준편차 값도 커집니다.

- **Standard deviation 공식**

$$\sigma = \sqrt{\frac{\Sigma(x-m)^2}{N}} = \frac{\sqrt{\Sigma(x-m)^2}}{\sqrt{N}} = \frac{\Sigma|x-m|}{\sqrt{N}}$$

- **Standard deviation 구하는 방식**

(1) Find the arithmetic mean,

(2) Find the differences between the mean and each of the n numbers,

(3) Square each of the differences,

(4) Find the average of the squared differences, and

(5) Take the non-negative square root of this average.

Q: For the ten data {70, 70, 100, 90, 80, 70, 70, 80, 90, 80}, the standard deviation is ?

- First, the mean of the data is 80

- Second, the differences between the mean and each of the n numbers: -10, -10, 20, 10, 0, -10, -10, 0, 10, 0

- Third, square each of the differences: 100, 100, 400, 100, 0, 100, 100, 0, 100, 0

- Fourth, find the average of the squared differences = $\frac{1000}{10} = 100$

- Finally, non-negative square root of this average = $\sqrt{100} = 10$ (non-negative)

Exercise 5:

A = { 4, 5, 5, 6 }, B = {6, 4, 4, 6 } Question: A's SD < B's SD ?

Answer:

4)표준편차 (standard deviation) 특징

Adding or subtracting a constant to each value in a data set does not change the value of the standard deviation. (Why? 평균이 변하지 않는다)

	Mean	(Data – Mean)	Standard Deviation
A = { 3, 5, 7, 9}	6	{3, 1, 1, 3}	$\sqrt{5}$
B = {13, 15, 17, 19}	16	{3, 1, 1, 3}	$\sqrt{5}$

Multiplying each value in a data set by a constant also multiplies the standard deviation by that constant. (Why? 평균이 변한다)

	Mean	(Data – Mean)	Standard Deviation
A = { 3, 5, 7, 9}	6	{3, 1, 1, 3}	$\sqrt{5}$
B = { 6, 10, 14, 18}	12	{6, 2, 2, 6}	$2\sqrt{5}$

Exercise 6:

If the positive number d is the standard deviation of n, k and p then the standard deviation of n+1, k+1 and p+1 is

Answer:

Question 4

For each student in a certain class, a teacher adjusted the student's test score using the formula y = 0.8x + 20, where x is the student's original test score and y is the student's adjusted test score. If the standard deviation of the original test scores of the students in the class was 20, what was the standard deviation of the adjusted test scores of the students in the class?

Answer:

5) 정규분포 (normal distribution) 개념 및 특징

정규분포: 도수 분포 곡선이 평균값을 중앙으로 하여 좌우 대칭인 **종 모양**을 이루는 분포
정규분포는 다음과 같은 특성을 가지고 있습니다:

- 대칭인 종 모양입니다 (**symmetry about the center (mean)**
- 평균과 중앙값, 최빈값은 거의 같은 위치에 있습니다.

- 자료의 68%는 평균으로부터 오른쪽, 왼쪽으로 표준편차의 1 배 내에 있음.
- 자료의 95%는 평균으로부터 오른쪽, 왼쪽으로 표준편차의 2 배 내에 있음.
- 자료의 99.7%는 평균으로부터 오른쪽, 왼쪽으로 표준편차의 3 배 내에 있음.

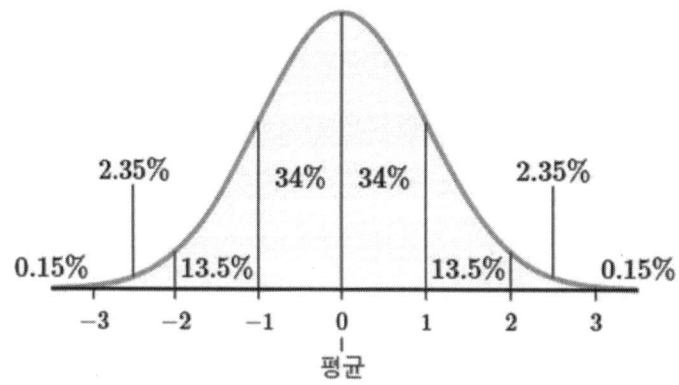

Question 5

특정 종류 소나무의 평균 몸통 지름은 150 cm 이고 표준편차는 30 cm 입니다. 숲의 특정 지역에 나무는 500 그루 있습니다. 지름이 120 cm 보다 작은 나무는 약 몇 그루인가요?

Answer.

Exercise 1	$\dfrac{17(10) + 20(20)}{10 + 20} = 19$
Exercise 2	the mode number of the list 의미는 5 와 6 이 등장한 횟수 ⇒ 2 회가 정답
Exercise 3	21 - 5 = 16.
Exercise 4	Interquartile range = Q3 – Q1 = 8.5 – 6 = 2.5
Exercise 5	A's SD < B's SD
Exercise 6	d

Question 1	**$126,000**
Question 2	**37 $\leq$ integers $\leq$ 50**
Question 3	**10**
Question 4	**16**
Question 5	120 cm 보다 작은 나무 = 16% (50 – 34 = 16%) 500 의 16 %가 몇 그루인지 계산 = 500×0.16 = 80

Chapter VI.
Sequence (수열)

	수열 문제를 풀 때 가장 중요한 것?
	"등차/등비 수열 공식만 암기하자"
1	▪ 등차 수열 sum 공식 활용 문제
2	▪ 등비수열에서 무한등비급수의 합은 어떻게?
3	▪ 기타 수열의 핵심은 패턴 찾기!

1. 등차수열

1) 등차수열 개념 및 일반항

등차수열 - 어떤 수에 차례로 일정한 수를 더하여 얻어지는 수열을 말함.

$$\{1, 5, 9, 13, 17, 21, 25, 29, 33, \ldots\}$$

첫째 항 $a_1 = 1$	공차(difference) = 4

- 등차수열의 일반항을 a_n 이라 하면

$$a_n = a + (n-1)d, \quad a_{n+1} - a_n = d$$

Exercise 1

$\{1, 5, 9, 13, 17, 21, 25, 29, 33, \ldots\}$ 33 는 몇 번째 항?

Answer.

---

2) 등차수열 합 공식

- 등차수열의 합 (암기 필요) $= \frac{n}{2}(a + l) = \frac{n}{2}(2a + (n-1)d)$ (a = 초항, l = 끝항)

- 자연수의 합 → $1 + 2 + 3 + \ldots + n = \frac{n(n+1)}{2}$

Question 1

What is the sum of all even integers between 17 and 99?

Answer:

2. 등비수열

1) 등비수열 개념 및 일반항

등비수열: A geometric sequence is a sequence of numbers where each term after the first is found by **multiplying** the previous one by a fixed non-zero number called the common **ratio**.

- 첫째 항 a, 공비(ratio) **r** (≠ 0)인 등비수열의 일반항을 a_n 이라 하면

$$a_n = ar^{n-1}, \quad a_{n+1} = r \times a_n$$

Exercise _2_

In the sequence 1, 2, 4, 8, 16, 32, ..., each term after the first is twice the previous term. What is the sum of the 16th, 17th, and 18th terms in the sequence?

Answer.

2) 등비수열 합 공식

등비수열 합 공식 (암기 필수)
첫째 항 **a**, 공비 **r** (≠ 0)인 이라 하면: $S_n = \dfrac{a(r^n - 1)}{r - 1}$
If $-1 < r < 1$, then $\displaystyle\lim_{n=\infty} r^n = 0$ ⇒ 무한등비급수 $S_n = \dfrac{a}{1-r}$ $(-1 < r < 1)$

Question 2

For every integer n from 1 to 200, inclusive, the nth term of a certain sequence is given by $(-1)^n \left(\dfrac{1}{2^n}\right)$. If N is the sum of the first 200 terms in the sequence, then N is

Answer:

3. 기타 특별한 수열

계차 수열	두 항의 차가 규칙있게 나열되는 수열
	For example, 2, 4, 7, 11, 16, 22, ... (차가, +2, +3, +4, +5, +6, ...)
조화 수열	등차수열의 각 항의 역수로 이루어진 수열
<u>피보나치 수열</u>	연속한 두 수의 합이 그 다음 수가 되는 수열

기타 수열 문제의 핵심은: a_n= ? or sum = ? **규칙성(패턴) 찾기**

Question 3

For every positive integer n, the nth term of sequence is given by $a_n = \frac{1}{n} - \frac{1}{n+1}$. What is the sum of the first 100 terms?

Answer:

Chapter 6 Answer Sheet

Exercise 1	공식 활용: 33 = 1 + (n-1)4 ⟶ n = 9
Exercise 2	$7(2^{15})$

Question 1	2,378
Question 2	Sum $\approx -\dfrac{1}{3}$
Question 3	Sum $= 1 - \dfrac{1}{101} = \dfrac{100}{101}$

Chapter VII.
Algebra (대수학)

	Algebra 문제를 풀 때 가장 중요한 팩트?	
	"Algebra 범위가 엄청 넓죠! 아래 GMAT 기출 포인트만 기억하세요"	
1	▪	영어 표현을 into Math!
2	▪	근의공식
3	▪	2 차 함수 꼭지점 (vertex)
4	▪	절대값과 완전 제곱근
5	▪	이중 절대값 방정식

1. Algebraic Expressions

1) 정의

Algebra is based on the operation of arithmetic and on the concept of an **unknown quantity (미지수)**, or <u>variables</u>. Letters such as **x** or *n* are used to represent unknown quantities. Numerical expressions are used to represent known quantities called *constants*. A combination of variables, constants, and arithmetical operations is called an *algebraic expression*.

The expression *19x² − 6x +3* consists of *19 x²*, *-6x*, and 3, where 19 is the <u>coefficient</u> (계수) of *x²*, -6 is the coefficient of *x¹*, and 3 is a <u>constant term (상수)</u>. Such an expression is called a second degree (or quadratic) polynomial in *x* since the highest power of *x* is 2. The expression of F + 5 is a first degree (or linear) polynomial in F since the highest power of F is 1.

2) Algebraic Expressions 1(수학 표현)

Algebraic Expressions	Mathematical Operations
1) 3 less than x	• $x - 3$
2) 1 is less than 2	• $1 < 2$
3) x more than y	• $x + y$
4) x greater than y	• $x > y$
5) 2x and 3x	• Twice x and triple x
6) x² and x³	• x squared and x cubed
7) *xy*	• the product of x and y; **x times y**
8) *xʸ*	• x to the power of y; x to the yth power
9) ratio of x to y	• x: y = $^x/_y$
10) $\frac{35}{100}$	• Thirty-five hundredths

Exercise 1

Three-fifths of x is 14 less than twice y squared.

Answer:

3 Algebraic Expressions 2

Algebraic Expressions	Mathematical Operations
1) A is half as many as B	• a = ½ b
2) A is 3 times as many as	• a = 3b
3) X is no more than Y	• $x \leq y$
4) No number was chosen by more than 3 people.	Selected numbers (1, 2, or 3) $\leq \mathbf{3}$
5) X is no less than Y	• $x \geq y$
6) At most 100 students study GMAT	• $x \leq 100$ (최대값)
7) At least 100 students study GMAT.	• $x \geq 100$ (최소값)

2. 방정식 (Equation)

1)1 차 방정식 (Linear Equation)

1) 1 차 방정식 + 미지수 1 개: 5x − 2 = 9 − x	$x = \frac{11}{6}$
2) 1 차 방정식 + 미지수 2 개: 3x + 1 = y - 2	x = ? (구할 수 없음)

3) 1 차 빙정식 2 개 + 미지수 2 개
   (1) 6x + 5y = 29
   (2) 4x - 3y = -6
	$x = \frac{3}{2}$, y = 4.

* **고난이도 문제 출제 포인트**

1 차 방정식 + 미지수 2 개 ⇒ condition 따라 value 구할 수 있음 (아래 연습 문제에서 확인)

Question 1 (Data Sufficiency)

Martha bought several pencils. If each pencil was either a 23 cent pencil or a 21 pencil, how many 23 cent pencils did Martha buy?

(1) Martha bought a total of 6 pencils
(2) The total value of the pencils Martha bought was 130 cents.

Answer:

---

2) 연립 방정식 (equivalent equations)

Case 1: 1 차식 + 1 차식	Case 2: 1 차식 + 2 차식
1) $6x + 5y = 29$ 2) $4x - 3y = -6$	1) $x - y = 0$ 2) $x^2 + y^2 = 4$
⬇	⬇
1) $18x + 15y = 87$ 2) $20x - 15y = -30$	1 차식을 2 차식에 대입
▪ $x = {}^3/_2 \ y = 4$	$(\sqrt{2}, \sqrt{2})$ or $(-\sqrt{2}, -\sqrt{2})$

3) 2 차 방정식 (Quadratic Equations)

일부 2 차 방정식은 인수분해 (factoring)로 근을 찾을 수 있음.

Factoring (인수 분해) = A×B

$$acx^2 + (ad + bc)x + bd = (ax + b)(cx + d)$$

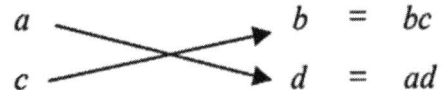

Exercise 2	x² + 6x + 5 = 0	**Answer:**
Exercise 3	$6x^2 + (17)x + 10 = 0$	**Answer:**

Question 2

By how much does the larger root of the equation 2x² + 5x = 12 exceed the smaller root?

Answer:

---

4) 인수분해 곱셈공식 활용법

$a^2 \pm 2ab + b^2 = (a \pm b)^2$	$a^2 - b^2 = (a + b)(a - b)$

1	x² - 6x + 9 = 0	(x – 3)² = 0 ⇒ x = 3
2	9x² - 25 = 0	(3x + 5)(3x –5) = 0 ⇒ $x = \frac{5}{3}, or -\frac{5}{3}$

Exercise 4 (곱셈공식 활용을 통한 문제 유형)

If a − b = 2, ab = 3, then a + b = ?

포인트: $(a − b)^2 = 4$ 식을 변경해서 (a + b)를 구할 수 있는 형태로 수정

Answer:

Question 3

If (a + b) = 4, and ab = $\frac{7}{4}$, what is the value of $a^2 − b^2$?

Answer:

5) 근의 공식 활용법

If 2 차 방정식 인수 분해 안 되면, then 근의 공식 사용

$$For \; ax^2 + bx + c = 0,$$

$$x = \frac{-b \pm \sqrt{b^2 - 4ac}}{2a} \; unless \; b^2 - 4ac \leq 0$$

Quadratic Formula (근의공식) 응용 문제 출제 포인트	
If $a + \sqrt{b}$ is one of the roots of a quadratic equation, then the other root is	$a - \sqrt{b}$
비에트의 공식 (Vieta's Theorem): 이차 방정식 $ax^2 + bx + c = 0$의 두 근을 α, β라 하면	• $\alpha + \beta = -\dfrac{b}{a}$ • $\alpha \times \beta = \dfrac{c}{a}$
If 이차 방정식의 두 근: $a + \sqrt{b}$, $a - \sqrt{b}$	$x^2 - 2ax + (a + \sqrt{b})(a - \sqrt{b}) = 0$

Question 4

Which of the following equation has $1 + \sqrt{2}$ as one of its roots?

○ $x^2 + 2x - 1 = 0$
○ $x^2 - 2x + 1 = 0$
○ $x^2 + 2x + 1 = 0$
○ $x^2 - 2x - 1 = 0$
○ $x^2 - x - 1 = 0$

Answer:

3. 부등식 (Inequalities)

An inequality is a statement that uses one of the following symbols:

<	**less than**
>	**greater than**
≥	**no fewer than (= greater than or equal to)**
≤	**no more than (= less than or equal to)**

1) 1차 부등식 (Linear Inequalities)

1) 3x − 2 > 5		• $x > \frac{7}{3}$
2) $\frac{5x-1}{-2} < 3$	양변에 -2 곱하기 (부등호 방향 바뀜)	• **5x −1 > -6 ⇒ x > -1**

2) 2차 부등식 (Quadratic Inequalities)

Exercise 5

To find the ranges of x for $x^2 − 4x + 3 < 0$

1) Intersection points (1, 3) are the roots of the equation

2) "<" means in which range of x the graph is below x-axis.

Answer:

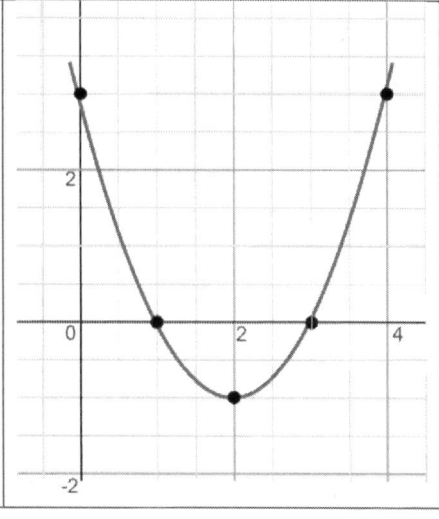

> **Question 5**
>
> If y − 2x ≤ 2 and 2y + 2x ≤ 12, what is the maximum possible value of y?
>
> **Answer:**

4. 함수 (function)

두 집합 X, Y 에 대해서 X 의 각 원소에 Y의 원소가 오직 하나씩 "대응"할 때, 이 대응을 function 이라 하고, 기호로는 $y = f(x)$

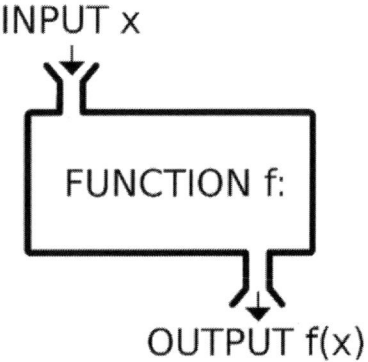

1) 일차 함수 (Linear Function)

Linear Function (1 차 함수) $\Rightarrow f(x) = ax + b$

2) 일차 함수 기울기 구하기

두 점 given (3, -3), (-2, 4): 기울기 (slope), x intercept and y intercept 구하기	
• Slope $= \dfrac{y_1 - y2_1}{x_1 - x_2}$	Slope $= -\dfrac{7}{5}$
• $y = -\dfrac{7}{5}x + b \Rightarrow$ (3, -3) or (-2, 4) 대입	b $= \dfrac{4}{5}$ (y intercept)
• $y = -\dfrac{7}{5}x + \dfrac{4}{5} \Rightarrow$ y = 0 대입	x $= \dfrac{4}{7}$ (x intercept)

3) 이차 함수 (quadratic function) 기본 형태

이차함수 기본형	$y = ax^2$
이차함수 Standard Form	$y = ax^2 + bx + c$

4) 이차 함수 (quadratic function) 꼭지점 찾기

Q: $y = ax^2 + bx + c$ 의 꼭지점을 찾아라?
•   Step 1: 이차함수 완전제곱 꼴로 수정 $\Rightarrow a^2 \pm 2ab + b^2 = (a \pm b)^2$ •   Step 2: $y = a(x + p)^2 + q$ •   Step 3: 꼭지점의 좌표 $(-p, q)$ 즉, 꼭지점 $(0, 0)$에서 $(-p, q)$ 수평 이동

Q: 꼭지점 $(-p, q)$가 주어진 이차함수 표준형은?
A: $y = a(x + p)^2 + q$

Exercise *6*
Find the vertex form of a quadratic function: $y = x^2 + 4x + 2$ **Answer:**

5) 함수 (function) 응용 문제 – 단위 전환

Type 1: 단위 전환 without Formulas (상식으로 알 수 있는 단위 전환은 formula 주어지지 않음)	• From kilometers to meters, vice versa • From Per second to per hour, vice versa
Type 2: 단위 전환 with Formulas (공식 없이는 알 수 없는 단위전환은 formular 주어짐)	• The formula $C = \frac{9}{5}(F - 32)$: temperature in degrees Celsius (C) and degrees Fahrenheit (F). • Currency exchange rates • From mph (mile per hour) to kph (kilometer per hour)

Exercise 7

If an object travels 100 feet in 2 seconds, what is the object's approximate speed in miles per hour? (Note: 1 mile = 5280 feet)

Answer:

Question 6

The temperature in degrees Celsius (C) can be converted to temperature in degrees Fahrenheit (F) by the formula $F = \frac{9}{5}C + 32$. What is the temperature at which F = C?

Answer:

5. 절대값 (absolute value)

1) 절대값 개념

- 절대값: 두 점 사이의 거리를 나타내는 값

$$|a - b| = |b - a| = c \quad \Rightarrow \quad a\text{ 와 } b\text{ 까지의 거리는 } c$$

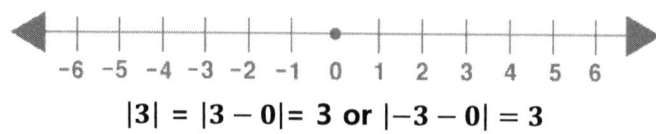

$$|3| = |3 - 0| = 3 \text{ or } |-3 - 0| = 3$$

Exercise 8

$|x - 3| = 2$

Answer:

---

2) 절대값과 제곱근 관계

중요 특징: $|x| = \sqrt{x^2}$

$|3| = \sqrt{(3)^2} = 3, |-3| = \sqrt{(-3)^2} = 3$

Question 7

If $x < 0$, then $\sqrt{(-x \times |x|)}$ is ?

Answer:

3) 이중 절대값

절대값이 두 개인 방정식 or 부등식

두 개의 절대값의 구간을 3 개의 구간으로 나누어서 문제 접근 필요

Exercise 9	
$\lvert x-3 \rvert = \lvert 3x+2 \rvert - 1$	
1) $x \geq 3$	
2) $-\dfrac{2}{3} \leq x < 3$	
3) $x < -\dfrac{2}{3}$	
Answer	

Question 8
$2 < \lvert x-8 \rvert < \lvert x-9 \rvert$, 만족하는 해를 구하여라?
Answer:

Chapter 7 Algebra Answer Sheet

Exercise 1	$\frac{3}{5}x = 2y^2 - 14$
Exercise 2	(x +1)(x + 5) = 0 ⇒ x = -1 or x = -5
Exercise 3	$(x + 2)(6x + 5) \Rightarrow x = -2$ or $x = -\frac{5}{6}$
Exercise 4	a + b = ± 4
Exercise 5	1 < x < 3
Exercise 6	(-2, -2)
Exercise 7	Speed ≈ 34 mph
Exercise 8	x = 5, 1
Exercise 9	$x = -3, \frac{1}{2}$

Question 1	B
Question 2	$\frac{3}{2} - (-4) = \frac{11}{2}$
Question 3	$a^2 - b^2 = \pm 12$
Question 4	D ($x^2 - 2x - 1 = 0$)
Question 5	$y = \frac{14}{3}$
Question 6	C = - 40
Question 7	$-x$
Question 8	**x < 6**

Chapter VIII.
Word Problems

Word Problems 문제를 풀 때 가장 중요한 것?	
"기출 문제 유형을 완전 습득 후 기출 변형문제 유형에 적응하자"	

1	공식 (formula) 사용 문제 유형: • Work rate, speed, interest rates, profit, mixture 문제유형 • 기출 변형문제 출제
2	NO Formula 문제 유형 • 융합형 문제 (A+B+C) • 식만들기 문제유형
3	• 빠르고 정확한 독해 • Making equations ⇒ 연립방정식 or 부등식 풀이

1. Work Rates 문제 유형

1) 정의 및 공식

개념: "단위시간 당 한 일의 양 "	공식:
• How fast certain individuals work • How fast they work together	$$Work\,(한\,일) = work\,rate \times Time$$ $$Work\,Rate = \frac{Work}{Time}$$

2) 합의 공식

Work Rate 문제 구성	
조건 1: Ram 혼자 작업 시간 = r	조건 2: Sam 혼자 작업 시간 = s
Question: Ram 과 Sam 이 공동 작업 시간 h =?	
Answer: $\frac{1}{r} + \frac{1}{s} = \frac{1}{h}$	

Question 1

Working simultaneously at their respective constant rates, Machines A and B produce 800 nails in x hours. Working alone at its constant rate, Machine A produces 800 nails in y hours. In terms of x and y, how many hours does it take Machine B, working alone at its constant rate, to produce 800 nails?

Answer:

2. Speed 문제 유형

1) 정의

정의: "단위시간 당 이동한 거리"	$Speed = \dfrac{Distance}{Time}$ $Distance = Speed \times Time$

Exercise 1

A passenger train leaves the train depot 2 hours after a freight train left the same depot. The freight train is traveling 20 mph slower than the passenger train. Find the speed of the passenger train, if it overtakes the freight train in three hours.

Answer:

---

2) 연비 (consumption)

정의: Fuel consumption measures the amount of fuel a car consumes to go a specific distance.	$\textbf{Fuel consumption} = \dfrac{Distance}{the\ amount\ of\ fuel\ used}$ $Distance = fuel\ consumption \times fuel\ used$

Question 2

For a 30-mile trip, the fuel consumption of a certain car was 15 miles per gallon for the first 10 miles and 45 miles per gallon for the rest of the trip. What was the car's fuel consumption for the trip, in miles per gallon?

Answer:

3. 이자 (Interest Rates) 문제 유형

1) 기본 개념 및 공식

이자 소득 구하기	
단리 (Simple interest rates)	복리 (Compounded interest rates)
최초 원금(principle)에 이자가 붙음	원금에서 발생한 이자에 대한 이자도 계산:
⬇	⬇
단리 이자 소득= (원금)×(interest rate)×time	복리 최종 금액 = principle × (1 + interest rate)^{time} (time = 기간)

Exercise 2

A total of $36,000 was invested for one month in a new money market account that paid simple annual interest at the rate of r percent. If the investment earned $360 in interest for the month, what is the value of r ?

Answer:

---

2) 복리 공식

$$A \text{ (원리 합계)} = P(1 + \frac{r}{n})^{nt}$$

A final amount **r** annual interest rate

P 원금(initial principal balance) **t** time (in years)

n the number of times that interest is compounded per unit t

- n = 1 년에 이자가 집행되는 횟수
- If annually, then n =1. If quarterly, then n = 4. If monthly, then n = 12

Question 3

On January 1, 1994, Jill invested P dollars in an account that pays interest at a rate of 8 percent per year, compounded annually on December 31. If there were no other deposits or withdrawals in the account, how many dollars were in the account on January 1, 1998, in terms of P?

Answer:

4. 혼합 (mixture) 문제 유형

혼합 문제 유형	
Type 1: single mixture	**Type 2: Two mixtures**
1 mixture + 새로운 것을 추가	**1 mixture + 2 mixture = 3 mixture**
⬇	⬇
문제 조건에서 반드시 equation 만들 수 있는 조건 제공 ⇒ 그 조건을 활용해서 미지수 찾으면 됨.	**A + B = C 의 equation 활용**

Exercise 3

You have a 200 liter mixture that is 90% water and 10% bleach and ask **how much water** you would need to add to make it 5% bleach.

Answer:

Question 4

In what ratio should a 20% methyl alcohol solution be mixed with a 50% methyl alcohol solution so that the resultant solution has 40% methyl alcohol in it?

Answer:

5. Percent 증가/감소 문제 유형

1) 기본 개념 및 공식

To find the percent increase, first find the amount of the increase; then divide this increase by the original amount, and express this quotient as a percent.

$$\textbf{Percent change} = \frac{new - old}{old} \times 100$$

2) Percent 두 수 비교하기

Q: A 는 B 의 몇%인가?

영어 표현: A is what percent of B = $\frac{A}{B}$

Exercise 4

한 반에 boys = 15 명, girls = 12 명, 남자의 수는 여자의 수 보다 몇 % 더 큰가?

Answer:

Question 5

The percent change from 29 to 43 is approximately what percent of the percent change from 43 to 57?

Answer:

6. Profit (이윤) 문제 유형

Profit 문제는 주어진 data 따라서 어떤 공식을 사용할지 결정 가능합니다.	
Gross Profit	**= revenues - expenses**
	= selling price - costs

Question 6

The profit P, in dollars, for any given month at a certain company is defined by P= I — C, where I represents total income, in dollars, and C represents total costs, in dollars, for the month. For each of the first 4 months of the year, C = I + 32,000; and for each of the next 3 months, I = C + 36,000. If I = C + 10,000 for each of the 5 remaining months of the year, what was the company's total profit for the 12-month year?

Answer:

Chapter 8 Word Problems Answer Sheet

Exercise 1	x = 50
Exercise 2	r = 12
Exercise 3	x = 200
Exercise 4	25% 더 큼.

Question 1	$b = \dfrac{xy}{y-x}$
Question 2	Fuel consumption = 27
Question 3	$(1.08)^4 P$
Question 4	x : y = 1 : 2
Question 5	150%
Question 6	Profit sum = -32,000×4 + 36,000×3 + 10,000×5 = $30,000

Chapter IX.
Integers (정수)

Integers 문제를 풀 때 가장 중요한 것?	
"이론은 미약하나, 문제 난이도는 창대한 유형에 적응하자"	
1	▪ 정수의 세밀한 특징 (연속된 정수, 배수 판단)
2	▪ Prime numbers 특징을 활용한 개념 – factors, 소인수분해, 최대공약수, 최소공배수
3	▪ 나머지 (remainder) 결합 문제

1. 정수 Overview

1) 정수 정의

Integers (정수)- A number that can be written without fractional component

    i.   **Positive Integers, Natural Numbers (양의 정수)**

    ii.   **Zero (0)**

    iii.   **Negative Integers** (음의 정수)

2) 정수의 곱의 법칙

a × b = Even	At least one even
a × b = odd	All odds

3) 정수의 합의 법칙

정수의 합의 결과는 홀수 (odd)의 숫자로 결정	
• Even + odd =	Odd
• Even + odd + odd =	Even
• Even + odd + odd + odd =	Odd
If the number of odds = Odd	**If the number of odds = Even**

Question 1

If x is an integer, which of the following must be an even integer?

○ $x^2 - x - 1$

○ $x^2 - 4x + 6$

○ $x^2 - 5x + 5$

○ $x^2 + 3x + 8$

○ $x^2 + 2x + 10$

Answer:

4) 연속된 정수 (consecutive integers) 특징

연속된 정수: [n, n+1, n+2, n+3,...]

The product of *n* consecutive integers 는 n! 반드시 나누어짐.		
The product of 3 consecutive integers	(1)(2)(3), (2)(3)(4), (3)(4)(5)	3! = 6 으로 나누어 짐
The product of 4 consecutive integers	(1)(2)(3)(4), (2)(3)(4)(5), (3)(4)(5)(6)	4! = 24 으로 나누어 짐

Exercise 1

If T is a set of 35 consecutive integers, of which 17 are negative, what is the sum of all the integers in T?

Answer:

Question 2

n=1234567891011.........499500

The digits of the integer n above are the digits of the integers from 1 to 500 written in consecutive order. How many digits does n have?

Answer:

2. 약수 (factors or divisors)

1) 약수 개념

n 의 약수 (divisors or factors): n = 정수×정수

For example, 12 의 약수 ⇒ 12 = 정수 ×정수 ⇒ 1×12, 2×6, 3×4 ⇒ 총 6 개

n = km (m is a factor of n)

2) 소수 개념

소수 (prime number) = 1 × itself 정수
For example, **3 의 약수 ⇒ 1×3 = 3**

- All prime numbers above 3 are of the form (6n -1) or (6n +1)
- 25 is an exception.

3) 소인수분해 개념

소인수분해 (Prime Factorization) = (prime)×(prime)×(prime)

For example, Prime Factorization of 12 ⇒12 = 2 × 2 × 3 = $2^2 × 3$

Question 3

Given that N is an integer greater than 1,000, the number of prime numbers that are greater than N and less than N + 15 is greater than 6 ?

Answer:

4) 약수의 개수 구하기

약수 (factors or divisors) 개수 구하기	
x number prime factorization = $a^x \times b^y \times c^z$	x 약수의 개수 = $(x+1)(y+1)(z+1)$

	1	2	2^2	2^3
1				
5				
5^2				

Exercise 2. 200 약수의 개수?
•   Step 1: 200 = $2^3 \times 5^2$
•   Step 2: (지수 + 1)(지수 + 1)
•   Step 3: (3+1) ×(2+1) = 12

3. 배수 (multiples)

1) 배수 개념

• $y = x \times (0)$(단 배수는 $x \times 0$ 가능)
If y is divisible by x, y is a multiple of x
For example, multiple of 3 = 0, 3,6,9,12,15,...
3 에 0, 1, 2, 3, 4, ...를 곱하면, 0, 3, 6, 9, 12,...가 된다. 이와 같이, 어떤 정수 (0 또는 어떤 자연수)에 자연수가 곱해진 수를 처음 수의 배수라고 한다.

2) 3 의 배수 판단

3 의 배수: 각 자리의 합이 3 의 배수	
Q: 567 은 3 의 배수?	A: 5 + 6 + 7 = 18 ⟶ 18 ÷3 = 6

3) 2, 4, 8 의 배수 판별

2 의 배수	1000a + 100b + 10c + **d**	(abc×5)×2 + d 로 2 의 배수 판단
4 의 배수	1000a + 100b + **10c + d**	(ab×25)×4 + (10c + d) 로 4 의 배수 판단
8 의 배수	1000a + **100b + 10c + d**	(a×125)×8 + (100b + 10c + d) 로 8 의 배수 판단

Question 4

What is the number closest to 823467897 that is a multiple of 8?

○   823,467,904

○   823,467,898

○   823,467,896

○   823,467,894

○   823,467,892

4) 최대공약수 & 최소공배수

- 최대 공약수(Greatest Common Divisor) – 공약수 가운데 차수가 가장 높은 것을 최대공약수

- 최소 공배수 (Least Common Multiple)- 공배수 가운데 차수가 가장 낮은 것을 최소공배수

- (최대공약수)× (최소공배수) = the product of two numbers **(출제 포인트)**

Exercise 3

Find GCD and LCM of 3,780 and 4,950.

Answer:

Exercise 4

The product of the least common multiple and the greatest common factor of 36 and m is 1728. What is the value of m?

Answer:

Question 5

Let y = 105n, where n is a positive integer. If y is both the square of an integer and y is divisible by 30, what is the least possible value of n?

Answer:

5) 나머지 (remainders)

When y is divisible by x, the remainder is R

$$y = xQ + R \quad (Q = quotient) \quad 0 \leq R < x$$

For example. when 15 is divided by 6, 15 = 6×2 + 3 (2 = quotient, 3 = remainder)

Question 6

What is the remainder when 3^{75} is divided by 5?

Answer:

Algebra approach 필요한 고난이도 문제 다수

Question 7

A positive integer N leaves a remainder of 4 when divided by 33. How many different remainders can N have, when N is divided by 55?

Answer:

Exercise 1	Sum = 0
Exercise 2	**12**
Exercise 3	GCD= 2 x 3^2 x 5 = 90, LCM= 2^2 x 3^3 x 5^2 x 7 x 11
Exercise 4	**$1728 = 36 \times m \rightarrow$ m = 48**

Question 1	D
Question 2	**Sum = 9 + 180 + 1203 = 1392**
Question 3	Less than 6
Question 4	C
Question 5	**2×2×3×5×7 = 420**
Question 6	2
Question 7	만족하는 $z \Rightarrow 0 \leq z \leq 4$

Chapter X.
Real numbers (실수)

Real Numbers 문제를 풀 때 가장 중요한 것?	
"절대적으로 넓은 범위를 차지하지만, GMAT 시험은 한국 수능과 출제 포인트가 다릅니다. 선택과 집중이 필요합니다"	

1	▪ Decimals 관련 개념 응용 문제
2	▪ 지수 법칙을 기반으로 한 문제 꾸준히 등장 ▪ 지수와 연관 개념 - 절대값
3	▪ 분수 & 소수 개념이 연결된 percent, ratio, proportion

1. 실수 (Real Numbers) 정의

1) 실수 범위

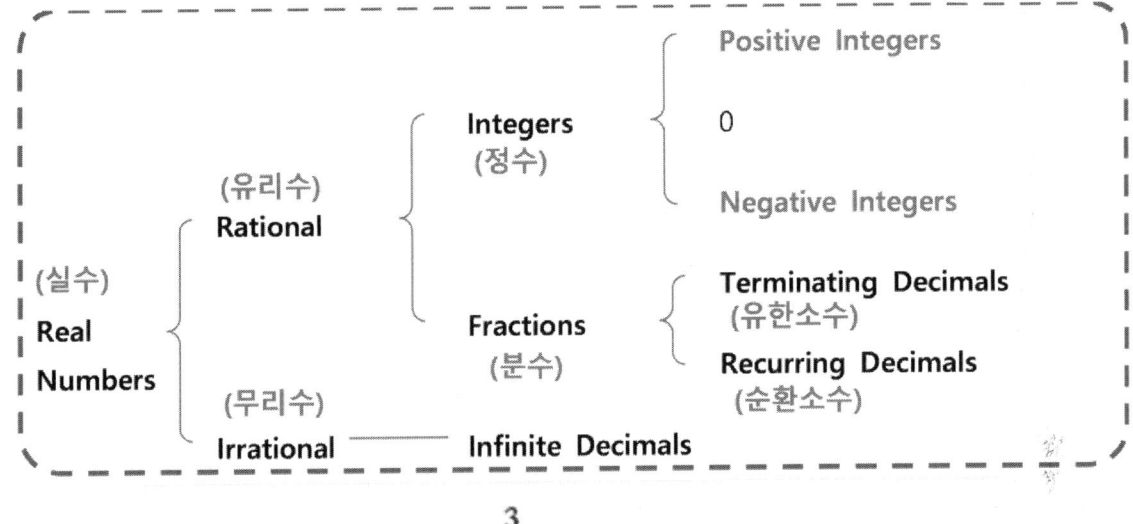

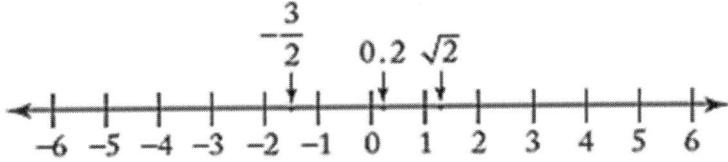

2) Decimals 출제포인트

In the decimal system, the position of the period or *decimal point* determines the *place values* of the digits.

Example: The digits in the number **7,654.321** have the following place values:

Thousands		Hundreds	Tens	Ones or units		Tenths	Hundredths	Thousandths
7	,	6	5	4	.	3	2	1

Question 1

If $\frac{k}{60125} = 0.001$, what is the units digit of k?

Answer:

3) 유한소수 (terminating decimals)

유한 소수 - 분모의 소인수는 2 or 5, 또는 both 2 and 5

$$0.3 = \frac{3}{10} = \frac{3}{10^1} = \frac{3}{2^1 \times 5^1}$$

Question 2

Which of the following fractions has a decimal equivalent that is a terminating decimal?

○ $\frac{10}{189}$

○ $\frac{15}{196}$

○ $\frac{16}{225}$

○ $\frac{25}{144}$

○ $\frac{39}{128}$

Answer:

4) 반올림 (rounding) , 올림, 내림

ROUND (반올림):

구하는 자리보다 한 자리 아래의 숫자가 1) 4 이하이면 버리고, 2) 5 or 5 higher

면 10 으로 올림

Exercise 1: To round 7651.4 to the nearest hundred	**7651.4** ⇒
Exercise 2: To round 0.43248 to the nearest thousandth (thousandth ⇒ 소수점 셋째 자리 = 1/1,000)	**0.43248** ⇒

5) 올림 (rounding Up) & 내림 (rounding Down)

올림 (rounding Up)	내림 (rounding Down)
* 어떤 숫자가 오더라도, 무조건 올림 * Ceiling function (천장 함수)	* 어떤 숫자가 오더라도, 무조건 내림 * Floor function (바닥 함수)
The least integer greater than or equal to a number x is represented as $\lceil x \rceil$	The greatest integer less than or equal to a number x is represented as $\lfloor x \rfloor$
Exercise 3 $\lceil 2.1 \rceil = $ *round up*	**Exercise 6** $\lfloor 2.1 \rfloor = $ *round down*
Exercise 4 $\lceil -2.1 \rceil = $ *round up*	**Exercise 7** $\lfloor -2.1 \rfloor = $ *round down*
Exercise 5 $\lceil 2 \rceil = $ *round up*	**Exercise 8** $\lfloor 2 \rfloor = $ *round down*

Question 3

If $\lfloor x \rfloor$ is the greatest integer less than or equal to a number x, what is the value of $\lfloor -1.6 \rfloor + \lfloor 3.4 \rfloor + \lfloor 2.7 \rfloor$?

Answer:

6) Percent to Decimal

$$Percent = \frac{Part}{Whole} \times 100$$

A percent may be represented as **a decimal** by moving the decimal point in the percent **two places to the left.** To convert a percentage to a decimal, divide by 100.

Fraction	Decimal	Percent
1/2	0.5	50%
1/3	0.3333...	33.3%
1/4	0.25	25%
1/5	0.2	20%

A percent may be represented as a fraction in which the percent number is the numerator over a denominator of 100.

Percent Expression	
A is *x* percent of (or greater than) b	$\dfrac{a}{b} = \dfrac{x}{100}$

Exercise 9

330 is what percent of 11?

Answer:

2. 지수 (Exponents)

1) 지수 법칙

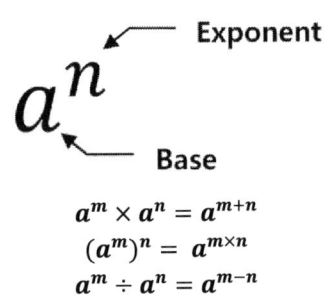

$$a^m \times a^n = a^{m+n}$$
$$(a^m)^n = a^{m \times n}$$
$$a^m \div a^n = a^{m-n}$$

Question 4

What is the smallest integer n for which $25^n > 5^{12}$?

Answer:

---

2) 지수 확장 법칙

Exponent (지수)가 정수 (음의 정수)로 확장 (a≠ 0)	$a^{-m} = \dfrac{1}{a^m}$

Question 5

If $m^{-1} = -\frac{1}{3}$, then m^{-2} is equal to

Answer:

3. 제곱근 (square roots)

1) 제곱근 개념

어떤 수 $x^2 = a$ 가 될 때	→ x 를 a 의 제곱근
• Example: $x^2 = 3$	• $x = \pm\sqrt{3}$
어떤 수 $x^n = a$ 가 될 때	→ x 를 a 의 n 제곱근

2) 제곱근 공식

$\sqrt{a} \times \sqrt{b} = \sqrt{ab}$	$\sqrt[n]{a} \times \sqrt[n]{b} = \sqrt[n]{ab}$
$\dfrac{\sqrt{a}}{\sqrt{b}} = \sqrt{\dfrac{a}{b}} \qquad \dfrac{\sqrt[n]{a}}{\sqrt[n]{b}} = \sqrt[n]{\dfrac{a}{b}}$	$\sqrt[n]{\sqrt[m]{a}} = \sqrt[nm]{a}$

3) 제곱근과 절대값

• $\sqrt{x^2} = |x|$ (출제) $\left(\sqrt{x}\right)^2 = x$	1) when $x \leqq 0$, $\sqrt{x^2} = -x$, 2) when $x \geqq 0$, $\sqrt{x^2} = x$,

---

Question 6

If $\sqrt{(x+4)^2} = 3$, which of the following could be the value of x - 4?

Answer:

---

4) 제곱근과 지수확장

Exponent (지수)가 유리수로 확장 (base > 0)		
▪ $x^{\frac{1}{n}} = \sqrt[n]{x}$ (x > 0)		▪ $x^{\frac{m}{n}} = \sqrt[n]{x^m}$
$x^{\frac{1}{2}} = \sqrt{x}$	$x^{\frac{1}{3}} = \sqrt[3]{x}$	$x^{\frac{7}{3}} = \sqrt[3]{x^7}$

Question 7

If $x > 0$, $x^2 = 2^{64}$, and $x^x = 2^y$, what is the value of y ?

Answer:

---

4. Ratio & Proportion

1) Ratio 출제 포인트

The ratio of the number **a** to the number **b** (b≠ 0)	a: b or $\frac{a}{b}$

2) Three Numbers Ratio 출세 포인트

Ratio (3 Factors) 접근방법: To calculate a ratio of 3 numbers

- Step 1: Find the total number of parts in the ratio by adding the numbers in the ratio together.
- Step 2: Find the value of each part in the ratio by dividing the given amount by the total number of parts.

- Step 3: Multiply the original ratio by the value of each part.

Exercise 10

Share $48 in the ratio 3:1:2.

Answer:

Question 8

The initial ratio of three variables x,y, and z is 3:24:100. Values of x,y and z are changed such that the ratio of x to z is doubled while the ratio of y to z is halved. If the new value of x is 24, what is the new value of y?

Answer:

3) Proportion 표현

If a : b = c : d, then a, b, c, d are said to be in proportion		
• A:B = C: D	A:B = C: D $\leftrightarrow \frac{A}{B} = \frac{C}{D}$	• A:B = C: D $\leftrightarrow$ AD = BC

Exercise 11

In a certain graph, 1 cm represents 12 km of the actual distance. If the distance between point A and point B is 96 km, what is their distance on map?

Answer:

Exercise 1	$\underline{7}651.4 \Rightarrow 7,700$
Exercise 2	$0.43\underline{2}48 \Rightarrow 0.432$
Exercise 3	$[2.1] = 3$
Exercise 4	$[-2.1] = -2$
Exercise 5	$[2] = 2$
Exercise 6	$[2.1] = 2$
Exercise 7	$[-2.1] = -3$
Exercise 8	$[2] = 2$
Exercise 9	1) $x = \frac{330}{11} \dashrightarrow x = 30$ 2) Decimal 을 percent 전환: 오른쪽으로 두 자리 옮기기: $30 \dashrightarrow 3,000$ percent 정답: 3,000 percent
Exercise 10	$3x + x + 2x = 48 \Rightarrow 6x = 48 \Rightarrow x = 8 \Rightarrow 24: 8: 16$
Exercise 11	$1: 12 = x : 96 \dashrightarrow x = 8$

Question 1	the units digit: 0
Question 2	E
Question 3	세 수의 합: -2 + 3 + 2 = 3
Question 4	최소 정수 = 7
Question 5	$m^{-2} = \frac{1}{m^2} = \frac{1}{9}$
Question 6	$x - 4 = -5, -11$
Question 7	$y = 2^{37}$
Question 8	$x: y : z = 24: 48: 400$

PART II
Data Insights(DI)

Data Insights(DI)

Chapter I.
DI Introduction

1. DI Overview

1) DI 시험 정보

Data Insights	
Questions	20 questions
Time	45 minutes
Type of Question	Data Sufficiency
	Multi-Source Reasoning
	Table Analysis
	Graphics Interpretation
	Two-Part Analysis

2) DI Exam Structure

각 section 에서 출제되는 문제수는 문제 유형에 따라 달라질 수 있습니다.

Type 1		Type 2	
Table analysis	2	Table analysis	2
Graphics interpretation	3	Graphics interpretation	3
Two-part analysis	5	Two-part analysis	4
Multi-source reasoning	3	Multi-source reasoning	6
Data sufficiency	7	Data sufficiency	5
Total	**20**	**Total**	**20**

2. Data Sufficiency 시험 정보

1) GMAT Exam 시험 정보

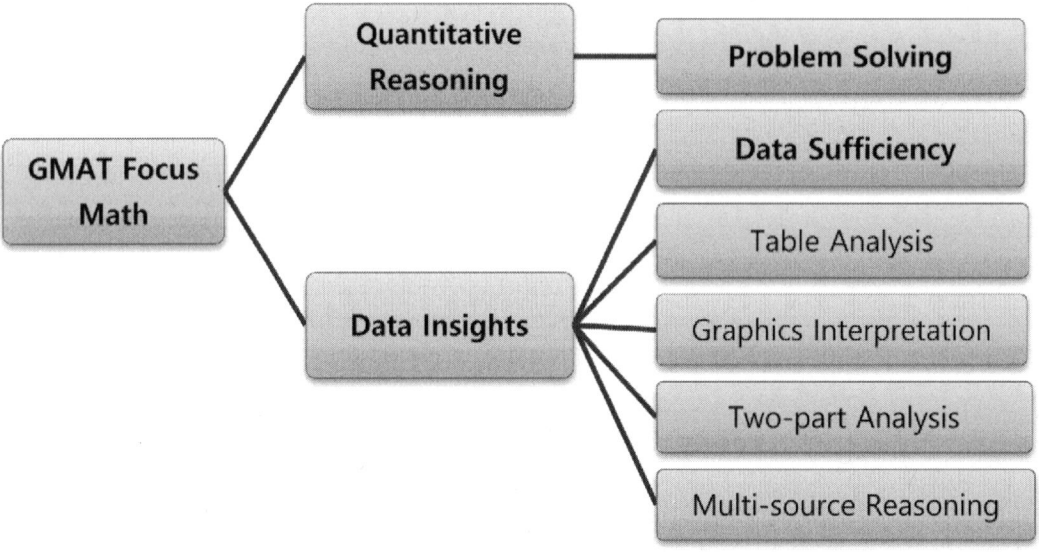

2) Old GMAT & GMT Focus 변동 사항

Old GMAT	• Old GMAT Math 문제유형 = problem solving + Data Sufficiency • **시험 범위**: problem solving and Data Sufficiency almost 동일
GMAT Focus **(new test)**	• GMAT Focus 시험에서는 data sufficiency 가 ⇒ Data Insights 이동 • Data sufficiency 현 소속: Data Insights 속함. • Data Sufficiency 시험 범위: Quantitative Reasoning 거의 동일

3) Data Sufficiency 정보

Directions

This data sufficiency problem consists of a question and two statements, labeled (1) and (2), in which certain data are given. You have to decide whether the data given in the statements are sufficient for answering the question. Using the data given in the statements, plus your knowledge of mathematics and everyday facts (such as the number of days in July or the meaning of the word counterclockwise), you must indicate whether:

- Statement (1) ALONE is sufficient, but statement (2) alone is not sufficient to answer the question asked.
- Statement (2) ALONE is sufficient, but statement (1) alone is not sufficient to answer the question asked.
- BOTH statements (1) and (2) TOGETHER are sufficient to answer the question asked, but NEITHER statement ALONE is sufficient to answer the question asked.
- EACH statement ALONE is sufficient to answer the question asked.
- Statements (1) and (2) TOGETHER are NOT sufficient to answer the question asked, and additional data specific to the problem are needed.

4) Data Sufficiency – sample question

If a real estate agent received a commission of 6 percent of the selling price of a certain house, what was the selling price of the house?
(1) The selling price minus the real estate agent's commission was $84,600.
(2) The selling price was 250 percent of the original purchase price of $36,000.

(A) Statement (1) ALONE is sufficient, but statement (2) alone is not sufficient.
(B) Statement (2) ALONE is sufficient, but statement (1) alone is not sufficient.
(C) BOTH statements TOGETHER are sufficient, but NEITHER statement ALONE is sufficient.

(D) EACH statement ALONE is sufficient.

(E) Statements (1) and (2) TOGETHER are NOT sufficient.

Answer: (D)

5) Data Sufficiency 문제 유형

Data Sufficiency	
■　부등식 문제	■　방정식 문제
문제에 대해 YES, NO 로 답하는 문제	x 의 값은 오직 1 개 (uniqueness)
1. x > 0 인가? (1) x = -1 (2) x = 1	1. $x = ?$ (1) $x^3 - x^2 - 6x = 0$ (2) $x = -x$
2. x > 0 인가? (1) x = ± 1 (2) x = -1, -2, -3	2. $x = ?$ (1) x = -1 (2) x = ± 1

6) Data Sufficiency – C-Trap 유형

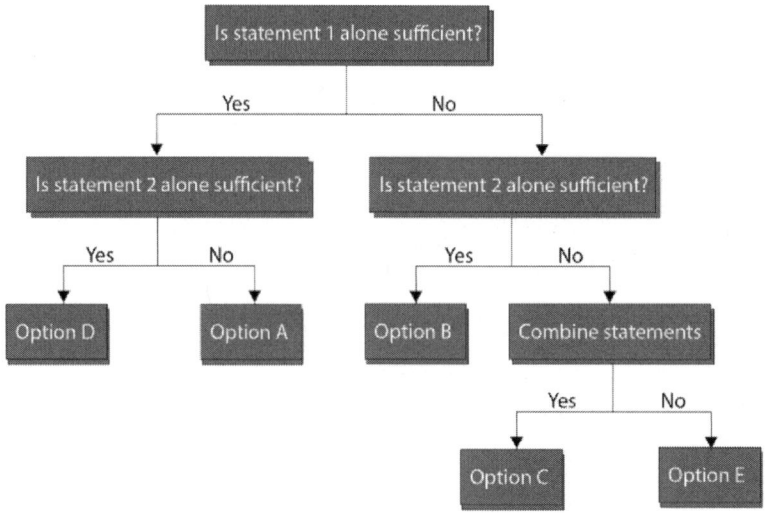

3. Table Analysis 문제 유형

1) Table Analysis 기본 정보

문항수	2~3 문제 출제
난이도	Data Insights 문제 중에서 가장 Easy level 문제가 출제
문제 유형	주로 table 의 data 분석, 추론 문제 중심으로 출제

2) Table Analysis Sample Question

This table displays data on Brazilian agricultural products in 2009.

Commodity	Production, world share(%)	Production, world rank	Exports, world share (%)	Exports, world rank
Beef	16	2	22	1
Chickens	15	3	38	1
Coffee	40	1	32	1
Corn	8	4	10	2
Cotton	5	5	10	4
Orange juice	56	1	82	1
Pork	4	4	12	4
Soybeans	27	2	40	2
Sugar	21	1	44	1

For each of the following statements, select *Yes* if the statement can be shown to be true based on the information in the table. Otherwise select *No*.

○ Yes ○ No No individual country produces more than one-fourth of the world's sugar.

○ Yes ○ No There are countries that export a greater percent of their coffee crops than does Brazil.

○ Yes ○ No Of the commodities in the table for which Brazil ranks first in world exports, Brazil produces more than 20% of the world's supply.

○ Yes ○ No If Brazil produces more than 20% of the world's supply of a commodity, it must be the world's top exporter of that commodity.

4. Graphics Interpretation 문제 유형

1) Graphics Interpretation 기본 정보

문항수	3 ~ 4 문제 출제
난이도	Data Insights 문제 중에서 Easy and Medium level 문제 출제
문제 유형	Chart types 에 따라서 문제 유형이 조금씩 달라짐.

2) Graphics Interpretation Sample Question

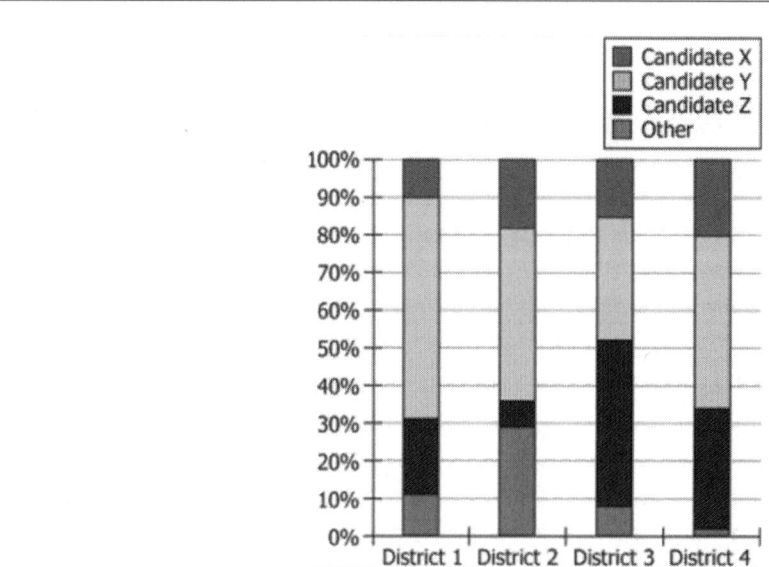

For each of four voting districts (Districts 1 through 4), the graph shows the percent of the voters in that district who voted for each of the three major candidates (Candidates X, Y, and Z) for mayor of a certain town, and the percent who voted for a candidate other than these three.

Select from the drop-down menus the options that create the most accurate statement based on the information provided.

Voters in District 4 were more than three times as likely as voters in District **Select One: (1), (2), (3)** to have voted for Candidate **Select One: (X), (Y), (Z).**

5. Two-part Analysis 문제 유형

1) Two-part Analysis 기본 정보

문항수	4 ~ 6 문제 출제
난이도	Data Insights 문제 중에서 the most difficult level 문제 출제
문제 유형	• Math-based questions • Verbal-based questions • Logic-based questions

2) Two-part Analysis Sample Question

Ethics board member: All actions that are permissible under the code of ethics are also legal in all of the jurisdictions in which our company operates. Furthermore, regardless of whether it has been determined if an action is legal, it is always permissible to ask the ethics board to review the action for conformity to the code of ethics.

Statements: Without exception, an action is permissible under the code of ethics ___1___ it is legal in all of the jurisdictions in which the company operates. Furthermore, one is permitted to ask the ethics board to review an action for conformity to the code of ethics ___2___ the legality of the action has been established.

Select for *1* and for *2* the two different options that complete the statements so that they most accurately paraphrase the Ethics board member's assertions. Make only two selections, one in each column.

1	2	
○	○	if
○	○	only if
○	○	unless
○	○	whether or not
○	○	or

6. Multi-source Reasoning 문제 유형

1) Multi-source Reasoning 기본 정보

문항수	3 ~ 6 문제 출제
난이도	Data Insights 문제 중에서 Easy and Medium 문제 출제
문제 유형	• **Two values 선택** • **Multiple choice**

2) Multi-source Reasoning Sample Question

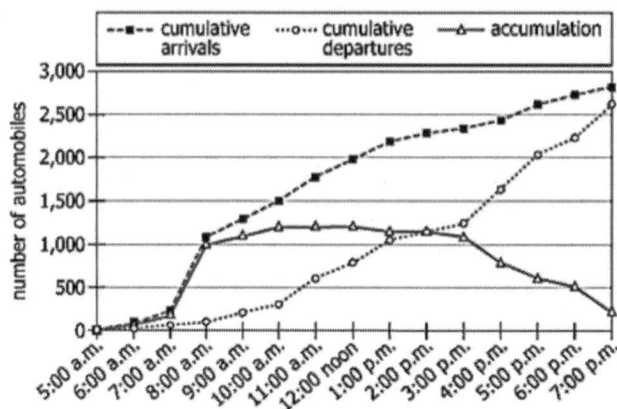

Parking Study   Second   Third

City X conducted a one-day study of accumulation patterns in a city-owned parking garage that contains a total of 1,200 parking spaces. The graph summarizes the cumulative arrivals (number of automobiles that had arrived at the garage), cumulative departures (number of automobiles that had departed the garage), and accumulation (number of automobiles occupying the garage) at one-hour intervals from 5:00 a.m. to 7:00 p.m. on the day of the study.

Parking Garage Accumulation Patterns

Each of the following options describes a condition that occurred at least once between 5:00 a.m. and 7:00 p.m. on the day of the parking study. For each option, select *Before 1:00 p.m.* if the first such occurrence was before 1:00 p.m. Otherwise, select *1:00 p.m. or later*.

○ Before 1:00 p.m.	○ 1:00 p.m. or later	Cumulative arrivals were greater than accumulation.
○ Before 1:00 p.m.	○ 1:00 p.m. or later	Cumulative arrivals were greater than 2 times cumulative departures.
○ Before 1:00 p.m.	○ 1:00 p.m. or later	Cumulative departures were greater than accumulation.

Chapter II.
Data Set Introduction

1. Data Types 정보

A data set is an organized collection of data about a specific topic.

Data Types	
Quantitative Data	**Qualitative Data**
⬇	⬇
• Numbers	• Nominal data: Name of people, nationalities
• Logarithmic data (로그 스케일)	• Ordinal data: Education level, income level
• Ratio data	• Binary data: Yes and No, True and False

2. Data Display 정보

Data 보여주는 방식에 따라서 구분

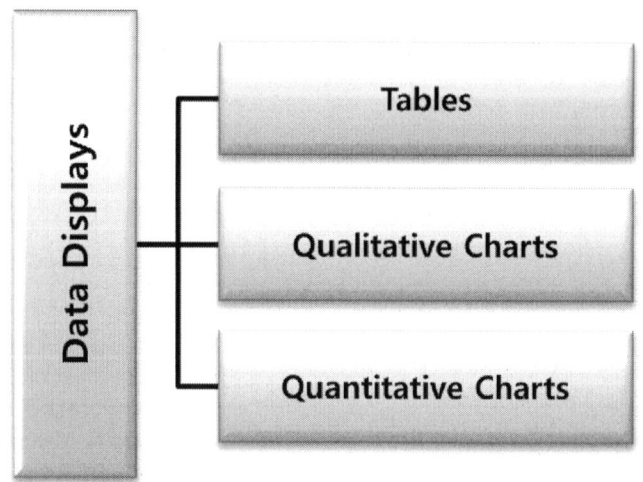

3. Table 정보

Village Shoppe	Revenue	Expense	Profit
Mapleton branch			
January-June	125000	40000	85000
April-December	90000	35000	55000
Elmville branch			
January-June	85000	30000	55000
April-December	115000	25000	90000
Annual grand totals	**415000**	**130000**	**285000**

4. Qualitative Charts 정보

1) Network Diagram

- **정의: lines connecting small circles or other shapes**
- **출제포인트: 문제의 주어진 조건(아래 그림에서는 화살표 or double-headed arrows) 중심으로 문제 풀이**

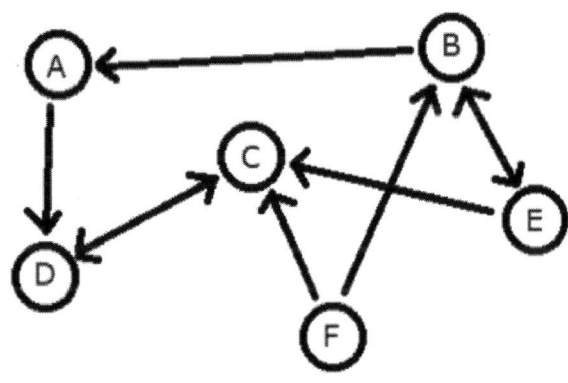

2) Tree Diagram

- 정의: **organizational structures, ancestral relationships, or conditional probabilities**
- 출제포인트: **관계 중심으로 경우의 수 or 확률 문제 풀이**

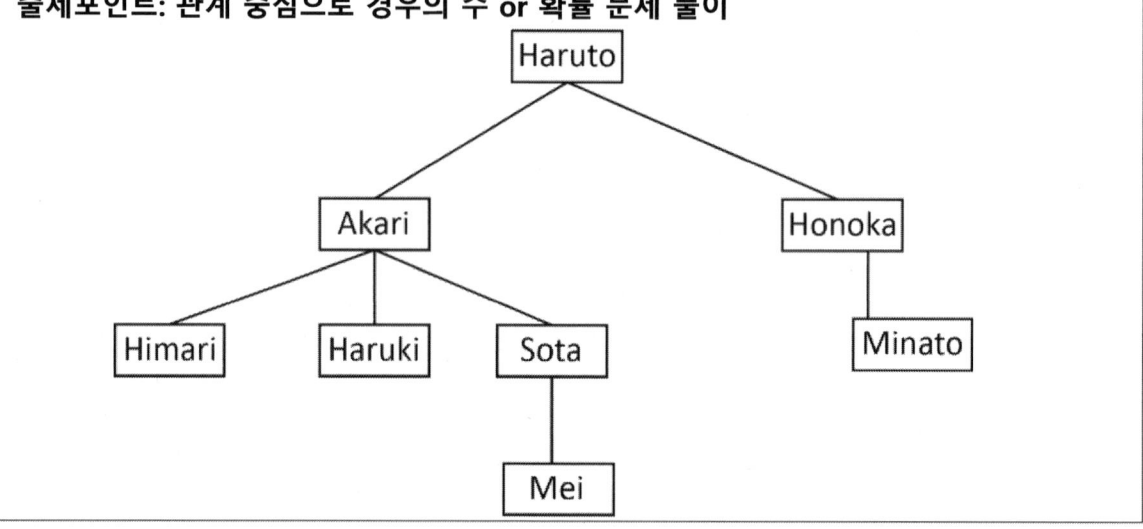

3) Flowchart 유형

- 정의: **steps in a process 보여줌.**
- 출제포인트: **probability or 경우의 수 문제가 등장할 가능성 높음**

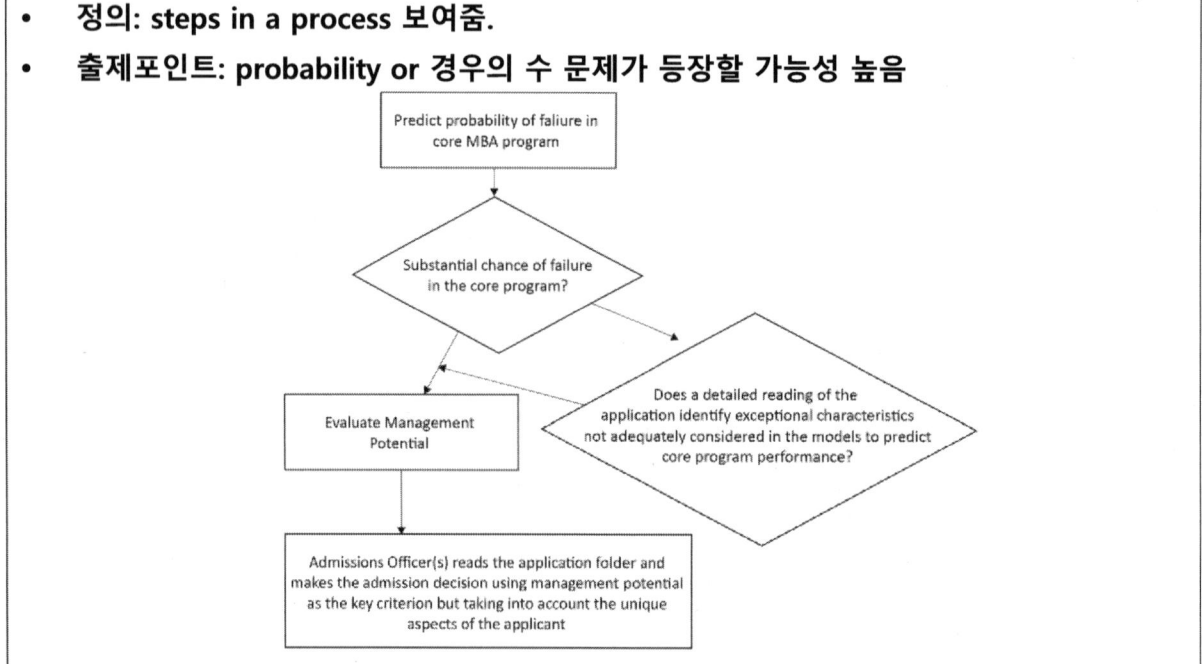

5. Quantitative Charts 정보

1) Pie Chart 유형

- **개념:** A *pie chart* has a circle divided into sections like pie slices. The sections make up the whole circle without overlapping.
- **포인트:** 1) pie chart 의 total value = 100%, 2) Sum of all the data = 360 도

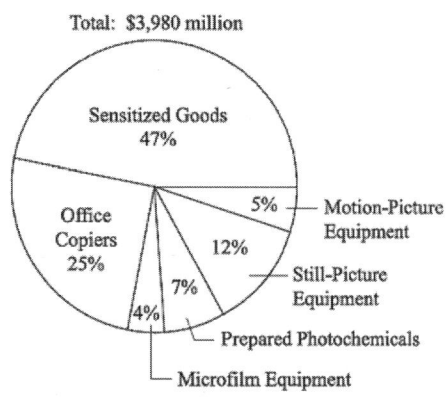

| Photochemicals: 7% | • 360×0.07 = 25 degrees |
| | • **$3,980 ×0.07 = 278.6 million** |

2) Bar Chart 유형

- **개념:** rectangular bars are used to represent the categories of the data
- **포인트: Bar char 는 each bar = different category 특징이라서 비교 문제가 자주 등장**

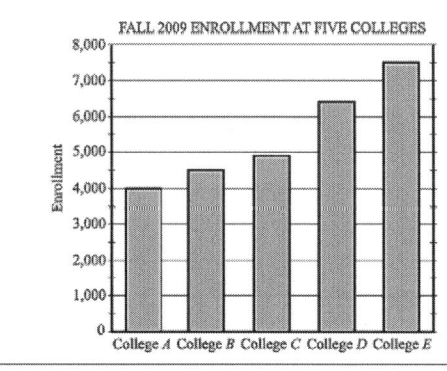
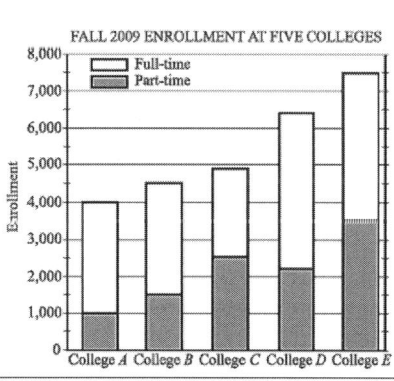

3) Histogram 유형

- **개념**: the graphical representation of numerical data.
- **포인트**: Histogram is useful for identifying the shape of a <u>distribution of data</u>. 따라서 통계 관련 문제로 출제

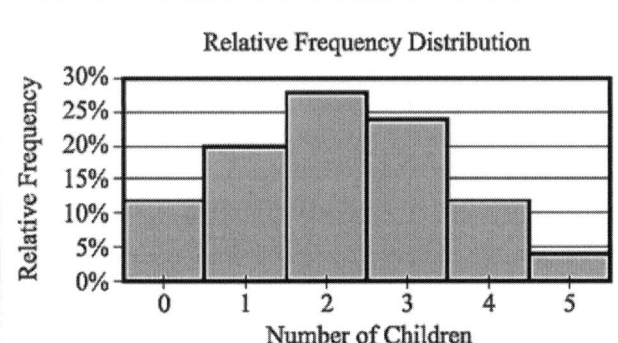

4) Line Charts 유형

- **개념**: It shows how the values of one or more quantitative variables change over time - trends and correlations
- 출제포인트: 1) Slope 비교 문제, 2) Percent change 비교 문제

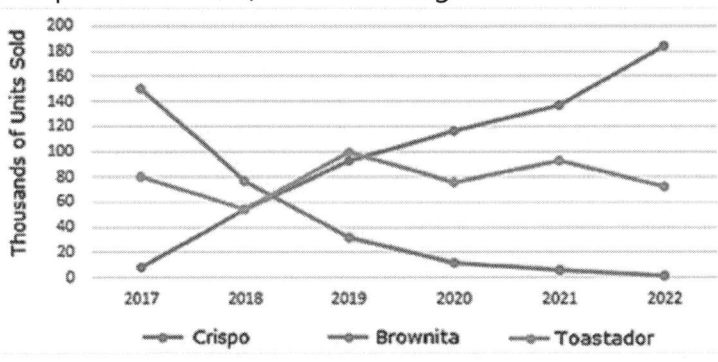

5) Scatterplot 유형

- **개념**: to observe relationships between two numeric variables.
- **포인트**: overall trend in the data 판단 문제 – 1) positive corelated, or 2) negative corelated.

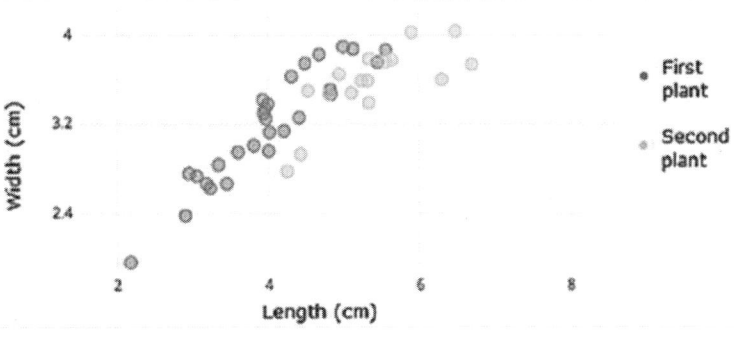

Chapter III.
논리와 명제

	논리와 명제 관련 문제를 풀 때 가장 중요한 것?
	"개념 이해 후 기출 문제에서 어떻게 구현되는지 확인하자"
1	▪ 충분 조건, 필요 조건 이해 필수
2	▪ 명제 역, 대우, 삼단논법 개념
3	▪ 기출 명제 표현 이해 및 암기 필수

1. 명제 (proposition)

1) 명제 정의

True or False 를 판단할 수 있는 문장 or 조건

2) 명제 표현

조건 p, q 에 대하여	• p 이면 q 이다 • If p, then q.	p (가정) → q (결론)

3) 참인 명제 정의

참인 명제 (true): p ⇒ q	집합 표현: P ⊂ Q 

4) 충분 조건 & 필요 조건

P: If A is 충주 시민, Q: then A is 대한민국 국민이다.	
충분 조건	필요 조건
• P 는 Q 가 되기 위한 충분조건 (sufficient conditions) • P is sufficient for Q = sufficient conditions • 충분 조건 표현: 명제 표현에서 확인	• Q 는 P 가 되기 위한 필요조건 (necessary conditions)Q is necessary for P = necessary conditions • 필요 조건 표현: 명제 표현에서 확인

5) 필요충분 조건 정의

• 필요충분 조건: P = Q	• 영어표현: P is **if and only if** Q.
예문: A number n is even <u>if and only if</u> there exists an integer k such that n = 2k.	

6) 명제 역 (conversion)

• **명제**: 충주 시민 (p), then 대한민국 국민 (q)	If P, then Q ⇒ True
• **명제 역**: If 대한민국 국민이면(q), then 충주시민(p).	If Q, then P ⇒ False
• 명제의 역 (the converse of the statement) ⇒ True or False 가능	

7) 명제 대우 (contraposition)

명제: 충주 시민 (p), then 대한민국 국민 (q)	If P, then Q ⇒ True
명제 대우: 대한민국 국민이 아니면(~Q), 충주시민이 아니다(~P)	If not Q, then not P ⇒ True
• 명제의 대우 (the converse of the statement) ⇒ **Always True**	

▪ **GMAT 시험 출제 구문**: No (not) X unless Y (unless = if not)
▪ 변경 구문: If not Y, then no X ⇒ 대우: If X, then Y.

Exercise 1:
I <u>can't</u> go to the beach <u>unless</u> I find my sunscreen.
Answer:

8) 삼단논법 (syllogism)

정의: **If the following two statements are true, then we can derive a third true statement.**

• 대전제 (major premise)	P ⇒ Q (True)
• 소전제 (minor premise)	Q ⇒ R (True)
• 결론 (conclusion) inference	P ⇒ R (True)

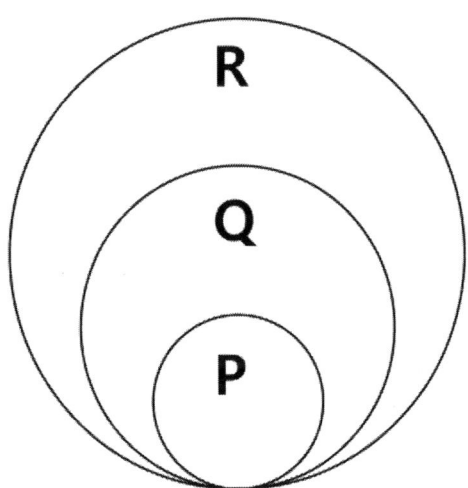

Exercise 2

If the following statements are true, use the Law of Syllogism to derive a new true statement.

1) If it snows today, then I will wear my gloves.

2) If I wear my gloves, my fingers will get itchy.

Answer:

(1) 결론 찾기 명제 유형

(1) All A is B (2) All A is C	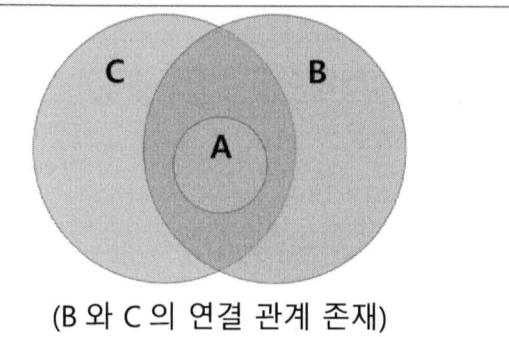
결론 Inference: • some B is C, or some C is B	(B와 C의 연결 관계 존재)

(1) All A is B (2) Some A is C (=some C is A)	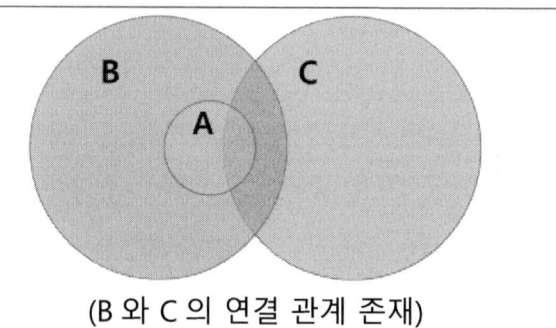
결론 Inference: • some B is C, or or some C is B	(B와 C의 연결 관계 존재)

(2) 전제 찾기 명제 유형

(1) All A is B **(2) All C is B**	주어진 조건으로 결론을 도출할 수 없는 문제는 결론이 주어진 문제 유형으로 전제를 추론하는 관점으로 문제를 해결
전제 Inference: • All C is A.	

2. 명제 (proposition) 표현

1) 명제 표현 (conditional statements)

충분조건: X is sufficient for Y (sufficient conditions)= X ⊂ Y	필요조건: X is necessary for X (necessary conditions) = X ⊂ Y

	Statements	Explanation
Exercise 3	People can feel secure <u>if</u> they are governed by laws that are not vague.	• Y if X If 절 후치 ⇒ NO 의미변화 • **Revised**:
Exercise 4	<u>Every</u> student who walks to school goes home for lunch.	• Every (all)) X is Y ⇒ X ⊂ Y • **Revised**:
Exercise 5	<u>Any</u> moon, by definition, orbits a planet	• Any X is Y ⇒ X ⊂ Y • **Revised**:
Exercise 6	I wear a hat <u>only if</u> it's sunny.	• Only if : A 되기 위한 필요조건 • X only if Y (출제 빈도 최상)= = If X, then Y. • **Revised**:
Exercise 7	<u>Only</u> sunny days will get me to wear a hat.	• Only Y is X ⇒ X ⊂ Y • **Revised**:
Exercise 8	Ann would <u>not</u> quit <u>unless</u> she were offered a fellowship.	• No (or not) X unless Y. If not Y, then no X ⇒ 명제 대우: If X, then Y. • **Revised**:

| Exercise 9 | Without self-understanding, it is impossible to understand others. | • Without Y, there is no X ⇒ Y is necessary for X
• **Revised:** |

2) 추가 명제 표현 (conditional statements)

	Statements	Explanation
Exercise 10	Y happens whenever or wherever X happens	• **X 충분** • **X Y**
Exercise 11	In order for X to be true, Y must be true	• **X 충분** • **X Y**
Exercise 12	X depends on Y	• **Y 필요** • **X Y**

Exercise 1	If no sunscreen, then no beach ⇒ 대우: If beach, then sunscreen.
Exercise 2	If it snows today (P), my fingers will get itchy (R).
Exercise 3	If not vague laws, then feel secure
Exercise 4	If walk to school, then go home for lunch
Exercise 5	moon ⇒ orbit planet
Exercise 6	A: Hat ⇒ sunny
Exercise 7	A: Hat ⇒ sunny
Exercise 8	A: If Ann quit, then Ann was offered a fellowship.
Exercise 9	A: understand others ⇒ self-understanding
Exercise 10	X ⊂ Y
Exercise 11	X ⊂ Y
Exercise 12	X ⊂ Y

Chapter IV.

Table Analysis

	Table Analysis 문제를 풀 때 가장 중요한 것?
	"주어진 *table* 의 데이터를 어떤 식으로 활용할 지 판단하는 것이다"
1	▪ Data 찾기 + 판단
2	▪ Data 찾기 + 활용 + 수학 계산 + 판단
3	▪ Data 찾기 + Inference + 판단

1. Table Analysis Overview

1) Table Analysis 문제 구성

This table displays data on Brazilian agricultural products in 2009.

Commodity	Production, world share(%)	Production, world rank	Exports, world share (%)	Exports, world rank
Beef	16	2	22	1
Chickens	15	3	38	1
Coffee	40	1	32	1
Corn	8	4	10	2
Cotton	5	5	10	4
Orange juice	56	1	82	1
Pork	4	4	12	4
Soybeans	27	2	40	2
Sugar	21	1	44	1

For each of the following statements, select *Yes* if the statement can be shown to be true based on the Information In the table. Otherwise select *No*.

○ Yes   ○ No   No individual country produces more than one-fourth of the world's sugar.

○ Yes   ○ No   If Brazil produces less than 20% of the world's supply of any commodity listed in the table, Brazil is not the world's top exporter of that commodity.

○ Yes   ○ No   Of the commodities in the table for which Brazil ranks first In world exports, Brazil produces more than 20% of the world's supply.

Table Analysis 구성	• Table (sortable table)	1) Quantilative data	2)Qualitative data
	• Question (문제의 condition 제공)	1) Yes or No 선택형	2)binary (이진) data 선택
	• Statements	• Each statement ⇒ table 자료 근거 ⇒ 문제에서 요구하는 선택하면 끝!	

2) Table Analysis 문제 접근

Step 1: 문제 유형 파악	**Yes/No 유형** • select *Yes* if the statement is true based on the information provided; otherwise select *No*. **Other binary data (이진 데이터) 유형: 주어진 two options 정체를 알고 문제를 풀기** • select *Positively correlated* if the data given for those two age ranges are positively correlated. Otherwise, select *Not positively correlated*.
Step 2: statements 핵심 파악	**Careful Reading 필요한 타임** • statements 원하는 핵심 내용을 찾는 것이 가장 중요함 • **빈출 내용**: 최대값 찾기, 최소값 찾기, 두 집합의 대소 관계 판단, 통계 표현, 그 외 수 많은 algebraic expressions 등장 • for example: Q: $A > B$?
Step 3: Tables – Data 확인	**문제 풀이에서 가장 중요한 단계** 테이블에서 문제에서 요구하는 내용을 바로 찾을 수도 있고, 수학적 계산이 필요할 수도 있고, 추론이 필요할 수도 있음. • Type 1: table data 로 **data 찾기** (난이도 하) • Type 2: table **data 찾기 + 활용 + 수학** (난이도 중) • Type 3: table **data 찾기** + inference (난이도 상)
Step 4: 최종 결정	• **주어진 statements 모두 correct ⇒ 포인트 주어짐.**

2. Table Analysis – Sample Question 1

1) Question

Date	Type	Amount (€)	Balance (€)
1-Mar	withdrawal	-84.85	2,946.03
3-Mar	deposit	815.00	3,761.03
3-Mar	withdrawal	-87.82	3,673.21
6-Mar	draft	-235.12	3,438.09
7-Mar	bank fee	-20.00	3,418.09
7-Mar	withdrawal	-321.85	3,096.24
10-Mar	deposit	702.10	3,798.34

The table shows all of the transactions for a small business's checking account from March 1 to March 10 of a certain year. The transactions are classified as being one of four mutually exclusive types—bank fee, deposit, draft (payout by check), or withdrawal. In each row, the balance shown is the account balance, in euros (€), immediately after the transaction occurred. The account balance did not change except during the transactions shown

For each of the following statements about this bank account during the period shown, select *Yes* if the statement accurately reflects the information provided. Otherwise, select *No*.

○ Yes ○ No On March 3, the account balance immediately prior to the first transaction of the day was less than that immediately after the last transaction of the day.

○ Yes ○ No The greatest account balance occurred on the day when the greatest deposit was made.

○ Yes ○ No The lowest account balance occurred on the same day as the withdrawal that decreased the account balance by the least amount.

2) 해설

Q 1) On March 3, the account balance immediately prior to the first transaction of the day was less than that immediately after the last transaction of the day.

Table data 근거:

- the account balance immediately prior to the first transaction of the day = 2,946 (Mar.1 자료)

- that immediately after the last transaction of the day = 3673 (Mar.3 마지막 자료) 2,946 < 3673 ⇒ Yes

---

Q 2) The greatest account balance occurred on the day when the greatest deposit was made.

- The greatest account balance = March 10

- the greatest deposit was made = March 3

- 최종적으로 March 10 ≠ March 3 ⇒ No

Q 3) The lowest account balance occurred on the same day as the withdrawal that decreased the account balance by the least amount.

- lowest account balance (€2,946.03) = March 1

- Withdrawal 발생은 3 회: 84.85 (1-Mar), 235,12(6-Mar), 321.85 (7-Mar)

- 그 중 least amount = Mar.1

- 따라서 March 1 = Mar.1 ⇒ Yes

3. Table Analysis – Sample Question 2

1) Question

For each of 5 different materials commonly used in residential roofing applications, the table lists the estimated longevity, in years, and gives ratings in each of 5 different categories.

Roofing material	Longevity (years)	Fire resistance	Energy savings	Maintenance	Initial cost	long-term cost
Asphalt (premium)	50	average	excellent	medium	average	low
Asphalt (standard)	15	average	poor	poor	low	high
Metal	100	excellent	excellent	excellent	high	very low
Slate	100	excellent	poor	medium	very high	very low
Wood shake	15	poor	poor	poor	very high	high

For each of the following statements, select *Yes* if that statement accurately reflects the information provided. Otherwise, select *No*.

○ Yes   ○ No   Each of the materials rated high for long-term cost also has the least longevity.

○ Yes   ○ No   Each of the materials rated excellent for energy savings is also rated excellent for maintenance.

○ Yes   ○ No   Each of the materials rated very high for initial cost is also rated excellent for fire resistance.

2) 해설

Q 1: Each of the materials rated high for long-term cost also has the least longevity.

- each = all 의미
- high for long-term cost: asphalt (standard) and wood shake
- asphalt (standard) and wood shake 의 longevity = 15 ⋯→ the least
- 따라서 Yes 판단 가능

Q 2: Each of the materials rated excellent for energy savings is also rated excellent for maintenance.

- Excellent energy saving: asphalt (premium) and Metal
- asphalt (premium)의 maintenance = medium ⋯→ not excellent
- 따라서 NO 판단 가능

Q 3: Each of the materials rated very high for initial cost is also rated excellent for fire resistance.

- Vert High for initial cost: slate and wood shake
- Wood shake 의 fire resistance = poor ⋯→ not excellent
- 따라서 NO 판단 가능

Chapter V.
Graphics Interpretation

Graphics Interpretation 문제를 풀 때 가장 중요한 것?		
"charts 유형에 따라서 요구하는 문제의 해심을		
파악해서 문제를 풀자"		
1	▪	**Quantitative charts**
2	▪	**Pictograph charts**
3	▪	**Qualitative charts**

1. Graphics Interpretation Overview

1) Graphics Interpretation 문제 구성

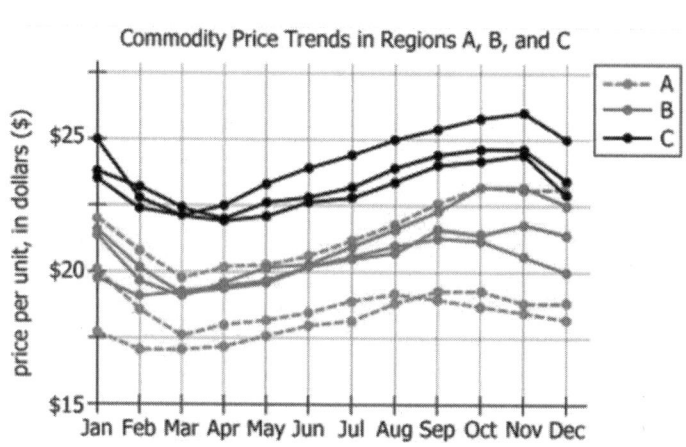

Text

Over the last three years, a certain commodity was regularly sold in Regions A, B, and C. For each of the three regions, the graph shows the trend within each year of the monthly average price per unit of the commodity.

Based on the information provided, **select from each drop-down menu** the option that creates the most accurate statement.

Question

On the assumption that the trends in the graph would continue, someone seeking to sell this commodity at the highest possible price would likely try to sell the commodity in Region **Select one**: (A), (B), (C), in either **Select one**: (February or March), (June or July), (October or November).

Graphics Interpretation 구성	• Text (차트 설명)	**Text: clarity the meaning of the graph**	
		• Text 많은 경우: charts 에 분명히 설명이 필요한 것이 있다는 증거이고, 이 부분에서 문제의 핵심 조건이 출제	
	• **Charts**	1) Quantitative charts (numbers 파악)	2) Qualitative charts (process or relationship 파악)
	• **Question**	**Two drop-down menu 문제**	
		• 정답은 주어진 options 중에서 the option that best completes the statement 선택	

2) Graphics Interpretation 차트 유형에 따른 접근

Quantitative charts	차트에 등장하는 numbers 중심 (가장 친숙한 형태의 챠트) • **출제 난이도**: Easy, Medium • **출제 빈도**: 상	
	• data 찾기 + 비교	• data 찾기 + 활용 + 수학
Pictograph charts (아래 그림) 	Representing the data using images or symbols (numbers 를 이미지로 준 챠트 형태) • **출제 난이도**: Medium, Hard • **출제 빈도**: 하	
	• Math 문제 출제	• sets, or probability
Qualitative charts (Diagram or flowcharts)	이 차트의 핵심은 주어진 elements 간의 relationship or 전체 process 흐름을 찾는 것 • **출제 난이도**: Hard • **출제 빈도**: 하	
	• 경우의 수	• probability 문제

3) Graphics Interpretation 문제 접근

Step 1: charts 유형 파악	Graphics Interpretation 문제가 등장하면 the first step 은 charts 유형을 판단하는 것 • Quantitative charts • Pictograph charts • Qualitative charts
Step 2: 문제 확인 Two Drop-down	이제는 문제 (statements)를 scanning 한 후 charts 에서 무엇을 찾을지를 판단하는 것 (careful reading 필요한 단계) 1) One statement 에 two drop-down questions 등장: 두 문제를 한 번에 or 동시에 풀 수 있음. 앞 뒤 순서는 상관없음. 2) Two statements 에 each drop-down question 등장: 다른 문제로 인식할 필요가 있음.
Step 3: 문제 풀이 Charts 확인	문제 풀이에서 가장 중요한 단계 (챠트 유형에 따라서 요구하는 문제의 스타일도 다양함) • data 찾기 + 비교 (난이도 하) • data 찾기 + 활용 + 수학 (난이도 중/상) • Math 문제 출제 (난이도 중/상) • 경우의 수 (난이도 상) • Relationship or process 파악 후 문제 풀이 (난이도 상)
Step 4: 최종 결정	• 정답은 the option that best completes the statement 선택

2. Graphics Interpretation Sample Question 1

1) Question

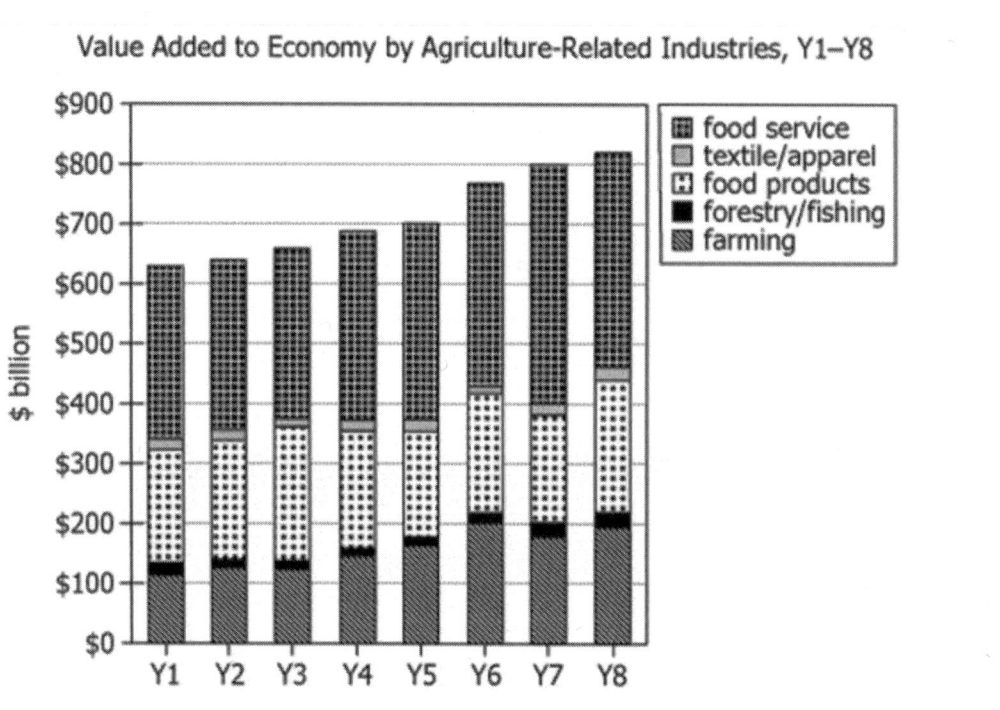

Value Added to Economy by Agriculture-Related Industries, Y1–Y8

An economic council evaluated the agriculture-related industries of a certain country's overall economy. The stacked-bar graph shows for each of eight consecutive years (Y1–Y8) the value added to the country's economy by each of five agriculture-related industries: food service, textile/apparel, food products, forestry/fishing, and farming.

From each drop-down menu, select the option that creates the most accurate statement according to the information provided.

For Y1 through Y8, the greatest of the yearly values added to the country's economy by a single agriculture-related industry was added by the **Select one**: (food service), (food product), (farming) industry in **Select one**: (Y6), (Y7), (Y8).

2) 해설

Question

For Y1 through Y8, the greatest of the yearly values added to the country's economy by a single agriculture-related industry was added by the **Select one**: (food service), (food product), (farming) industry in **Select one**: (Y6), (Y7), (Y8).

- **문제 유형: Quantitative charts + data 찾기 문제**
- **문제 포인트**: value 최대값 = the vertical bar 의 길이가 가장 큰 industry 찾기
- 정확한 numbers 로 대소관계를 파악할 필요는 없음. 그림의 size 에 근거해서 estimation 으로 충분히 답변 가능

해설(Explanation)

1) Food service bar 가 다른 industries 보가 확실히 longer
2) Among food service bars, Y7 의 food service = the longest

Answer: (food service), (Y7)

3. Graphics Interpretation Sample Question 2

1) Question

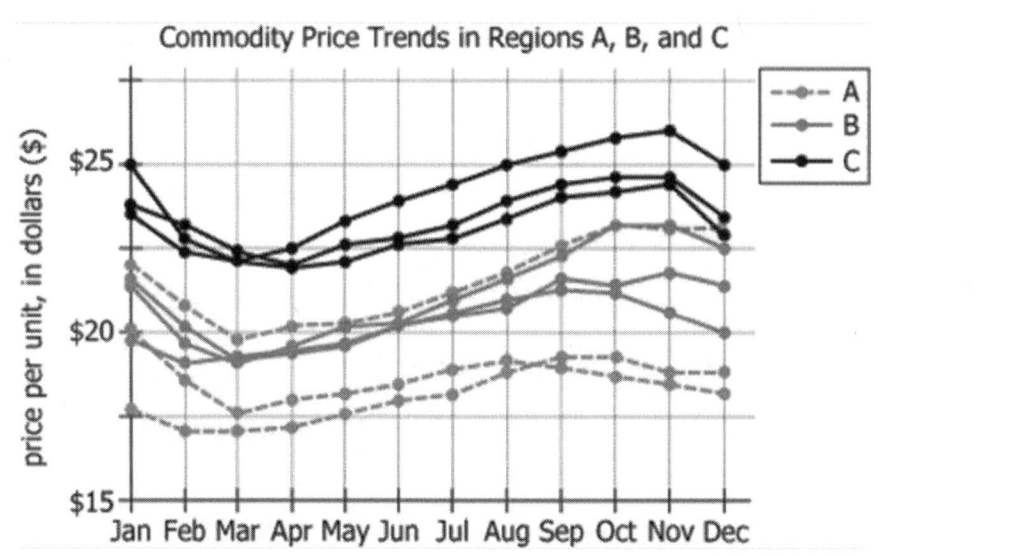

Over the last three years, a certain commodity was regularly sold in Regions A, B, and C. For each of the three regions, the graph shows the trend within each year of the monthly average price per unit of the commodity.

Based on the information provided, select from each drop-down menu the option that creates the most accurate statement.

On the assumption that the trends in the graph would continue, someone seeking to sell this commodity at the highest possible price would likely try to sell the commodity in Region **Select one: (A), (B), (C)**, in either **Select one: (February or March), (June or July), (October or November).**

2) 해설

Question On the assumption that the trends in the graph would continue, someone seeking to sell this commodity at the highest possible price would likely try to sell the commodity in Region **Select one:** (A), (B), (C) , in either **Select one**: (February or March), (June or July), (October or November).
<ul><li>**Quantitative charts (line charts) + data 찾기 문제**</li><li>**그래프**: the graph shows the trend within each year of the monthly average price per unit of the commodity</li><li>**문제 포인트**: A, B, or C 에서 average price 가 가장 높은 지역 = C</li><li>정확한 numbers 로 대소관계를 파악할 필요는 없음. 그래프에 근거해서 estimation 으로 충분히 답변 가능</li></ul>
해설(Explanation) 1) y 축 기준에서 가장 높은 지역은 C 2) Region C 에서 highest price = Nov.
<ul><li>**Answer: (C), (October or November)**</li></ul>

Chapter VI.
Two-part Analysis

	Two-part Analysis 문제를 풀 때 가장 중요한 것?	
	"문제 유형이 무엇인지 판단을 한 후, 각 유형에 최적화된 문제해결 능력을 발휘하는 것"	
1	▪ **Math-based questions**: Word problems or 다른 math 문제 풀이 방식과 거의 동일하게 문제 풀이	
2	▪ **Verbal-based questions**: CR 에서 사용하는 문제 풀이 방식과 거의 동일.	
3	▪ **Logic-based questions**: chapter 3 에서 학습한 명제와 논리의 이론을 십분 발휘	

1. Two-part Analysis Overview

1) Two-part Analysis 문제 구성

The Quasi JX is a new car model. Under ideal driving conditions, the Quasi JX's fuel economy is E kilometers per liter ($E\frac{km}{L}$) when its driving speed is constant at S kilometers per hour ($S\frac{km}{h}$).

In terms of the variables S and E, select the expression that represents the number of liters of fuel used in 1 hour of driving under ideal driving conditions at a constant speed S, and select the expression that represents the number of liters of fuel used in a 60 km drive under ideal driving conditions at a constant speed S. Make only two selections, one in each column.

Liters of fuel in 1 h	Liters of fuel in 60 km	
○	○	$\frac{S}{E}$
○	○	$\frac{E}{S}$
○	○	$\frac{60}{E}$
○	○	$\frac{60}{S}$
○	○	$\frac{S}{60}$
○	○	$\frac{E}{60}$

Two-part Analysis 구성	• Text (문제 설명)	• Written problem (No Table, No graphics) • Word problems 유형과 외관상 동일한 모습의 문제	
		1) Math 내용	2) Verbal 내용
	• Two Questions	• Make one choice. • Make another choice.	

2) Two-part Analysis 문제 유형에 따른 접근

Data insights 난이도 최상 난이도 문제 (고득점의 key!)

Math-based questions	특징: Solve complex math problems • Word problems 유사 문제 • **출제 난이도 중,상 & 출제 빈도 상**	
	Type 1: 경우의 수 & 조건	**Type 2:** 통계 활용 문제
Verbal-based questions	특징: CR 유형과 유사 문제 출제 • Analyze and evaluate arguments or statements • **출제 난이도 상 & 출제 빈도 하**	
	Type 1: Strengthen the argument	**Type 2:** Inference 가능 or 불가능 판단
Logic-based questions	특징: Apply logical reasoning skills to analyze arguments • Chapter 3(논리와 명제) 문제 다수 출제 • **출제 난이도 상 & 출제 빈도 하**	
	Type 1: Fill in the blanks	**Type 2:** Select an option

3) Two-part Analysis 문제 접근

Step 1: 문제 유형 파악	Two-part Analysis 문제가 등장하면 the first step 은 문제 유형을 판단하는 것 • Math-based questions • Verbal-based questions • Logic-based questions
Step 2: 문제 풀이	문제 유형에 따라서 문제 해결 스타일도 다름. • Math-based questions: Word problems or 다른 math 문제 풀이 방식과 거의 동일하게 문제 풀이 • Verbal-based questions: CR 에서 사용하는 문제 풀이 방식과 거의 동일. • Logic-based questions: chapter 3 에서 학습한 명제와 논리 이론을 십분 발휘
Step 3: 최종 결정	• 두 문제의 정답을 선택 • Make only two selections, one in each column.

2. Two-part Analysis Sample Question 1

1) Question

A corporation uses a model of diminishing returns to make predictions about the expected returns on research investment. For this model, in order to produce an x% increase in annual profits in subsequent years, the corporation must invest y% of annual profits into research, where $y = 2x^2$.

Select two different numbers that are jointly compatible with the information provided and could be the values for x and for y. Make only two selections, one in each column.

x	y	
○	○	1
○	○	3
○	○	5
○	○	20
○	○	50
○	○	80

2)해설

문제 유형	• Math 유형
문제 포인트	• Select two different numbers that are jointly compatible with the information provided and could be the values for x and for y. • $y = 2x^2$ 만족 시키는 여러 pairs 중에서 주어진 option 에서 (x, y) pair 찾기 문제
Solution	$y = 2x^2 \Rightarrow$ Option 에 있는 모든 x values 대입 | x	1	3	5	20	50	80
---	---	---	---	---	---	---
y	2	18	50	800	5,000	12,800	
Answer	**x = 5, y = 50**

3. Two-part Analysis Sample Question 2

1) Question

Four students from Mistville and four from Fogtown will attend school in New York City this year, and each group will rent an apartment.

Type A apartments are each 1,390 square feet, have 2 bedrooms, a 10-by-10-foot kitchen, and are 4 miles from the school. The price per square foot per month is $1.94.

Type B apartments are each 1,250 square feet, have 3 bedrooms, an 11-by-11-foot kitchen, and are 3 miles from the school. The rent is $2,250 per month.

Type C apartments are each 1,210 square feet, have 2 bedrooms, a 7-by-9-foot kitchen, and are 4.5 miles from the school. The rent is $2,190 per month.

The Mistville students choose a type C apartment and **the Fogtown students** choose a type A apartment.

Assume, for each group of students, that the group's choice of apartment type was based solely on an accurate assessment, using only the information above, of which apartment type met a particular criterion listed in the table. For each group, select that group's criterion. Make only two selections, one in each column.

Mistville students	Fogtown students	
O	O	Lowest rent
O	O	Largest kitchen (square footage)
O	O	Greatest number of bedrooms
O	O	Largest total square footage
O	O	Fewest miles from school
O	O	Lowest price per square foot

2)해설

문제 유형	• Verbal + Math 융합 유형
문제 포인트	• Mistville group: type C apartment • Fogtown group: type A apartment • Assume, for each group of students, that the group's choice of apartment type was based solely on an accurate assessment, using only the information above, of which apartment type met a particular criterion listed in the table. For each group, select that group's criterion. • Each group 선택 기준
Solution	Mistville group: type C apartment • type C apartment ⋯→ \$ 2,190 ⋯→ lowest rent • Type A rent per month = \$1.94× 1,390 = \$2,696 Fogtown group: type A apartment • 1,390 square feet = largest total square footage (length × width = area)
Answer	**Mistville**: lowest rent **Fogtown**: largest total square footage

Chapter VII.
Multi-source Reasoning

Multi-source Reasoning 문제를 풀 때 가장 중요한 것? *"일반 reading 접근과 다르게, data-oriented reading 을 통해서 문제를 해결하는 것"*	
1	▪ 일반 reading passage 의 핵심은 main point 를 파악한 후 details 이해를 통한 문제 풀이
2	▪ But, multi-source reasoning 의 중심은 text 가 아니라 Data! ▪ 즉 전체 tabs 에 등장하는 data 해석 및 추론을 통해서 문제 풀이 가능

1. Multi-source Reasoning Overview

1) Multi-source Reasoning 문제 구성

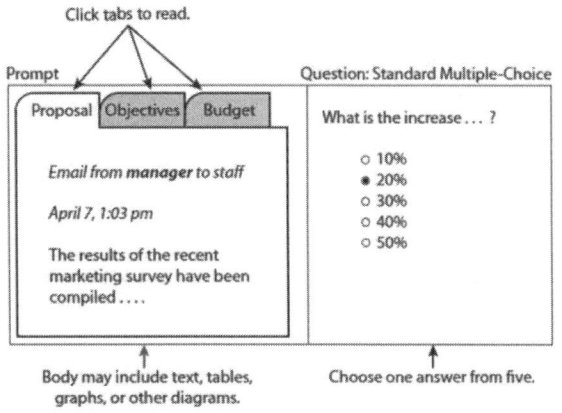

Multi-source Reasoning 구성	• **Tabs**	• 주로 Three Tabs 주어짐
		• 화면에는 one tab 의 내용만 보임, 따라서 다른 tabs 을 click 하면 보여지는 방식
		• 문제 화면에서 왼쪽에 등장
		1) Text (설명) ⎮ 2) tables or graphics 포함
	• **Questions**	• multi-source reasoning = 3 questions
		• 문제 화면에서 오른쪽에 등장
		• 문제 유형은 주로 2 개의 유형으로 나누어짐
		Type 1: [Two Values] 선택 • Table analysis 등장한 [Yes/No] 유형과 동일 • But, 차이점은 multi-source reasoning 은 근거할 facts (text + graphics)가 table analysis 보다 넓다는 것.
		Type 2: Multiple choice • Reading 문제 유형과 유사 • text 정보 근거 ⇒ 질문 답변

2) Multi-source Reasoning 문제 접근

Step 1: Tabs 전체 리뷰	Multi-source reasoning 문제가 등장하면 the first step 은 지문의 전체 tabs 을 Quick Review 하는 것입니다. • Tabs 의 메인 소재가 무엇인지? • 일반 reading 지문 읽는 것과의 가장 큰 차이점은 Multi-source reasoning 은 **data-oriented reading** • 모든 문제의 중심은 지문에 등장하는 data with tables or graphics • 나머지 text 는 data 를 back-up 하는 용도임.
Step 2: 1번 문제 풀이	• 실전 문제에서는 왼쪽에 지문이 있고 오른쪽에 한 문제가 보여집니다. • 따라서 first reading time ⇒ 1 문제 내용에 최대한 집중하면서 리딩을 하는 것을 권장합니다.
Step 3: 최종 문제 풀이	• Second and third question 은 first question 보다 난이도가 more difficult 하는 것이 일반적인 현상 • 따라서, second reading 은 문제에 맞춰서 필요한 부분을 다시 하는 것을 추천합니다.

2. Multi-source Reasoning Sample Passage

Parking Study   **Second**   **Third**

City X conducted a one-day study of accumulation patterns in a city-owned parking garage that contains a total of 1,200 parking spaces. The graph summarizes the cumulative arrivals (number of automobiles that had arrived at the garage), cumulative departures (number of automobiles that had departed the garage), and accumulation (number of automobiles occupying the garage) at one-hour intervals from 5:00 a.m. to 7:00 p.m. on the day of the study.

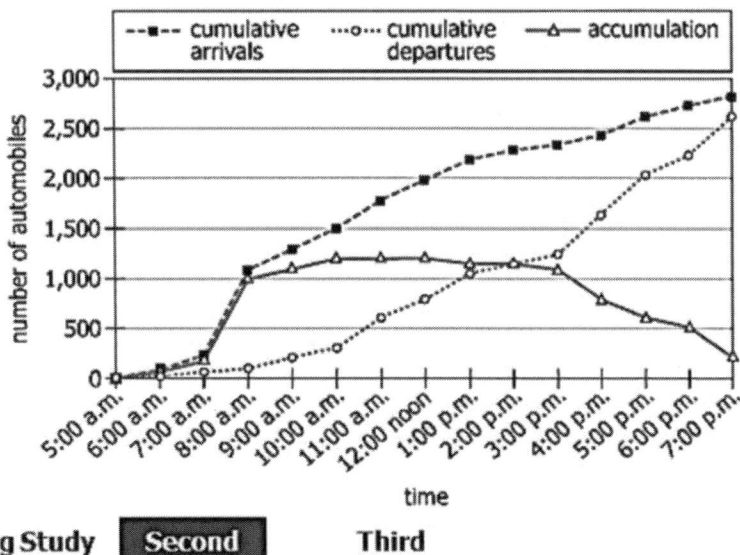

Parking Garage Accumulation Patterns

Parking Study   **Second**   **Third**

To monitor congestion, especially during the morning, City X is considering installation of a detection system at the parking garage. The system's components include detectors at each of the garage's 1,200 parking spaces, together with software and hardware to communicate real-time parking data to city residents via the Internet. In particular, the detection system communicates three types of parking alerts: a Green Alert is in effect whenever accumulation is in the range 0–500; a Yellow Alert is in effect whenever accumulation is in the range 501–1,000; and a Red Alert is in effect whenever accumulation is greater than 1,000. For the detection system in this parking garage, City X estimates that the *capital cost*—the total cost associated with initial construction and implementation—would be $6,000,000, while the annual operating cost would be $800,000.

Parking Study   **Second**   **Third**

City X is also considering **building a new parking garage** to ease congestion at the existing garage. For the new parking garage, the city estimates the average (arithmetic mean) capital cost per parking space would be $15,000 and the annual average operating cost per parking space would be $400. The estimated life span of the new garage is 30 years, at which time major reconstruction or replacement would be necessary.

Question 1

Each of the following options describes a condition that occurred at least once between 5:00 a.m. and 7:00 p.m. on the day of the parking study. For each option, select *Before 1:00 p.m.* if the first such occurrence was before 1:00 p.m. Otherwise, select *1:00 p.m. or later*.

Before 1:00 p.m.	1:00 p.m. or later	
○ Before 1:00 p.m.	○ 1:00 p.m. or later	Cumulative arrivals were greater than accumulation.
○ Before 1:00 p.m.	○ 1:00 p.m. or later	Cumulative arrivals were greater than 2 times cumulative departures.
○ Before 1:00 p.m.	○ 1:00 p.m. or later	Cumulative departures were greater than accumulation.

Question 2

If the detection system had been in operation on the day of the parking study, at which one of the following times would a Red Alert have been in effect?

O   3:00 p.m.

O   4:00 p.m.

O   5:00 p.m.

O   6:00 p.m.

O   7:00 p.m.

Sample Question 해설:

Question 1:

문제 유형: Two options 선택형	
Each of the following options describes a condition that occurred at least once between 5:00 a.m. and 7:00 p.m. on the day of the parking study. For each option, select *Before 1:00 p.m.* if the first such occurrence was before 1:00 p.m. Otherwise, select *1:00 p.m. or later.*	
1) Cumulative arrivals were greater than accumulation.	**Q: Cumulative arrivals > accumulation (before 1:00 발생?)** • **정답 근거**: first tab 에 등장하는 graph 참고 • 처음 발생은 before 1:00 p.m. 전에 있음 • **Answer**: before 1:00 p.m.
2) Cumulative arrivals were greater than 2 times cumulative departures.	Q: Cumulative arrivals > 2 cumulative departures • **정답 근거**: first tab 에 등장하는 graph 참고 • cumulative arrivals (greater than 1,000) • cumulative departures (less than 500) • **Answer**: before 1:00 p.m.
3) Cumulative departures were greater than accumulation.	Q: Cumulative departures > accumulation 비교 • **정답 근거**: first tab 에 등장하는 graph 참고 • 2:00 pm ⇒ Cumulative departures > accumulation • **Answer**: 1:00 p.m. or later

Question 2:

If the detection system had been in operation on the day of the parking study, at which one of the following times would a Red Alert have been in effect?
정보 찾기: detection system + Red Alert ⋯→ Second Tab • Red Alert: greater than 1,000 accumulation 두 번째 정보 찾기: The *Parking Study* tab 에서 above 1,000 on accumulation curve • from about 8:00 a.m. to a few minutes after 3:00 p.m.
Answer: 3: 00 p.m.

PART III
Critical Reasoning(CR)

GMAT CR은 총 9문제로 구성된다. 이를 유형별로 분류하면

1. Weaken, Strengthen, Evaluation(4문제 전후)
2. Assumption(2문제 전후)
3. Conclusion & Inference(1~2문제)
4. Explain(1~2문제)
5. Boldic(1~2문제)
6. Completion(1~2문제)
7. Logic Types(1~2문제)

와 같이 출제되는 게 일반적이다. 따라서, 처음 CR공부를 접근할 때에 Weaken,Strengthen에 대한 올바른 접근법과 Assumption의 개념을 정확히 이해하는 것이 매우 중요하다. 본서에서도 이런 문제 비중을 감안하여 설명을 전개하였다.

Critical Reasoning

Chapter I.
CR Intro

1. CRITICAL REASONING Summary :

본문의 내용을 문제 특징에 맞추어 알기 쉽게 재구성해야 한다.

대분류	논리 분석	문제 초점 요약
Weaken, Strengthen, Evaluation, Assumption (Critical)	1) 결과 예측 2) 인과관계 분석 3) 본문을 T분석용으로 재구성한다. Conclusion Premise | Gap	1) Focus on the conclusion 　– 문제를 푸는 초점은 본문 논리 전개 과정에서 파악된 conclusion(main point)에 초점을 맞추어야 한다. 　– 성격상 Conclusion의 역할을 하는 내용은 반드시 Guessing이 가미된다. 　– Signal : therefore, as a result, suggests, indicates, accordingly, so, consequently, thus, hence, it follows that, clearly, obviously, probably,　to V(목적의미), evidence that 등 2) 문제 요구사항을 정확히 파악할 것 　– Weaken=Less Likely 　– Strengthen=More Believable 　– Evaluation=Relevant Question
Conclusion &Inference (Positive)	1) 본문을 참이라고 간주한다 2) 본문을 나열형 정보로 재구성한다.	– 본문과 일치(must be true,연역적 접근) – 답지를 보고 나서 본문이 이해되는지 따지는 문제가 아니다 – 답지는 본문 안에서 도출되어야 한다
Explain (모순해소)	3) 본문을 T분석용으로 재구성한다. 모순점 fact | 해소점	– 본문 밖에서 본문의 모순에 대한 해결점을 찾아내야 한다 – 답지를 보고 사실일 때 본문이 이해되는지로 판단한다(귀납적 접근)
Completion	빈칸 채우기	– 빈칸 역할 규명을 통한 문제요구 파악
Boldic & Logic	본문을 pros&cons 표로 재구성한다.	– 결론 파악 후 결론과 대비한 boldic의 역할정리
2인간 대화	양자 의견 대립	– 반박논점 파악

2. CR 기본 개념

GMAT CR에서 나오는 논증은 개별적 사실로부터 일반적인 결론을 추정하는 방식이며 전제와 결론의 관계가 개연적이라는 특징을 지닌다. 즉, 전제는 사실이더라도 결론이 반드시 참인 것은 아니다.

1) Analysis of Argument

(1) 본문의 Argument를 Conclusion(the main point of the argument)과 이를 뒷받침하기 위한 Premise(stated pieces of information or evidence necessary to reach the given conclusion)로 나누어 분석한다.

▶결론부분에서 자주 사용되는 표현들 : therefore, as a result, suggests, indicates, accordingly, so, consequently, thus, hence, it follows that, clearly, obviously, probably, perhaps, to Verb(목적의 의미) strong tone(should, quite foolish), evidence that 등

▶ 전제부분에서 자주 사용되는 표현들 : since, because, given that 등

▶ 본문을 아래와 같이 T chart모양으로 재구성하면, 논리 구조가 한 눈에 들어온다.

Conclusion

Premise | Gap 인식

▶ since나 because 절이 결론과 연관해서 나오면, since/because절의 내용을 T-chart Premise 자리에 대입하고, 주절의 내용을 Conclusion 자리에 대입한 후, since/because절과 주절 사이에 존재하는 내용상의 Gap에 초점을 맞추면서 답지를 바라보는 습관을 가진다.

▶ 결론과 전제라는 Boundary를 정확히 이해하면서 그 Boundary 안에 답지가 들어갔을 때 어떤 영향을 주는가라는 관점으로 접근해야 한다.

(2) CR Weaken, Strengthen, Assumption 문제에서 나오는 본문의 내용에서 Conclusion과 이를 뒷받침하기 위한 Premise의 관계는 개연적이다. 따라서, 본문을 Critical한 시각으로 바라보면서 그 결론과 전제 사이의 연결고리 역할을 하는 Assumption(unstated yet necessary premises to reach the given conclusion)을 찾아본다.

2) Weaken·Strengthen에 대한 정확한 접근방법을 학습한다.

(1) 본문의 내용에서 사실(Fact: Statements known to be true and that can be shown to be true)로 제시된 내용과 작가가 추정(Guessing)한 내용을 구분해야 한다. CR의 가장 기본적인 문제가 Weaken, Strengthen문제인데 이 때 Weaken이나 Strengthen의 대상으로 삼을 수 있는 부분은 본문 내용 중 Guessing으로 제한시켜야 한다. 그런 관점에서 일단 본문 주장의 핵심인 결론(conclusion)에 대해 weaken·strength의 대상으로 삼는다.

(2) 답지의 내용에 대해 판단을 할 때에는 답지의 내용을 그대로 해석하여 본문에 추가되었을 때 본문의 Guessing에 미치는 영향을 객관적으로 가려내야 한다. 이 때 답지의 내용을 토대로 본인의 경험과 상식에 의거한 유추를 해서는 안 된다.

(3) Weaken이나 Strengthen문제에서는 "which of the following, if true," 라는 조건으로 문제를 출제한다. 따라서 답지의 내용에 대해 의문을 가져서는 안 된다.

(4) CR에서 Weaken의 개념은 논리를 100% 반박하는 것뿐만 아니라 반론의 제기 가능성을 보여주는 것까지를 포함한다. 또한, Strengthen의 개념도 논리를 100% 입증하는 것뿐만 아니라 논리를 보다 합리화시킬 수 있는 내용까지를 포함한다.
 (A valid weakener need not disprove an argument–it need only make the conclusion **less likely**, whereas a valid strengthener need not prove an argument–it simply must make the conclusion **more believable**.)

(5) 답지 2개 중 어떤 게 답인지 고민되는 경우가 있다. 이 때 막연하게 어떤 게 더 강할까라는 관점으로 답을 고르기보다는 전제-결론-답지의 scope관계를 정확히 따져 보면, 대부분 답지 둘 중 하나는 Out of scope으로 귀결되면서, 명확하게 답지의 O/X가 판명된다.

(6) T 분석법을 적극적으로 활용한다.

$$\frac{\text{Conclusion}}{\text{Premise} \mid \text{Gap}}$$

3) 정확한 Inference 개념을 학습한다.

(1) Inference(추론)은 본문에 주어진 정보로부터 확실하게 뒷받침되는 답지를 고르는 문제이다.

(2) An **inference** is something that must be true based on one sentence or a combination of sentences from the text.

(3) 본문의 정보를 나열형으로 정리한 후 "3단 논법의 조합"과 "paraphrase 답지"에 대비한다.

4) 정확한 Assumption 개념을 학습한다.

Assumption은 작가의 전제와 결론의 연결을 위해 **없어서는 안될 숨은 전제**를 말한다. 따라서, Assumption은 작가의 결론을 위해 ⅰ) **꼭 필요한 말이면서도, ⅱ) 겉으로 드러나지 않은 전제**의 성격이 있다. (An **assumption** is an unstated yet necessary premise (piece of evidence) without which the argument is incomplete and invalid.)

(1) Necessary Premise인지 여부 검증방법

① Conclusion이 성립되기 위해서는 Assumption은 반드시 사실로 성립되어야만 한다.
(conclusion → assumption(필요조건))

- 결론이 성립된다고 보았을 때 답지에서 나오는 전제가 must be true이어야만 하는지를 판단해 본다. 결론이 성립된다고 하더라도 전제가 굳이 must be true인게 아니라면, necessary premise가 아니다.

- 긍정문 형태의 assumption은 전제-결론의 연결관계가 답지에서 그대로 표현되므로 답지를 보는 순간 strengthen의 느낌을 받게 되므로, 답지의 인식은 용이하다. 그러나, 주의할 점을 strengthen의 역할을 하는 모든 전제가 assumption이 되는 것은 아니라는 점이다. 즉, necessary라는 조건에 부합되는 전제만 assumption으로 간주될 수 있다.

② Negation Test(Assumption의 부정 → Conclusion의 약화)

- 답지의 문장 내용을 부정했을 때 결론이 부정되는지 여부를 확인해 보는 것이다. 만약 답지의 내용이 Assumption의 성격에 부합된다면 답지내용의 부정은 결론을 약화시켜야만 한다.

- 부정문 형태의 assumption은 문장 형태상 전제-결론을 직접 연결하는 역할을 할 수가 없다. 다만, 전제-결론 연결에 대한 시비거리를 삭제함으로써 전제-결론이 이어지는 토대를 마련하게 된다. 논리전개를 위해서는 이런 시비거리 삭제 역할이 꼭 필요함에도 불구하고, 시비거리 삭제가 결론의 완결로 연결되는 것은 아니기 때문에 답지의 인식이 쉽지 않다. 따라서, 부정문 답지의 경우 Negation test를 적극적으로 활용할 필요성이 커진다.

(2) Assumption은 필요조건 (not the unique one but one of many)

반면 Assumption은 충분 조건을 의미하는 것은 아니기 때문에 결론을 어떠한 Assumption하나로 도출시킬 필요는 없다. 즉 결론을 위해 **꼭 일단 필요한 여러가지 전제들 중 하나**이지 그 하나로 인해 결론이 완벽하게 도출되는 것은 아니다.

(3) 오답에서 자주 사용되는 pattern들

– Extreme words의 사용: only, 최상급 등

논리가 성립되기 위해 "only"나 "최상급"과 같은 극단적인 표현이 꼭 필요한 상황이 많지는 않다. 따라서, 답지에서 이런 표현이 제시되면 과연 그런 표현이 들어가는 전제가 꼭 필요한지를 중점적으로 따져보아야 한다.

– Out of scope: 전제와 결론의 범위에서 벗어난 논점 지적

Sample Question #1

최근 유가상승으로 인해 대체에너지에 대한 관심이 높아지면서, 옥수수를 활용한 바이오 연료에 대한 관심이 커졌다. 또한, 한우의 축산량 증가에 따라 사료로서의 옥수수에 대한 수요 또한 많아졌다. 이런 요인들이 복합적으로 작용하면서 한국에서 옥수수 가격은 가파른 상승세를 보이고 있다. 따라서, 한국에서의 옥수수 재배면적이 급격히 늘어날 것으로 보인다.

Q 1 : Which of the following, if true, weakens the argument above?

(A) 한미 쇠고기 협상 타결을 예상하여 많은 한우 농가들이 다른 업종으로 전업해왔다.

(B) 한국정부의 규제 완화책에 맞추어 옥수수에 대한 수입규제가 풀리면서 최근 한국으로의 옥수수 수입량이 급격히 증가해왔다.

(C) 쌀 생산량 증가를 유도하기 위해 한국 정부는 옥수수에서 벼농사로 전환하거나 새롭게 쌀을 생산하는 농부들에게 대규모의 지원금을 제공하기로 결정했다.

(D) 전세계적으로 유가 안정을 위한 공조 정책을 추진해왔으나 번번이 무산되어 왔다.

Q 2 : Which of the following can be inferred from the argument above?

(A) 바이오 연료를 위한 옥수수 소비가 사료로 소비되는 양을 조만간 능가할 것이다.

(B) 옥수수 가격의 상승은 한우 농가의 생계를 위협하는 가장 심각한 요인이다.

(C) 옥수수에 대한 수요증가는 향후 장기적인 추세로 이어질 것이다.

(D) 옥수수 가격 변화는 일부 한국 농가의 재배 작물 결정에 영향을 미칠 수 있다.

(E) 한국 정부는 조만간 옥수수를 생필품 물가지수에 포함시켜 적극적인 가격통제에 나설 것이다.

Q 3 : Which of the following is an assumption on which the argument depends on?

(A) 옥수수 시장가격은 한국 농부들의 재배 작물 결정에 영향을 주는 유일한 요인이다.

(B) 한우 축산량은 한미 쇠고기 협상 타결에도 불구하고 앞으로도 10배 이상 늘어날 것으로 예상된다.

(C) 과거에는 옥수수 경작에 따른 이윤이 밀 경작에 따른 이윤보다 훨씬 작았다.

(D) 한국에서는 맥주가격의 급등으로 인해 옥수수 농지를 보리 농지로 전환시키고자 하는 욕구가 현저하게 늘어나지는 않을 것이다.

(E) 한국에서 길러지는 농산물 중 옥수수 가격 상승 속도가 가장 빠를 것이다.

Answer

T-Chart 정리:

Conclusion 한국에서의 옥수수 재배면적이 급격히 늘어날 것으로 보인다.	
Premise 한국에서 옥수수 가격은 가파른 상승세를 보이고 있다	Gap

바이오 연료 및 축산 사료로서 옥수수에 대한 수요가 늘면서 한국에서 옥수수 가격이 급상승하고 있으므로, 한국의 옥수수 재배 면적이 늘 것으로 추정하고 있다.

문제 1)
(A) 본문 논리 전개와는 무관하다.
(B) 옥수수 수입량이 늘었음에도 옥수수 가격이 급등하고 있다면, 옥수수 수요가 폭발적으로 늘어나는 게 반증되는 셈이고, 이에 따라 옥수수 재배면적이 늘 것이라는 작가의 추정은 강화된다.
(C) 정답
    쌀 농사에 대한 지원금 규모에 따라 농부들의 재배작물 결정에 영향을 줄 수 있으므로 옥수수 재배 면적이 늘 것이라는 추정은 약화된다.
(D) 본문 논리 전개와는 무관하다.
(E) 본문 논리 전개와는 무관하다.

문제 2)
Inference는 본문으로부터 반드시 도출될 수 있는 내용이어야 한다. 따라서, 정답은 D가 된다. 다른 내용은 본문에서 다른 추정이 추가될 때만 도출이 될 수 있는 내용이기 때문에 오답이 된다.

문제 3)
(A) 본문의 논리를 위해 "옥수수시장 가격이 재배작물 결정에 영향을 주는 유일한 요인"일 필요는 굳이 없다. 따라서, 이는 논리를 위해 꼭 필요한 전제는 아니다.
(B) 본문의 논리를 위해 "한우 축사량이 10배 이상 늘어난다"라는 전제가 꼭 필요한 것은 아니다.
(C) 본문 논리와는 무관하다.
(D) 정답
    답지 D를 부정하면, "옥수수 농지를 보리 농지로 전환하고자 하는 욕구가 현저하게 늘어날 것이다"가 되어 옥수수 재배 면적이 늘 것이라는 추정이 약화되어진다. 따라서, 답지 D는 없어서는 안될 전제이다.
(E) 본문 논리를 위해 꼭 필요한 전제는 아니다.

Chapter II.
Weaken & Strengthen

1. Weaken & Strengthen 기본 문제 분석

1) 본문을 T-chart 모형으로 재구성한다.

T-Chart 정리:

Conclusion
_____
Premise | Gap

2) Weaken & Strengthen의 대상

본문의 내용 중 Fact로 제시된 내용은 절대로 Weaken & Strengthen의 대상으로 삼아서는 안된다. Weaken & Strengthen 대상의 선정이 잘못되면 답지가 수행하는 역할을 잘못 판단할 수 있다. Weaken이나 Strengthen의 대상으로 삼을 수 있는 부분은 본문 내용 중 Guessing으로 제한시켜야 한다. 특히, Weaken & Strengthen 본문 내용 중 결론은 추측이 가미되어지므로, 결론에 초점을 맞추면서 접근한다.

– 결론부분에서 자주 사용되는 표현들 : therefore, as a result, suggests, indicates, accordingly, so, consequently, thus, hence, it follows that, clearly, obviously, probably, perhaps, to Verb(목적의 의미) strong tone(should, quite foolish), evidence that 등

3) 답지는 전혀 새로운 정보로 제시되었더라도 무조건 TRUE로 인정해야 한다.

4) 본문의 내용에 경험과 상식을 덧붙여 주관적인 판단을 내리지 말아야 한다.

아울러 답지의 내용을 판단하는 것도 전제와 결본 사이에서 "Weaken or Strengthen or Out of Scope" 중 어떤 역할을 하는지를 객관적으로 결정하는 것이지 답지의 내용에 주관적인 경험과 상식을 덧붙이거나 여러 답지를 결합시켜서 추론하는 확대 해석을 하지 말아야 한다.

5) CR에서 Weaken/Strengthen의 개념

CR에서 Weaken의 개념은 논리를 100% 반박하는 것뿐만 아니라 반론의 제기 가능성을 보여주는 것까지를 포함한다. 또한, Strengthen의 개념도 논리를 100% 입증하는 것뿐만 아니라 논리를 보다 합리화시킬 수 있는 내용까지를 포함한다.

(A valid weakener need not disprove an argument-it need only make the conclusion **less likely**, whereas a valid strengthener need not prove an argument-it simply must make the conclusion **more believable**.)

6) 기본 논리 유형 익히기

(1) Pattern drilling

논리유형	논리구조	분석의 초점
Generalization	research subjects, study, experiment, survey, poll 등에서 제시된 일부 현상을 근거로 전체 대상으로 확대 해석하는 구조 EX) I have received over 2,000 letters on this issue, and the vast majority of them support my current position. These letters prove that most of the people in the country agree with me.	– 전제에서 제시된 대상이 결론의 대상을 represent할 수 있는 지 여부 – 실험이나 여론조사 과정에 bias가 개입될 여지가 없었는 지 여부 – 결론 부분의 any,every,always,--ever generally,typically 등의 단어유의
Analogy	전제와 결론에서 나오는 대상/시간/장소 등이 바뀌어지면서 논리를 전개해가는 구조 EX) Child's World, **a chain of toy stores,** has relied on a "supermarket concept"	– 두 대상/시간/장소 등에 있어 차이점이 존재하지 않는가?

	of computerized inventory control and customer self-service to eliminate the category of sales clerks from its force of employees. It now plans to employ the same concept in selling **children's clothes.**	
Cause Analysis & Causal Fallacy	비교관계나 선후관계를 전제로 인과관계를 추측하는 구조 EX) People who marry have a **longer average life span** than do people who never marry. Therefore, **marry and live longer.**	– 비교대상의 동질성 – 인과관계의 역전 가능성 – 다른 원인의 존재 가능성

(2) 전형적인 Weaken 방법

- 새로운 증거를 통해 논리의 Assumption을 공격한다.
- 결론의 추측을 직접 공격한다.
- Question 예시

    Which of the following, if true, most seriously weakens the argument?
    Which of the following, if true, most strongly supports the view that the drug treatment will NOT be successful?

(3) 전형적인 Strengthen 방법

- 결론의 약점을 보완한다.
- 논리의 Assumption 타당성 보완한다.
- 추가적인 증거를 제시한다.
- Question 예시

    Which of the following, if true, most strengthens the argument above?
    Which of the following, if true, most strongly supports the scientists' hypothesis?
    Which of the following provides the strongest reason to expect that the plan will be successful?

EXERCISE

E

Q 1 : A researcher recently studied two sets of students. The members of one set spent 15 or more hours per week playing football, and the members of the other set spent 2 hours or less per week playing football. A significantly greater proportion of the students in the first group exhibited aggressive behavior during the period of the study. Obviously, playing football caused the aggressive behavior.

Which of the following, if true, of the teenagers in the study, provides the strongest challenge to the sociologist's conclusion?

(A) Some students who played football more than 15 hours per week behaved less aggressively than others in the same group of students.

(B) Some students who played football 2 hours did not behave aggressively.

(C) Some students voluntarily stopped playing football after being victims of violence.

(D) Some students played football on weekends, while others did so in weekdays.

(E) Many of the students in the first group exhibited aggressive behavior before the study began.

비교 집단의 동질성

Q 2 : Rapid industrial growth in Korea has generated many environmental problems but, factories in Korea are not willing to spend a lot of money on pollution-control systems. The government of Korea is developing a green growth plan that includes environmental regulations that will require the installation of such systems. Since no companies in Korea currently produce pollution-control systems, the plan, if implemented, will create significant opportunities for foreign exporters to market pollution-control systems.

Which of the following, if true, most seriously weakens the argument?

(A) Most Koreans prefer economic growth to the preservation of environment, objecting to the government's plan.

(B) The plan includes several incentives for Korean businesses to develop and manufacture pollution-control devices.

(C) Foreign exporters are ready to export pollution-control systems to Korea.

(D) Many Korean workers are suffering heath problems resulting from pollution.

(E) The regulations that Korea plans to implement are much less strict than those in

Analogy Fallacy : 두 시점의 차이점 부각을 통해 Weaken이 가능하다.

Q 3 : In a survey conducted by MBC, 70% of respondents favored tax increase that will contribute to assisting disabled workers. This result indicates that most people in Korea are willing to sacrifice their own money for the good of others.

Which of the following, if true, most strongly supports the argument above?

(A) Many people in the survey pretended to be altruistic.

(B) People interested in the wealth of disabled workers were more willing to respond to the survey.

(C) The subjects were also questioned about the political issues.

(D) Awareness of sufferings of disabled workers is higher among the general population than it was among the respondents.

전제와 결론의 연결 과정에서 대상의 확대가 이루어지면 그 전제가 결론의 대상에 대해 **representative**한지 확인해본다.

EXERCISE 해설 & 정답　　　A

1 **본문 해설 :**

한 연구자가 최근 두 집단의 학생들을 연구했다. 한 집단은 주당 15시간 이상을 축구하는데 쓰는 반면, 다른 집단의 학생들은 주당 축구하는 시간이 채 2시간이 되지 않았다. 연구 기간 동안 공격적인 행동을 보여주는 학생들의 비율이 전자 집단에서 훨씬 높게 나타났다. 명백하게도 축구 경기를 하는 것이 공격적인 행동을 일으켰다.

Reasoning Summary:

주당 축구 경기 시간이 보다 많은 학생 집단에서 공격적 학생 비율이 높다는 점을 근거로, 축구 경기로 인해 공격적인 행동이 일으켜진다는 인과관계를 추정하고 있음

(A) 함정이다. 공격적인 행동을 보여주는 학생들의 비율에 대한 비교가 확인되었기 때문에 전자의 집단 학생 내에서 조금 더 공격적인 학생들과 덜 공격적인 학생들이 섞여 있다는 사실이 논리전개에 아무런 영향을 주지 못한다.

(B) "후자의 집단에 속한 학생들 중 일부가 공격적인 행동을 보여주지 못했다"는 점은 논리 전개에 아무런 영향을 주지 못한다.

(C) "자발적인 축구 중단"은 논리전개와 무관한다.

(D) 축구 경기를 하는 요일 차는 논리전개와 무관하다.

(E) 정답

"전자 집단에 속한 많은 학생들이 연구 시작 이전부터 공격적인 행동을 보여주었다"가 사실이면, 애초 비교 십단 설정시 전자 집단에 공격적인 학생들이 몰려 있었을 가능성이 제기된다. 따라서, 두 집단 비교의 논리적 의미가 약화되면서, 본문 사실이 "공격석인 성향의 학생들이 축구 경기 시간을 보다 많이 갖는다"라고 본문 인과관계와는 반대되는 인과관계 설정이 가능해지게 되면서 본문 논리 전개가 약화된다.

2 **본문 해설 :**

한국에서의 급격한 산업 성장은 많은 환경문제를 야기해왔으나, 한국에 있는 공장들은 오염 억제 시스템에 많은 돈을 지불할 의지가 없다. 한국 정부는 그런 오염 억제 시스템 설치를 의무화하게 될 환경 규제를 포함하는 청정성장 계획을 마련하고 있다. 현재, 한국에 있는 회사들 중 오염 억제 시스템을 만드는 회사가 없기 때문에 그 계획이 만약 실행된다면, 외국 수출업자들이 오염 억제 시스템을 판매할 수 있는 현저한 기회를 제공할 것이다.

Reasoning Summary:

현재 한국에서 오염억제 시스템을 만드는 회사가 없다는 사실을 근거로, 정부가 그 계획을 실천에 옮기더라도, 한국 회사들 중에는 오염 억제 시스템을 만들 회사가 없을 것으로 추정하면서, 그 계획이 실천될 경우 외국 회사 제품의 판매 기회로 연결될 것이라고 추정하고 있음.

(A) 한국인들의 선호 문제는 논리전개와는 무관하다.

(B) 정답

"그 계획에는 한국 업체들이 오염 억제 시스템을 개발하고 제작할 수 있는 많은 유인책들을 포함하고 있다"가 사실이라면, 현재와 달리 그 계획이 실행될 시점에서는 한국 업체들도 오염 억제 시스템 제작에 참여할 가능성이 커지게 된다. 따라서, 외국 회사 제품의 판매 기회로 연결될 가능성은 약화된다.

(C) "외국업체가 오염억제시스템을 판매할 준비가 되어 있다"라고 한다면, 실제 계획 실행시 외국업체 제품의 판매 증대 가능성이 오히려 강화될 수 있다.

(D) 한국인들의 건강 문제는 본문 논리 전개와 무관하다.

(E) 일본과의 규제 강도 비교는 본문 논리 전개와 무관하다.

3 **본문 해설 :**

최근 MBC조사에 따르면, 응답자의 70%가 신체 장애 노동자들을 지원하는 데 기여할 세금 증가에 찬성하였다. 이러한 결과는 한국에 있는 대부분의 사람들이 타인의 복리를 위해 자신의 돈을 희생할 용의가 있음을 나타내어 준다.

Reasoning Summary:

MBC여론조사의 결과를 한국에 있는 대부분 사람들의 의견으로 일반화시키고 있다.

(A) "조사참가자들이 이타적인 척하였다"라고 한다면, 조사 결과에 대한 일반화를 어렵게 할 뿐이다.

(B) "신체 장애 노동자 복리에 관심있는 사람들이 설문 조사 응답에 보다 적극적이었다"라고 한다면, 설문 조사 결과를 일반인들의 생각으로 확대해석하기는 보다 어려워진다.

(C) 다른 항목에 대한 설문 조사여부는 본문 논리 전개와 무관하다.

(D) 정답

"신체 장애 노동자들에 대한 인식이 응답자들보다 일반인구 사이에서 보다 높다"라고 한다면, 응답자들에 비해 일반인구의 사람들은 신체 장애 노동자들에 대해 고려할 가능성이 더욱 높아진다. 따라서, 설문조사 결과를 좀더 확대하여 해석할 수 있는 개연성이 더욱 강화된다.

(E) 외국 노동자 비율은 본문 논리 전개와 무관하다.

2. Weaken & Strengthen 고급 문제 접근 분석

1) 본문을 T-chart 모형으로 재구성한다.

CR문제의 난이도가 올라가면, 본문이 길어지면서 결론을 내리기 위한 전제가 좀 더 치밀해지는 경향이 있다. 이런 문제의 경우 전제-결론의 Gap을 발견하기가 어려워지고, 오히려 본문 논리 흐름에 동화가 되어버리는 경우를 종종 보게 된다. Weaken & Strengthen문제를 풀기 위해서는 본문의 논리상 헛점 즉, 전제-결론의 Gap을 발견해야만 하므로, 이런 문제를 마주칠 경우 전제-결론의 단어들을 일일이 대응하면서 Gap을 찾아내야 한다. 이런 문제의 경우 T-chart 모형으로 본문을 재구성하면, 특히 효과적이다.

T-Chart 정리:

	Conclusion	
Premise		Gap

2) 전제-결론-답지의 Scope관계를 정확히 따진다.

CR문제를 풀다 보면 종종 답지 2개 중 어떤 것이 답인지 고민되는 경우가 있다. 이 때 막연하게 어떤 게 더 강할까라는 관점으로 답을 골라서는 안된다. 대부분 이런 경우 전제-결론-답지의 Scope관계를 정확히 따져 보면, 답지 둘 중 하나는 Out of scope으로 귀결되면서, 명확하게 답지의 O/X가 판명된다. 틀린 문제를 Review할 때에는 이런 관점을 인식하여 답지 하나하나에 대해 O/X를 판명해본다. 이렇게 O/X를 구분하기 위해서는 Conclusion의 Boundary를 정확히 확인해야 한다. 이어지는 Boundary Key Words 들을 잘 익혀서 난이도 높은 문제에 대한 적응력을 키워나간다.

3) Boundary Key Words

본문에서 결론을 찾아내는 과정이 Targeting 설정 과정이었다면, 답지 하나하나에 대해 그 Targeting에 정확히 적절한 지를 따져나가는 데 있어 논리와 답지의 Boundary 설정에 중요한 역할을 하는 표현들을 정확히 인식해야 한다.

(1) many(= more than one), some(= at least one), on average, most(=more than half), only, all, every, any 등의 범위설정 표현들과 비교/최상급 등의 표현들

a. Weaken·strengthen문제 본문에서 most, many, on average 등의 범위를 설정한 경우 답지에서 이와 상충되는 some의 경우를 드는 것은 Out of scope이 된다

b. 반면, Weaken·strengthen문제 본문에서 all, any, every 등의 범위에 대해 추측한 경우 답지에서 some의 경우를 드는 것도 적절할 수 있다.

EX A researcher studying drug addicts found that, on average, they tend to manipulate other people a great deal more than nonaddicts do. The researcher concluded that people who frequently manipulate other people are likely to become addicts.

– Some nonaddicts manipulate other people more than some addicts do.
(out of scope: 비교 관계는 상대적인 빈도를 비교하는 것이기 때문에 빈도 낮은 쪽의 몇가지 예를 제시하는 것은 논리의 초점과 무관한다.)

(2) "to 부정사"를 사용하여 글쓴이가 목적을 설정한 경우 그 목적 범위는 논리의 범위와 직결된다.

EX A lot of discount stores in Korea now provide shopping carts for their customers. Since the introduction of these carts, most of these stores are experiencing strong sales growth because customers using shopping carts tend to buy more than those without shopping carts. Therefore, in order to boost sales, managers of Gallaria premier department store are planning to purchase shopping carts.

Which of the following, if true, most seriously undermines the plan's effectiveness?

A. Introducing shopping carts will increase cost because the store has to hire people to retrieve the carts from parking areas.

(Out of scope: 본문에서 to boost sales함으로써 논리의 범위를 sales로만 제안시켰기 때문에 cost관련 내용은 논리의 초점에서 벗어나다)

(3) 동사·형용사·부사의 범위(예를 들면, eliminate와 reduce는 범위가 다르다), 명사지 칭범위(예를 들면 fatality는 치명적 사고를 의미하기 때문에 accident와는 범위가 다 르다)

EX In Korea, although the population of driving age has increased for the past ten years, the annual number of traffic fatalities has declined. Clearly, therefore, the driving-age population of Korea consists of more skillful drivers now than ten years ago.

Which of the following, if true, weakens the argument EXCEPT:

The number of hospital emergency facilities in Korea has tripled in the last seven years.

(Weaken: 응급 병원 시설이 늘어나면, 사고 감소요인은 아니지만, 치명적인 fatalities의 감소에 대한 다른 요인이 될 수 있으므로, 본문 논리의 원인 분석은 약화된다)

(4) 전치사구나 관계사 수식구를 통한 범위 설정

EX Of the Japanese people taking holidays overseas, the percentage who spent their holidays in Korea has decreased by five percentage points over the past two years. Since many Korean businesses cater to Japanese tourists, this decline is likely to have a noticeably negative economic effect on these businesses.

Which of the following, if true, most seriously weakens the argument?

In Korea, the number of manufacturing businesses is far greater than that of tourist businesses.

(본문 "on these businesses"를 참조하면 본문 논리의 범위는 tourist businesses에 한정됨을 알 수 있다. 따라서, manufacturing businesses에 대한 언급은 본문 논리와 무관한다)

(5) 본문논리와 답지의 시점상의 상관관계

답지의 현재(완료) 표현에 특히 유의해야 한다. 대부분 논리에서, 미래에 대한 추측이 결론으로 전개되는 경우가 많기 때문에 답지의 시제도 미래로 인식되는 경우가 많다.

따라서, 답지의 시점이 현재(완료)로 표현되는 경우 그 시점을 인식하여 해석하면서, 본문 논리에 대한 영향을 파악해야 한다. 종종, 현재 시점을 미래 시점으로 착각하여 해석하면, weaken·strengthen의 영향이 거꾸로 판단되는 경우가 종종 있다.

(6) 특정 조건 설정 하에서의 논리를 전개할 경우 조건 자체의 성립 여부는 Weaken·Strengthen의 대상이 아니다.

조건설정표현:<u>if(once S V), unless, until, when, by ~ing,</u> 동명사 주어, 분사나 관계사절 수식 등

EX Rapid industrial growth in Korea has confronted many environmental problems but, factories in Korea are not willing to spend a lot of money on pollution-control systems. The government of Korea is developing a green growth plan that includes environmental regulations that will require the installation of such systems. Since no companies in Korea currently produce pollution-control systems, the plan, **if implemented**, will create significant opportunities for foreign exporters to market pollution-control systems.

– Most Koreans prefer economic growth to the preservation of environment, objecting to the government's plan.(out of scope: 본문에서 "그 계획이 실행된다면"이라고 조건을 설정하였기 때문에 그 조건의 실현여부는 논리의 초점이 아니다)

3. Weaken & Strengthen 문제 유형

Weaken & Strengthen 문제는 동전의 양면처럼 맞물려 있다. 즉 개별적 사실로부터 일반적인 결론을 도출하는 개연적인 논리 관계에서 개연성을 약화시키면서 결론 도출을 어렵게 하면 Weaken 문제의 답이 될 수 있고, 개연성을 강화시면서 결론 도출을 뒷받침하면 Strengthen의 답이 될 수 있다.

아래 설명에서는 이해의 편의를 위해 Weaken 관점 설명이 주로 이루어진다. 이를 뒤집어서 정리하면 Strengthen의 관점도 동시에 이해할 수 있을 것이다.

1) CR 문제 유형 대분류

CR의 본문과 문제에서는 다양한 상황을 다루게 된다. 이런 상황을 일일이 유형별로 정리하는 것은 쉽지 않고 그런 유형만을 신경쓰다가 정작 CR문제를 풀 수 있는 일관성 있는 핵심 개념을 놓치는 우를 범하기 쉽다. 다양한 상황 설정도 크게 보면 다음과 같은 두가지 Framework로 설정되므로 이를 염두에 두면서 모든 문제를 일관성 있게 접근함으로써 문제에 대한 적응력을 키워야 한다.

> (A) 앞으로 발생하게 될 결과에 대해 미리 예측하는 논리 유형
>
> (B) 이미 발생한 일에 대해 원인이 무엇일까를 분석하는 논리 유형

이 중 (A) 앞으로 발생하게 될 결과에 대해 미리 예측하는 논리 유형의 경우 그 결과가 실제로 일어날 것인가에 초점을 맞추면서 문제를 풀어나가는데 사실 대부분의 CR문제가 이런 범주에 속한다. 반면, (B) 이미 발생한 일에 대해 원인이 무엇일까를 분석하는 논리 유형의 경우 이미 발생한 일(Fact)에 대해서는 Weaken & Strengthen의 대상으로 삼지 말고 원인 분석에 대해 초점을 맞추어 문제를 풀어나가야 한다.

(1) 대분류 Example 비교

일반적으로, 이 두가지 Framework에 대한 혼동 때문에 많은 GMATter들이 답지의 Weaken,Strengthen역할을 잘못 인식하게 되는데 초반부에 이 부분을 명확하게 정리하면 CR이 훨씬 쉽게 이해된다. 다음 두가지 Example을 비교해보자.

| Example #1 –type (A) |

Koreans have been forced to eat the most expensive beef in the world these past four years. However, as Korean and U.S. delegates sealed a deal last week on Korea's full opening of its beef market to U.S. products, many consumers in Korea will enjoy cheaper beef.

답지1) **Strengthen**: Encouraged by tax cuts and a cheaper and easier supply of cattle feed for livestock farms, many Korean farmers will raise more cows.

답지2) **Weaken**: Many Korean farmers, expecting the tighter profit margins from the livestock business, will so hurriedly leave the business as to decrease beef supply.

(논리분석)

본문에서 한미간의 대표단이 한국 쇠고기 시장을 미국 제품에 전면적으로 개방하기로 협의했다는 사실(Fact)을 근거로 한국의 많은 소비자들이 보다 저렴한 쇠고기를 즐길 것이라고 추정(Guessing)하고 있다. 이런 논리의 경우 한국 쇠고기 가격이 내려갈 것이라는 앞으로 발생하게 될 결과 추정에 대해 Weaken & Strengthen의 초점이 맞추어진다.

(답지분석)

답지1) "세금감면과 축산농가들을 위한 가축 사료가 보다 쉽고 저렴하게 공급됨에 따라 많은 한국 농부들이 더 많은 소를 키울 것이다"가 사실이라면, 본문 논리의 추정(Guessing)-"한국의 많은 소비자들이 보다 저렴한 쇠고기를 즐길 것"-은 강화되어진다.

답지2) "많은 한국의 농부들은 축산업으로부터의 이익 감소를 예상하여 서둘러 축산업을 그만두면서 쇠고기 공급을 줄일 것이다"가 사실이라면, 본문 논리의 추정(Guessing)-"한국의 많은 소비자들이 보다 저렴한 쇠고기를 즐길 것"-은 약화되어진다.

Example #2-type (B)

Although Koreans were forced to eat the most expensive beef in the world 5 years ago, they are now enjoying much cheaper beef. Here, we see the benefit of the bilateral beef accord on Korea's full opening of its beef market to U.S.

답지1) **Weaken**: Encouraged by tax cuts and a cheaper and easier supply of cattle feed for livestock farms, many Korean farmers have increased their raising of cows for the recent 5 years.

답지2) **Strengthen**: Many Korean farmers, suffering from the tighter profit margins from the livestock business, have so hurriedly leave the business as to decrease beef supply.

(논리분석)

한국인들이 이제는 훨씬 저렴한 쇠고기를 즐기고 있다는 사실(Fact)과 한국의 쇠고기 시장을 미국 쇠고기 제품에 대해 전면적으로 개방하기로 한미간 쇠고기 협정을 맺었다는 사실(Fact)을 근거로 한국 쇠고기 가격 하락에서 한미간 쇠고기 협정의 혜택을 볼 수 있다라고 추정(Guessing)하고 있다. 이런 논리의 경우 한국 쇠고기 가격 하락이 한미간 쇠고기 협정 때문인가 즉, 본문에서 "see the benefit"라는 Guessing부분에 Weaken & Strengthen의 초점이 맞추어진다. Example #1과 비교했을 때 상황설정은 비슷하지만 Weaken & Strengthen의 대상 즉 본문의 Guessing부분이 전혀 달라져 있음을 인식해야 한다.

(답지분석)

답지1) "세금감면과 축산농가들을 위한 가축 사료가 보다 쉽고 저렴하게 공급됨에 따라 많은 한국 농부들이 최근 5년 동안 키우는 소의 수를 늘려왔다"가 사실이라면, 본문 논리의 추정(Guessing)–"한국쇠고기 가격 하락에서 한미간 쇠고기 협정의 혜택을 볼 수 있다"–는 약화되어진다. 답지 1) 분석시 주의할 점은 본문 내용 중 "한국인들이 이제는 훨씬 저렴한 쇠고기를 즐기고 있다"라는 Fact는 Weaken & Strengthen의 대상으로 삼지 말아야 한다는 점이다. 만약, 답지 1)을 이러한 Fact와 연관시키면 순간적으로 답지 1)이 Strengthen의 역할을 하는 것처럼 착각될 수 있다.

답지2) 많은 한국의 농부들은 축산업으로부터의 이익 감소를 예상하여 서둘러 축산업을 그만두면서 쇠고기 공급을 줄여왔다"가 사실이라면, 이렇게 한우 공급이 줄었음에도 한국 쇠고기 가격이 낮아졌다라고 이해 되기 때문에 본문 논리의 추정(Guessing)–"한국쇠고기 가격 하락에서 한미간 쇠고기 협정의 혜택을 볼 수 있다"–는 강화되어진다. 답지 2) 분석시 주의할 점은 본문 내용 중 "한국인들이 이제는 훨씬 저렴한 쇠고기를 즐기고 있다"라는 Fact는 Weaken & Strengthen의 대상으로 삼지 말아야 한다는 점이다. 만약, 답지 2)을 이러한 Fact와 연관시키면 순간적으로 답지 2)가 Weaken의 역할을 하는 것처럼 착각될 수 있다.

(2) 대분류 적용시 주의 사항

– 상기 두 가지 예를 비교하면서 이해했듯이 상황도 비슷하고 답지 내용도 비슷하더라도 본문 논리의 추정 부분이 바뀌어지면 비슷한 내용의 답지이더라도 Weaken, Strengthen의 역할이 달라짐을 알 수 있었다. 따라서, CR문제를 풀 때에는 항상 본문 논리의 추정 즉, Weaken & Strengthen의 대상인 추정(Guessing)이 어느 부분인지를 정확히 인식하면서 접근할 필요가 있다. 만약 해석적으로 Guessing의 구분이 힘들다면 일단 결론을 Targeting 초점으로 삼는다. 왜냐하면, Argument의 결론(Conclusion)은 항상 Guessing이 들어가기 때문이다.

– 그렇다고, 매번 결과 예측인가 원인 분석인가를 미리 염두에 두고 접근할 필요는 굳이 없다. 항상 일관되게 본문에서 추정(Guessing)한 부분을 정확히 찾아내는 데 초점을 맞춘다. 그리고, 그 추정이 결과 예측인지 원인 분석(due to, explain, result from 등의 표현이 자주 사용됨)인지를 구분하면 된다. 그리고, 본문 추정(Guessing)이 이처럼 원인분석(Cause Analysis)에 초점이 맞추어지면 Weaken관점에서 Alternate Cause가 제기될 수도 있다는 점을 인식할 필요가 있다.

2) Cause Analysis & Causal Fallacy

(1) 원인분석(Cause Analysis)

이미 발생한 일에 대한 원인분석(Cause Analysis)의 논리의 경우 Weaken관점에서 Alternate Cause를 제기하는 경우가 많다는 점을 예측해야 한다. 왜냐하면, Alternate Cause라는 framework을 예측하지 않으면, 그런 답지를 만났을 때 답으로서 인식하기보다는 Out of scope으로 착각하기가 쉽기 때문이다.

Sample Question

After 100 factory workers took part in a seminar, their productivity rose by 10 percent. Therefore, managers are recommending more workers to join the same seminar.
Which of the following, if true, weakens the manager's recommendation?

(A) The 100 workers performed precisely the same task as other workers.
(B) After the seminar, the company introduced productivity-related-pay system to the 100 workers.
(C) Nearly all workers had refused to take part in a seminar.
(D) Other companies are also recommending their workers to take part in the same seminar.
(E) Many of the workers who had taken part in the seminar reported that they liked the seminar.

답지분석:

정답:B

해설:100명의 노동자들이 세미나 참석 후 생산성이 10퍼센트 늘어났다는 선후관계를 근거로, 보다 많은 노동자들의 세미나 참석을 권고하고 있다. "정답 B:세미나 이후 회사가 생산성 연동형 급여 시스템을 도입했다"가 사실이라면, 생산성 증가의 원인이 세미나의 효과라기보다는 급여 시스템 변화 때문으로 설명될 수 있다. 따라서, 세미나 참석 권고의 타당성은 less likely해진다.

(2) Causal Fallacy Type

(A) 두 사건이 순차적으로 일어나면, 선행사건이 후행사건의 원인인 듯한 편견에 빠진다. 그러나, 사건의 선후 관계가 곧바로 인과관계를 입증하지는 않는다.

> **Ex**) According to a recent survey, marriage is fattening. Cited as evidence is the survey's finding that the average woman gains 23 pounds and the average man gains 18 pounds during 13 years of marriage.

논리분석: 본문에서는 "결혼 후 13년 동안 평균적으로 여성들 체중이 23파운드 늘고 남성들의 체중이 18파운드 늘었다는 사실을 근거로 결혼이 살을 찌우고 있다"라고 추정하고 있다. 그러나, 결혼 후 체중 증가가 결혼 때문에 체중이 늘어난다로 곧바로 해석될 수는 없다.

(B) 두 개의 사건이 동시에 발생할 때, 하나의 사건이 다른 사건의 원인이라는 편견에 빠진다. 두 개의 사건은 우연히 함께 발생하거나 2가지 사건 모두 제 3의 사건의 결과가 될 수도 있다.

특히, 비교관계로 확인된 두 가지 사실들은 일단 우연의 관계로 인식해야 한다. 즉 2가지 사실이 어떤 관계를 가지고 있는지는 별개로 확인해야 한다. 그럼에도 불구하고, CR에서는 아래와 같이 불합리하게 논리를 전개하는 경우가 많다.

> (FACT A, FACT B) → Conclusion: FACT A causes FACT B

이런 식의 논리 전개에서는 전형적으로 Weaken type이나 Assumption type의 문제가 종종 출제된다.

구체적으로 살펴보면, Weaken 유형에서는 주의할 점은

(i) 빈도비교가 확인된 상황에서 "빈도 낮은 예"의 제시는 Out of scope이라는 점이고,

(ii) 자주 나오는 답지 패턴은 ① FACT B causes FACT A, ② other things caused B (or A and B)이다.

한편 Assumption 유형은 "FACT B does not cause FACT A" 패턴의 답지가 많이 출제된다.

Example

A survey conducted in a high school has found that students who consume more than 3 cups of coffee a day are more likely to suffer from insomnia than those who do not. Among many ingredients in coffee is caffeine, which is known to have the effect of making people remain wakeful. So, obviously, consuming coffee causes insomnia.

Which of the following, if true, most seriously weakens the argument above?

답지1) Some aged people, who don't drink coffee at all, also suffer from insomnia.(out of scope:본문비교관계서술시some infrequent cases의제시는irrelevant)

답지2) Students suffering from insomnia usually drink a lot of coffee to get over the symptoms of drowsiness. (weaken:인과관계역전)

답지3) Students suffering from insomnia do not usually drink a lot of coffee to get over the symptoms of drowsiness. (assumption:인과관계역전가능성봉쇄)

Reasoning Summary :

한 고등학교 조사에서 하루 커피를 3잔 이상 마시는 학생들이 그렇지 않은 학생들에 비해 불면증에 시달릴 가능성이 높다는 사실과 커피속 성분중 하나인 카페인이 사람을 각성시킨다고 알려져있다는 사실을 전제로, 커피를 마시는게 불면증을 일으킨다라고 결론을 내림

답지 1) 본문의 전제로 제시된 전제는 커피를 3잔 이상 마시는 학생들이 그렇지 않은 학생들에 비해 불면증가능성이 크다는 비교관계이지 커피를 마시지 않은 사람 들은 전혀불면증이 없었다는 논리관계가 아니기 때문에, 간혹 커피를 마시지않는몇몇노인들도 불면증에 시달린다라고 해서, 논리에 끼치는 영향이 없는 바이답지는 out of scope이다.

답지 2) 답지 2)"불면증에 시달리는 학생들이 졸림의 증상을 극복하기 위해 다량의 커피를 마시곤 한다"가사실이면, 본문논리의인과 관계(커피 때문에 불면증 이유발됨)에 대해 반대방향의 해석(불면증 때문에 커피를 마시게 됨)의가능성이제기됨으로써 본문논리의 추정은 약화된다.

답지 3) 답지 3에서 not을 떼어내어 negation 하면 본문논리추정이 약화된다.
따라서, 답지 3)이 부정되면, 결론까지 부정되는 게 확인되는바, 본문결론이 가능하려면
답지 3) 은 반드시 필요한 assumption이다.

(3) Causal Fallacy에 대한 일반적 Weaken방법 정리는 다음과 같다.

(A) 진술된 결과를 일으키는 또 다른 원인(Alternate Cause)을 제시한다.

(B) 진술된 원인이 존재해도 결과가 발생하지 않는 경우를 보여준다.

(C) 진술된 원인 없이도 결과가 발생하는 경우를 보여준다.

(D) 진술된 인과관계가 역전되는 경우를 보여준다.

(E) 인과적 진술을 구성하기 위해 사용된 자료에 통계적 결함이 있음을 드러낸다.

Sample Question 해설: OG2025 Q665 ▼

본문 해설 :

평균적으로, 정기적으로 자원봉사 활동을 하는 사람들이 그렇지 않은 사람들보다 오래사는 경향이 있다. 자원봉사 활동을 포함하는 "선행활동"은 사람들에게 행복감을 느끼게 만드는 엔도르핀이라는 뇌의 자연적 최면 성분을 배출하게 만든다. 명백하게도, 정기적으로 엔도르핀을 배출하는 것이 사람들의 수명을 늘리는데 도움을 준다는 상관관계가 있다.

Reasoning Summary:

정기적으로 자원봉사 활동에 참여하는 사람들이 그렇지 않은 사람들에 비해 오래사는 경향이 있다는 사실과 자원봉사 활동시 엔도르핀이 배출된다는 사실을 통해, 자원봉사 때문에 엔도르핀이 배출된 결과로 수명이 늘게 된다는 인과관계 가능성을 추정하고 있다.

답지분석:

(A) 생계유지활동도 선행활동이라고 느낀다면 엔도르핀 배출이 늘어나도록 작용할 것인 바, 본문 추정의 약화와는 무관함

(B) 건강에 해가 될 수 있는 극단적 레벨의 엔도르핀은 자연적으로 도달할 수 없다면, 봉사활동을 통한 엔도르핀 배출은 건강에 도움이 될 가능성만을 시사하므로 본문 논리 추정 약화와는 무관함

(C) 본문 논리 대상은 정기적인 봉사활동에 참여하는 사람들(regular volunteer work)이었기 때문에, 비정기적으로 봉사활동에 참여하는 사람들이 많다는 사실은 본문 논리 추정 약화와는 무관함

(D) 정답

"사람들이 애초에 건강하고 에너지가 충분하지 않는다면, 정기적인 봉사활동에 참여하지 않는 경향이 있다"가 사실이라면, 본문의 "정기적인 자원봉사활동 때문에 건강해져 장수한다"라는 인과관계 추정이 "건강하기 때문에 정기적인 자원봉사 활동에 참여한다"라고 반대된 인과관계 설명(인과관계 역전)이 가능해지는 바, 본문 논리 추정은 약화됨

(E) 장거리 달리기 선수들의 행복감의 원인도 엔도르핀 배출이라는 사실은 본문 논리 추정 약화와는 무관함

3) NON-Confirmed Premises

일반적으로 대부분의 Weaken & Strengthen 문제에서는 결론에 초점을 맞추어 문제를 풀게 된다. 그러다 보니, 결론에 대한 전제는 무조건 사실 전제로서 받아들여야 되는 것처럼 착각이 일어날 수 있다. 그러나, 결론을 위한 전제에서도 추측의 가미될 수 있으며, 이 경우에는 그 추정전제의 진위 여부도 논란의 초점이 될 수 있다. 그러나, 이렇게 non-confirmed premises(추정전제)를 제시하고, 그 부분에 초점을 맞추는 문제 빈도가 높지는 않다. 따라서, 우리는 아래와 같이 문제 접근법을 정리한다.

Weaken·Strengthen의 Targeting 초점을 일단 Conclusion에 맞추되 답지의 내용이 본문의 전제와 상충되는 느낌이 드는 경우에는 전제의 성격을 따져서

1) 전제의 성격이 만약 사실 전제라면 전제의 내용과 답지가 둘다 맞다라고 보았을 때 본문의 Guessing에 어떤 영향을 주는가라고 접근한다.

2) 전제의 성격이 만약 추정 전제라면 그 전제의 내용에 대해서도 의구심을 제기할 수 있다는 점을 인식하면서 답지를 분석해야 한다.

Sample Question ▼

In response to a survey showing that many people are worried about overheating house prices, a candidate has proposed cutting realty-transfer tax. He reasons that since the measure will encourage more people to sell their houses, it will lower the house prices.

Which of the following statements, if true, weakens the candidate's reasoning?

(A) Even without the tax decrease, the economic downturn will lower house prices.

(B) Reducing realty-transfer tax will make people expect further measures, delaying their sales of houses.

(C) Most of the people currently do not own houses.

(D) Many people opposing the candidate's proposal have been worried about populism.

(E) Realty-transfer tax accounts for a significant proportion of government's revenue.

답지분석:

정답:B

해설:양도세 완화는 주택 매도를 늘릴 것이는 추측전제를 근거로, 양도세 완화조치가 집값을 하락시킬 것이라는 후보자의 주장에 대해 "답지 B:양도세를 줄이면 사람들은 추가조치를 기대하면서 그들의 주택 판매를 미룰 것이다"가 사실이라면, 양도세 완화가 주택 매도를 늘릴 것이라는 추측전제가 약화되면서, 결론 또한 less likely해진다.

4) 통계적 오류 : 수나 양의 증감과 비율의 증감이 항상 일치하는 것은 아니다.

Of the Japanese people taking holidays overseas, the percentage who spent their holidays in Korea has decreased by twenty percentage points over the past two years. Since many Korean businesses cater to Japanese tourists, this decline is likely to have a noticeably negative economic effect on these businesses.

(외국으로 휴가 떠나는 일본인 대비 한국의 선택 비율이 낮아진다고 해서, 한국으로 휴가오는 일본 관광객의 수가 꼭 줄어든 것은 아니다)

5) "Flawed" "Vulnerable" "Criticism" : 연역적 접근 필요

본문에서 논리에 대한 헛점을 정확히 인식하고 이를 표현하는 답지를 찾아내야 한다. 따라서, 통상적인 Weaken보다는 까다롭게 인식된다.

As skiing has become a relatively safe sports due to improvements in ski equipment, the number of ski injuries has decreased by 30 percent for the past 10 years. Clearly, however, there have not been decreases in the number of injuries in all categories. Although broken legs and ankle injuries have decreased by 30 percent, knee injuries now represent 20 percent of all ski injuries, up significantly from the 10 percent of 10 years ago.

The reasoning in the argument is vulnerable to which of the following criticism?

6) Assumption에 대한 반박(Weaken) & 보충 (Strengthen)

논리상 연결고리 역할을 하는 Assumption은 무수히 많다. 이는 어떤 Assumption을 반박하는 Weaken, 이를 보충하는 Strengthen의 내용도 무수히 많다는 점을 의미한다. 따라서, 미리 출제자가 예시하는 답지문장을 정확히 예측하기는 어렵다. 따라서, 답지 하나하나를 정확하게 해석하면서 본문의 Guessing부분에 어떤 영향을 주는지 따져야 하고, 이 과정에서 답지가 본문 논리에 대해 관련성이 있는지(In the scope) 혹은 무관한지(Out of scope)를 분명히 가려내어야 함정에 빠지지 않는다.

Sample Question

The number of people killed each year by sharks is about the same as the number of people electrocuted by electric blenders. So, sharks are about as dangerous as electric blenders.

Which one of the following, if true, most weakens the author's argument?
(A) Sharks feed on fish, affecting fishery resources.
(B) People are more afraid of sharks.
(C) Electric blenders greatly help people cook.
(D) Most people would rather take their chances with blenders than sharks.
(E) The number of times people use electric blenders each year far exceeds the number of times people have contacts with sharks.

답지분석:

정답:E

상어 습격으로 죽은 사람들의 숫자와 믹서기 감전사로 죽은 사람들의 숫자가 같다는 사실을 전제로, 위험성에 있어 상어와 믹서기가 비슷하다라고 결론을 내리고 있다. 만약 "답지 E:해마다 믹서기를 사용하는 사람들의 숫자가 상어와의 접촉 횟수보다 훨씬 많다"가 사실이라면, 사망자 숫자가 비슷하더라도 사망률은 상어습격으로 인한 사망률이 훨씬 더 크므로, 위험성이 비슷하다라는 본문 결론이 less likely해진다.

Sample Question 해설 #1 (OG2025 Q775) ▼

문제 type : strengthen

본문 논리 요약

계산서가 놓여지는 선반에 신용카드로고가 있을 때에, 놓여지는 팁의 규모가 보다 크다는 사실에 대해, 단순히 신용카드로고를 보기만해도, 사람들은 그들의 지출능력이 당장 지니고 있는 현금을 능가한다는 점이 상기되어지기 때문이라고 분석한다.

답지분석:

정답:"B:
신용카드채무로 인한 재정적 압박에 시달리는 고객들은 계산서가 놓여지는 선반에 신용카드 로고가 없을 때에 비해, 로고가 있을 때에 팁을 덜 놓는다"가 사실이면, 신용카드 로고가 신용카드 채무에 대해 상기시켰다고 해석이 가능한 바, 신용카드 로고로 인한 지출 능력 상기 효과 연결 개연성이 more believable해진다.

Sample Question 해설 #2 OG2025 Q785 ▼

문제 type : weaken

결론

전형적으로(typically), 1930년 이전 호텔들에서 일을 했던 목수들이 그 이후에 지어진 호텔들에서 일을 했던 목수들에 비해, 보다 좋은 기술, 큰 세심함, 많은 노력으로 작업을 했다.

전제

전국의 호텔을 돌아보면서 1930년 이전에 지어진 호텔들의 최초 목공일의 품질이 그 이후에 지어진 호텔들의 최초 목공일 품질보다 뛰어나다는 점을 주목해왔다.

답지분석:

정답: D

"건물 속 최초 목공일의 품질이 뛰어날수록, 건물이 못쓰게되고 철거될 가능성이 낮다"가 사실이라면, 시간이 지날수록 최초 목공일의 품질이 뛰어난 건물만 남게 되는 바, 1930년 이전 호텔들 중 지금까지 남아 있는 호텔들의 목공일 품질이 그 당시 호텔들의 전형적인 목공일 품질을 나타내는 대표적 건물로 보기가 어려워져 본문 논리가 약화된다.

7) 문제에서 나오는 Support 해석의 주의사항

문제 중에 "Above support Following"이 나오면 Inference type 이다. 일반적으로 Support란 말이 나오면 strengthen을 연상하기 쉬우나 Above support Following의 형태가 되면 사실상 본문과 일치하는 답을 고르는 문제임을 유의해야 한다.

Sample Question 해설 #1: OG2025 Q626 ▼

본문 해설 :

신경학자: 기억은 동물들로 하여금, 유사 상황에 대한 과거 경험을 활용함으로써 그들이 직면하는 상황에 대해 적절하게 대응하도록 도움을 준다. 그러나, 이러한 과정이 동물들로 하여금 그들의 모든 경험의 모든 상세한 부분을 완전하게 기억하도록 요구하지는 않는다. 오히려, 기억의 기능이 잘 이루어지려면 기억은 현재의 경험과 유사한 과거의 경험을 일반화시켜야 한다.

Reasoning Summary:

문제에서는 "신경학자의 문장들이 사실이라면, 다음 중 어떤 결론을 가장 잘 뒷받침하는가?"라고 묻고 있으므로 본문의 신경학자의 문장들과 일치하는 내용을 고를 것을 요구하고 있다.

답지분석:

(A) 적어도 한가지 과거 경험에 대한 모든 상세한 부분들을 완전하게 기억하는 동물들의 존재여부에 대한 언급이 없으므로 답지 A는 알 수 없는 내용이다.

(B) 본문에서는 "적절한 상황 대처를 위해서 굳이 과거 경험의 모든 상세한 부분을 완전히 기억하도록 요구하지는 않는다"고 하였으므로, "모든 과거 경험에 대한 상세한 내용을 모조리 기억하는 것이 그렇지 않았을 경우에 비해 보다 적절하게 상황을 대처하게 만든다"라고 결론내리기 어려워진다.

(C) 과거 경험으로부터의 일반화에 필요한 내용은 본문에서 언급된 바 없으므로 답지 C는 알 수 없는 내용이다.

(D) 모는 과거 경험에 대한 상세한 내용을 모조리 기억하는 것과 과거 경험에 대한 일반화가 양립될 수 있는지 여부는 본문에서 언급되지 않았던 내용인 바, 알 수 없는 내용이다.

㉤ 본문 첫 문장 "기억의 기능=과거 경험을 활용함으로써 직면하는 상황에 대해 보다 적절하게 대처하게 함"과 마지막 문장 "기억의 기능이 잘 이루어지려면 기억은 현재의 경험과 유사한 과거의 경험을 일반화시켜야 한다"를 3단 논법으로 결합하면 "과거 경험을 활용함으로써 직면하는 상황에 대해 보다 적절하게 대처하려면, 기억은 현재의 경험과 유사한 과거의 경험을 일반화시켜야 한다"가 도출된다. 따라서, 답지 "E:동물들은 유사 상황에 대한 과거 경험으로부터의 일반화에 의지한다면, 그렇지 않았을 때에 비해 그들이 직면하는 상황에 대해 보다 적절하게 반응을 할 수 있다"는 본문으로부터 도출가능한 결론이다.

EXERCISE E

Q1 : Unlike common people, many famous musicians are well developed in the absolute musical note. Among them, however, those who had started studying music before the age of 6 are generally far more proficient in the absolute musical note than those who started in later days. So, obviously, by beginning to study music before the age of 6, can one greatly enhance his or her sense of musical note.

Which of the following, if true, casts doubt on the argument above?

(A) Some musicians who had started studying music before the age of 6 are less developed in the absolute musical note than those who had started after the age of 6.

(B) Most of the musicians who begin to study music as children volunteer to do so.

(C) Those who are naturally gifted for the absolute musical note are far more willing to start studying music before they are 6 years old than others.

(D) Studying music before the age of 6 can prevent children from playing outdoors, inhibiting physical growth.

(E) Many children like to play music.

Q2 : A lot of discount stores in Korea now provide shopping carts for their customers. Since the introduction of these carts, most of these stores have experienced significant sales growth because customers using shopping carts tend to buy more than those without shopping carts. Therefore, in order to boost sales, managers of AVENUEL, a premier department store, are planning to introduce shopping carts.

Which of the following, if true, most seriously undermines the plan's effectiveness?

(A) Introducing shopping carts will increase cost because the store has to hire people to retrieve the carts from parking areas.

(B) AVENUEL, the premier department store, has suffered the recent, extended sales slump.

(C) Shopping carts connote low-quality discount stores, making it possible for AVENUEL's high-quality image to suffer if shopping carts are introduced.

(D) Some shoppers try to steal shopping carts even though they are not very expensive.

(E) Many department stores that did not make shopping carts available to their customers have had to close recently due to falling profits.

Q3 : Of the Japanese people taking holidays overseas, the percentage who spent their holidays in Korea has decreased by five percentage points over the past two years. Since many Korean businesses cater to Japanese tourists, this decline is likely to affect these businesses greatly.

Which of the following, if true, most seriously weakens the argument?

(A) In Korea, the number of manufacturing businesses is far greater than that of tourist businesses.

(B) Korea is the most popular place among Japanese holiday takers.

(C) There are more people who traveled to Japan than those who traveled to Korea.

(D) The value of Japanese yen has risen very rapidly since three years ago, increasing greatly the number of the Japanese people who took holidays overseas.

(E) The number of people who left Korea to spend their holidays in Japan was greater last year than it was two years ago.

Q4 : In Korea, although the population of driving age has increased for the past ten years, the annual number of traffic fatalities has declined. Clearly, therefore, the driving-age population of Korea consists of more skillful drivers now than ten years ago.

Which of the following, if true, weakens the argument EXCEPT:

(A) Seven years ago, a mandatory seat-belt law went into effect throughout Korea.

(B) The number of hospital emergency facilities in Korea has tripled in the last seven years.

(C) In response to an increase in traffic fatalities, Korea instituted a program of mandatory driver education seven years ago.

(D) Korea has implemented a major road repair project since eight years ago.

(E) Because of increase in the price of fuel, Koreans on average drive less each year than in the preceding year.

Q5 : Nowadays, fishermen are striking, marching on capitals and blockading ports all over Europe. Faced with the skyrocketing price of marine diesel, they complain that they cannot pass on their rising costs because of cheap imports. In fact, there are fewer fishing boats now than 10 years ago. So, if fishing boats continue to decrease, the amount of fish European fishermen catch will rapidly decrease.

Which of the following, if true, most seriously weakens the argument above?

(A) European governments have paid out a lot of subsidies to cut the price of marine diesel.

(B) In Europe, the fishing industry has political clout way beyond their size because fishing is concentrated in coastal regions with few other obvious jobs.

(C) Given in to the romanticism of European people about fishermen, European governments have made several steps to increase the number of fishing boats.

(D) Today's boats are more and more capable, with better engines and electronic gadgets, thus continuing to increase greatly their efficiency in term of tones caught per vessel.

(E) European herring fishermen burn 100 liters of fuel a ton, whereas Canadian herring fishermen burn 30 liters.

Q6 : Because there is only a limited supply of nitrogen out in the open ocean, additional amounts of it can have a huge stimulating effect. For example, the increased level of nitrogen has brought about new marine life in the open ocean. So, clearly, the global warming will be slowed down by releasing more nitrogen into the open ocean because marine life absorbs a lot of man-made carbon dioxide into the ocean and the more marine life there, the more absorption.

Which of the following, if true, most seriously undermines the argument above?

(A) Many countries have attempted to decrease the level of nitrogen in the ocean in an effort to reduce dead water.

(B) Nitrogen in the air is an inert gas.

(C) Nitrogen taken up by fish can cause respiratory ailments for humans when they consume such fish.

(D) The more marine life there is, the greater release of nitrous oxide, a potent greenhouse gas, will be made from the sea.

(E) Nitrogen oxides, released into the atmosphere, can fall back to earth as acid rain.

Q7 : Despite the approach of moving season, apartment prices are falling. Therefore, unless the government pushes ahead with its strong economic stimulus measures, the prices of multiplex houses are also likely to remain low.

Which of the following, if true, provides the most support for the conclusion above?

(A) Many experts predict that, fearful of inflationary pressure, the government will not take its strong economic stimulus measures.

(B) The potential buyers of multiplex houses can quickly and cheaply switch to purchasing apartment instead.

(C) Industry leaders and academics are advising the Bank of Korea to not raise its interest rate.

(D) Skyrocketing housing prices usually force out families with children and other people with low or even moderate incomes.

(E) Apartment prices are more likely to be affected by the government's economic stimulus measures than are the prices of multiplex houses.

EXERCISE 해설 & 정답

1 본문 해설 :

평범한 사람들과는 달리, 많은 유명한 음악가들은 절대 음감이 발달되어있다. 그런데 이런 음악가들 중에서도 일반적으로 6살 이전에 음악을 시작한 음악가들이 그 이후에 음악을 시작한 음악가들에 비해 절대음감이 훨씬 더 발달되어 있다. 따라서, 명백하게도, 6살 이전에 음악을 시작함으로써, 사람들은 자신의 절대음감을 발달시킬 수 있다.

Reasoning Summary:

평범한 사람들과는 달리, 많은 유명한 음악가들은 절대 음감이 발달되어있다. 그런데 이런 음악가들 중에서도 일반적으로 6살 이전에 음악을 시작한 음악가들이 그 이후에 음악을 시작한 음악가들에 비해 절대음감이 훨씬 더 발달되어 있다는 비교 사실관계를 근거로, 6살 이전에 음악을 시작함으로써 자신의 절대음감을 발달시킬 수 있다는 인과관계의 추정을 전개하고 있다.

(A) 함정이다. 본문은 상대적인 비교 관계를 근거로 제시한 것이기 때문에, 간혹 6살 이전에 시작한 음악가들 중에서도 6살 이후에 시작한 음악가보다도 음감이 나쁜 음악가가 있을 수 있다고 보고 있다. 따라서, 답지 A가 사실이더라도, 비교 관계의 변화는 없기 때문에 본문 논리 전개를 약화시킬 수 없다.

(B) 음악가들의 자발성 여부는 본문 논리 전개와 무관하.

(C) 정답

(D) 답지 "C:음감이 선천적으로 타고난 음악가가 다른 음악가들에 비해 6살 이전에 음악을 시작하려는 의지가 훨씬 강하다"가 사실이라면, 본문에서 제시되었던 "조기교육과 좋은 음감 간의 인과관계가 역전"되어져 본문논리가 약화되어진다.

(E) 육체적 발달 여부는 본문 논리 전개와 무관하다.

2 본문 해설 :

한국에 있는 많은 할인점들은 고객들에게 쇼핑카트를 제공하고 있다. 쇼핑카트를 활용하는 고객들은 그렇지 않은 손님보다 구매량이 많기 때문에, 이 가게들은 쇼핑카트 도입 이후, 급속한 매출 신장을 이루어왔다. 따라서, 명품 백화점 AVENUEL의 경영자들은 매출 증대를 위해 쇼핑 카드를 도입할 계획이다.

Reasoning Summary:

할인점 가계들이 쇼핑카트 도입을 통해 매출 증대를 이룬 점을 근거로, 명품 백화점인 AVENUEL에서도 쇼핑카트 도입을 통해 매출 증대가 이루어질 것으로 추정하고 있음.

(A) 함정이다. 본문 논리의 목적은 "이익증가"가 아니라, "매출증대"에 있으므로, 비용 발생은 본문 논리와 무관하다.

(B) AVENUEL의 최근 매출 상황은 본문 논리 전개와 무관하다.

(C) 정답

"쇼핑카트가 저품질 image를 떠올리게 하면서, AVENUEL의 고품격 이미지가 훼손되게 만든다"가 사실이라면, 할인점과 달리 명품백화점인 AVENUEL에서는 쇼핑카트가 매출 신장에 도움이 된다라고 주장하기 어려워진다.

(D) 일부 쇼핑카트의 도난 여부는 본문 논리 전개와 무관하다.

(E) 쇼핑카트를 도입하지 않은 가게들이 매출 부진을 격었다라고 한다면, 쇼핑카트 도입의 정당성이 오히려 강화된다.

3 본문 해설 :

해외에서 휴가를 보내는 일본인들 중에서 한국에서 휴가를 보내는 일본인들의 비율이 지난 2년 동안 5% 줄어왔다. 많은 한국의 기업들이 일본인 관광객을 대상으로 사업을 하기 때문에 이런 비율 감소는 한국의 일본인 대상 기업들에게 큰 타격을 줄 것이다.

Reasoning Summary:

해외에서 휴가를 보내는 일본인 대비, 한국에서 휴가를 보내는 일본인들의 비율 감소를근거로 한국에 찾아오는 일본인 관광객 숫자가 줄어들 것으로 추정하고 있다. 이런 숫자 감소 추정을 근거로, 한국의 일본인 대상 기업들의 타격을 예상하고 있음.

(A) 함정이다. 제조업체 숫자는 본문 논리 범위인 "한국에 있는 일본인 대상 기업들"에서 벗어난다.

(B) 일본인 관광객들 사이에서의 한국의 인기 순위는 본문논리와 무관하다.

(C) 일본으로 관광가는 사람들의 숫자와의 비교는 본문 논리와 무관하다.

(D) 정답

"3년전 이래로, 일본 엔화 가치가 급격하게 상승하여, 해외로 휴가를 떠나는쇼핑카트가 일본인들의 숫자가 급증하였다"가 사실이라면, 해외에서 휴가를 보내는 일본인 대비, 한국에서 휴가를 보내는 일본인들의 비율이 줄더라도, 한국에 찾아오는 일본인 관광객 숫자는 늘어날 수 있다. 따라서, 본문 논리 전개는 약화된다.

(E) 한국에서 일본으로 가는 관광객들의 숫자 변동은 본문 논리 전개와 무관하다.

4 본문 해설 :

한국에서는 지난 십년동안 운전 연령에 해당하는 인구가 늘어왔음에도 불구하고, 연간 치명적인교통사고 건수는 줄어왔다. 따라서, 한국의 운전 연령 인구 중에서 기술있는 운전자들의 비율이 10년 전에 비해 현재 더 높아졌음이 분명하다.

Reasoning Summary:

운전 연령 인구 증가에도 불구하고 치명적인 교통사고 건수가 줄어든 데 대해 기술있는 운전자 비율 증가 때문일 것으로 추정하고 있음

문제가 요구하는 바는 weaken이 아닌 것을 찾는 문제이다. 따라서, 이런 문제에서는 strengthen도 답이 되고, out of scope에 해당하는 내용도 답이 될 수 있다.

(A) 7년 전에 안전벨트 착용 의무법이 시행됐다"라고 하면, 치명적인 교통사고 건수 감소가 안전벨트 착용 의무법의 시행때문이라고 설명될 수 있기 때문에 본문 논리는 약화되어진다. 따라서, 답이 될 수 없다.

(B) 함정이다. 7년 동안 응급병원시설 수가 3배 늘었다"는 내용은 교통사고(accident) 건수자체와는 무관하지만, 본문에서 제시된 치명적인 교통사고(fatalities)의 감소는 설명할 수 있는 요인이 될 수 있다. 따라서, 치명적인 교통사고 건수의 감소를 응급병원 시설 수의 증가로 설명할 수 있기 때문에 본문 논리는 약화되어진다. 따라서, 답이 될 수 없다.

(C) 정답

"치명적인 교통사고 증가에 대응해서 한국은 7년 전 의무적인 운전자 교육프로그램을 제정했다"라고 하면, 운전자 기술 향상의 배경을 설명하게 되기 때문에 본문 논리는 오히려 강화되어진다. 따라서, weaken의 역할을 할 수 없는 답지이기 때문에 정답이다.

(D) 8년전부터 대대적인 도로보수작업을 실행해왔다"라고 하면, 치명적인 교통사고 건수의 감소가 도로보수 때문이라고 설명될 수 있기 때문에 본문 논리는 약화되어진다.

(E) "연료가격 상승 때문에 평균적으로 한국인들이 운전하는 거리가 해마다 줄어든다"라고 하면, 치명적인 교통사고 건수의 감소가 운전거리 감소 때문이라고 설명될 수 있기 때문에 본문 논리는

5 본문 해설 :

최근, 유럽 전역에서 어부들이 시위를 벌이면서 수도 도시에서 행진을 하기도 하고, 항구를 봉쇄하기도 한다. 치솟는 디젤연료가격을 직면한 상황에서 싸구려 수입품 때문에 이 연료가격 상승을 전가시킬 수 없다는 불만을 쏟아낸다. 사실, 10년전에 비해 현재 어선들의 수는 줄어 있다. 따라서, 보다 많은 보조금이 어업분야에 제공되지 않는다면, 유럽 어부들이 어획하는 물고기 양이 줄어들 것이고, 유

Reasoning Summary:

유럽지역의 어선들의 수가 줄어드는 상황을 보면서, 어획량 감소와 유럽 어부들의 쇠퇴를 추정하고 있다.

(A) 디젤연료가격을 낮추기 위해 보조금을 지급해왔다고 해서 디젤연료가격이 치솟는다는 사실이 바뀌지 않으므로 답지 A는 본문 논리와는 무관하다.

(B) 어업분야의 정치적 영향력은 본문 논리와 무관하다.

(C) 어선 숫자를 늘리기 위한 조치를 해왔다고 해서 어선수가 줄었다는 사실은 바뀌지 않으므로, 본문논리를 약화시킬 수 없다.

(D) 정답

"유럽어선들은 보다 나은 엔진과 전자 장비를 가지고서 능력이 좋아져서, 한 어선당 어획톤수라는 측면에서 효율성이 현저하게 늘것이다"라고 한다면, 어선 수 감소에 따라 어획량이 줄어들 것이라고 추정하기 어려워지면서 본문논리는 약화되어진다. 따라서, D가 정답이다.

(E) 본문 논리 약화와는 무관하다.

6 본문 해설 :

외양에 존재하는 질소공급량이 제한적이기 때문에 질소가 바다에 추가되는 것이 커다란 자극효과를 가져올 수 있다. 예를 들면, 질소수치가 늘면서 바다에서 새로운 해양 생명체가 출현해왔다. 해양생명체는 사람이 만들어내는 이산화탄소를 바다로 흡수하고 생명체가 많을수록 이산화탄소 흡수량이 많기 때문에, 바다 속에서 보다 많은 질소를 배출함으로써 지구 온난화가 늦추어질 것이 분명하다.

Reasoning Summary:

바다 속에 질소를 유입시켜서 바다생명체를 늘리고 이런 바다 생명체가 이산화탄소를 흡수해줌으로써 지구온난화를 늦출 수 있다는 추정을 하고 있음

(A) 많은 나라들이 질소수치를 줄이기 위한 시도를 해왔다고 해서 질소가 늘면서 새로운 해양 생명체가 출현해왔다는 fact가 바뀌는 것이 아니므로 답지 A는 본문 논리와 무관함

(B) 대기 중의 질소 성질은 본문 논리와 무관함

(C) 사람의 순환기 질환 여부는 본문 논리 초점과 무관함

(D) 정답

"해양 생명체가 많아질수록 강력한 온실 가스인 질산배출량이 늘어난다"가 사실이라면 질소 배출을 통해 해양생명체를 늘리는 것이 지구 온난화를 가속화시키는 면도 있으므로 본문 논리 추정은 약화되어진다. 따라서 D가 정답이다.

(E) 대기 중 질산이 산성비로 지구로 돌아온다는 것은 본문 논리와 무관하다.

7 **본문 해설 :**

이사철이 다가옴에도 불구하고, 아파트 가격은 하락하고 있다. 따라서, 정부가 강력한 경기부양책을 추진하지 않는다면, 다세대 주택 가격 또한 낮은 상태로 머물 것이다.

Reasoning Summary:

아파트 가격하락을 근거로, 다세대 주택 가격이 낮은 상태로 유지될 것이라고 추정하고 있다.

(A) "정부가 강력한 경기 부양책을 추진하지 않는다면"이라는 조건 하에서 추정이 성립되느냐가 논리성립 여부 판단의 초점이지 이 조건 자체의 성립 여부는 논리성립 여부 판단과는 무관하다.(Boundary Key Words ⑥번 참조)

(B) 정답

"다세대 주책의 잠재적 구매자들은 재빠르게 그리고 돈들이지 않고 아파트 구매로 전환할 수 있다"라고 한다면, 아파트 가격이 하락하는 상황에서 다세대 주택 가격이 상승하면, 구매자들이 아파트 구매로 전환할 것이다. 따라서, 아파트 가격 하락 상황에서는 다세대 주택가격이 낮게 유지될 것이라는 본문 논리는 강화되어진다.

(C) 전문가들의 금리인상 자체 촉구는 본문 논리 강화와는 무관하다.

(D) 집값 상승에 따른 폐해를 언급하는 것은 본문 논리 전개와는 무관하다.

(E) 경기 부양에 따른 영향 비교는 본문 논리 전개와는 무관하다.

Chapter III.

Evaluation

1. 핵심개념

본문의 논리에 대한 판단작업을 하는데 도움이 될 수 있는 질문을 고르는 문제이다. 답지에 나오는 해당질문에 대한 답변을 통해 결론의 약화가 되면, 본문 논리에 대해 부정적인 평가가 이루어지면서 평가에 도움이 되기 때문에 정답이 되고 답지의 질문에 대한 답변을 통해 결론의 강화가 이루어지면, 본문 논리에 대한 긍정적 평가가 이루어지면서 평가에 도움이 되기 때문에 정답이 된다. 따라서, 본문 논리에 대해 Relevant question을 골라내면 된다. 즉, 답지 질문에 대한 답변을 통해 논리에 대해 Weaken이나 Strengthen이 가해질 수 있으면 정답인 반면 답지 질문에 대한 답변을 하더라도 논리와는 out of scope에 해당하면 오답이다.

Sample Question 해설 #1 : OG2025 Q768 ▼

문제 Type : evaluate

본문 논리

잘못된 자세를 유지하면서, 장시간 컴퓨터를 사용하면서 발생하는 손과 손목 손상이 학생들 사이에서 빈번한데, 컴퓨터가 교과과정에서 중요하여 컴퓨터 사용 시간을 줄이기는 힘들기 때문에, 교사들은 학생들이 교실 내에서 컴퓨터를 사용할 때 학생들의 자세를 세심하게 모니터링함으로써, 상기 손과 손목 손상을 크게 줄이고자 계획하고 있다.

정답분석

정답 : C

손과 손목 손상을 입은 Harnville학생들 중 어느 정도 비율의 학생들이 교실 바깥에서 광범위하게 컴퓨터를 사용하는가?"에 대해 "그런 학생들의 비율이 높다"라고 답변하게 되면, 교실 내 컴퓨터 사용 자세를 모니터링하더라도, 교실 바깥에서 컴퓨터를 부적절한 자세로 사용함으로써 일어나는 손과 손목 손상을 막지는 못하게 되면서 본문 결론이 less likely해진다. 따라서, 답지 C가 논리평가에 유용한 질문이다.

EXERCISE

E

Q1 : SK chain of gasoline stations, despite the objection of other gasoline stations, had a temporary sales promotion last September. This event awarded any customer who made a purchase of 40 or more liters of gasoline a merchandise coupon in the form of OK cash-back. For the month of September, SK experienced a 15 percent increase in gasoline sales as compared to those in September the previous year. Clearly the promotion was very effective in boosting sales.

In evaluating the argument , it would be most helpful to answer which of the following ?

(A) Was the cash-back promotion approved by regulating bodies?

(B) How did the gasoline sales for GS chain of gasoline stations last September that operated in the same area but did not have the promotion compare with sales for the previous September?

(C) Was there any seasonality in gasoline sales of SK chain of gasoline stations?

(D) Did SK chain of gasoline stations have to pay a lot of money to initiate a cash-back promotion?

(E) Were there any customers who complained of the promotion because they had to purchase more gasoline for the benefit of the event?

Q2 : As Yeosoo Expo approaches, demand for hotel rooms in Yeosoo has recently increased significantly. Even after the event ended, this trend is expected to continue and thus the average price hotels charge for rooms is projected to rise. In order to increase its revenues from properties, a real estate developer in Yeosoo is considering a plan to convert several unoccupied office buildings into hotels.

Which of the following would it be most useful for evaluating the plan the real estate developer in Yeosoo is considering?

(A) Whether a lot of companies that will demand office space are expected to relocate to Yeosoo from other cities?

(B) Whether the tourists visiting Yeosoo Expo will spend more money on snacks and drinks than those who visit other cities?

(C) Whether hotels that have been created by converting office buildings have fewer guest rooms than do hotels that were built as hotels

(D) Whether the population growth of Yeosoo will exceed that of other cities?

(E) Whether Yeosoo Expo will have a spill-over effect on other industries?

1 본문 해설 :

SK주유소에는 지난 9월 일시적으로 판촉행사를 벌였다. 주유량이 40리터가 넘는 고객들에게는 OK cash-back형태의 쿠폰을 수여하였다. 판촉행사를 벌였던 작년 9월의 주유 매출은 재작년 9월 매출에 비해 주유 매출이 15% 늘었다. 명백하게도 판촉행사가 주유 매출 증가에 매우 효과적이었다.

Reasoning Summary:

주유 판촉 행사 후 주유 매출이 늘었음을 근거로, 판촉 행사 때문에 주유 매출이 늘었을 것으로 추정하고 있음.

(A) 판촉행사의 규제당국으로부터의 허가 여부는 본문 논리 전개와 무관하다.

(B) 정답

　　"동일 지역에서 영업을 하고 있으나 판촉행사를 하지 않은 GS주유소 체인점의 작년 9월 매출이 재작년 9월과 어떻게 비교되는가"에 대해 "작년 9월 매출이 보다 컸었다"라고 답변이 규명된다면, 작년 9월 매출의 증가는 SK주유소만의 독특한 현상이 아니므로, 판촉행사와 매출증가의 인과 관계 개연성은 약화된다.

(C) 똑같은 9월끼리의 매출비교가 근거였기 때문에 계절적 변동 요인은 본문 논리 전개와 무관하다.

(D) 본문 논리의 범위는 매출 증가에 대한 원인 규명이었으므로, 판촉행사에 따른 비용 발생 여부는 본문 논리 전개와 무관하다.

(E) 고객 불평 여부는 본문논리와 무관하다.

2 본문 해설 :

여수 Expo가 다가옴에 따라, 여수지역의 호텔방에 대한 수요가 최근 급증해왔다. 이런 추세는 엑스포가 끝난 후에도 지속될 것으로 예상되므로, 호텔 객실료 또한 계속 상승할 것으로 예상된다. 부동산으로부터의 수익을 증대시키기 위해, 여수에 있는 한 부동산 개발업체는 공실로 남아 있는 사무실

Reasoning Summary:

호텔 경기 활성화 예상을 근거로, 부동산으로부터의 수익 증대를 위해 공실로 비어 있는사무실을 호텔로 전환시키고자 계획하고 있음.

(A) 정답

"조만간, 사무실을 필요로 하는 수많은 회사들이 다른 도시에서 여수로 이전할 것인가"라는 질문에 대해 "예"라고 답변이 규명되면, 부동산으로부터의 수익 증대를 위해 사무실을 호텔로 전환시키려는 계획의 타당성이 약화된다. 따라서, 논리 규명을 위해 답지 A는 유용한 질문이다.

(B) 여수에 찾아오는 손님들이 다른 지역 방문 손님들에 비해 스낵과 음료 지출에 사용하는 금액이 큰가 여부는 본문 논리 전개와 무관하다.

(C) 사무실을 전용한 호텔과 호텔로 신축된 호텔의 방수 비교는 본문 논리와 무관하다.

(D) 다른 도시와의 인구 증가 비교는 본문 논리 전개와 무관하다.

(E) 다른 산업의 수혜 여부는 본문논리와 무관하다.

Chapter IV.
Assumption

1. Assumption 핵심개념

(1) 없어서는 안 될 전제 (반드시 필요한 전제)

(2) Necessary Premise: One of many Assumptions

(3) Negation Test: Negating Assumption will lead to the Weakening of the Argument

2. 긍정문 Assumption과 부정문 Assumption의 비교

(1) 긍정문 Assumption

- 본문 전제와 결론의 연결고리 역할이 그대로 답으로 기술된다. 따라서, 본문의 논리를 파악했으면 사전예측이 가능하고 답지에 대한 직관적 판단이 가능하다.

- 답지를 보는 순간 Strengthen의 느낌이 들기 때문에 답지를 놓칠 가능성은 적다.

- 그러나, strengthen but unnecessary한 오답을 제거해야 하기 때문에 "결론이 맞다라고 볼 때 답지의 내용이 must be true"인지 확인을 꼭 해야 한다.

- 이런 면에서 답지에 extreme expression이 들어가면 조금 더 조심스럽게 판단할 필요가 있다.

(2) 부정문 Assumption

- 부정문 형태의 assumption은 문장 형태상 전제-결론을 직접 연결하는 역할을 할 수가 없다.

- 다만, 전제-결론 연결에 대한 시비거리를 삭제함으로써 전제-결론이 이어지는 토대를 마련하게 된다. 논리전개를 위해서는 이런 시비거리 삭제 역할이 꼭 필요함에도 불구하고, 시비거리 삭제가 결론의 원결로 연결되는 것은 아니기 때문에 답지의 인식이 쉽지 않다.

- 따라서, 부정문 답지의 경우 negation test를 적극적으로 활용할 필요성이 커진다. 즉, 답지의 not을 제거했을 때 결론이 약화되는지 살펴봄으로써 necessary여부를 판단한다.

- 답지 문장 내 not이 여러 번 사용될 경우 무심코 모든 not을 제거해서는 안 된다. negation한다는 의미는 주절 동사를 부정한다는 의미이지, 조건절 및 수식구 내용의 변경을 일으켜서는 안된다.

Example

Investors from the Middle East are increasingly plowing petrodollars into the Seoul bourse despite a recent global credit crunch, market data showed yesterday. Moreover, some market observers predict many domestic investors will return to the stock market as the global financial problem ebbs. Therefore, Korean stock market will enjoy another rally.

Which of the following is an assumption the argument depends on?

- Money flowing into Seoul bourse will raise the value of some stocks in Korean market.(O)

- Many U.S. and European investors will not shed a massive amount of Korean shares as they continue to feel the pinch of the U.S. sub-prime mortgage loan crisis. (O)

두 답지 모두 Assumption의 답이 되지만 2번째 부정문 답지인 경우가 훨씬 예측이 어렵다는 것을 알 수 있다.

Sample Question 해설 #1: OG2025 Q776

문제 Type : assumption

본문 논리 분석

각각의 자원자에게 쉬운 임무와 어려운 임무의 선택권을 주면서, 다른 자원자에게는 그 자원자가 선택한 임무이외의 다른 임무가 주어질 것이라고 일러주는 한편, 상기 지원자에게 컴퓨터가 임무를 임의로 배정하게 할 수도 있는 선택권을 주었을 때, 대부분의 자원자는 자기 자신을 위해 쉬운 임무를 선택하였고, 이에 대해 질문을 받았을 때, 그들은 공정하게 행동했다라고 대답했던 반면, 상기 자원자들의 상황을 다른 그룹의 자원자들에게 알려주었을 때, 쉬운 임무 선택이 공정한 행위가 아니었다라고 대답하였음을 전제로, 대부분의 사람들은 타인에 대해 적용하는 도덕적 기준보다, 본인에 대해 적용하는 도덕적 기준이 보다 약하다라고 결론을 내린다.

정답해설 :

본문의 결론이 타당하려면, 자신의 행동이 공정한 행위였다라고 대답한 자원자들의 경우, 타인이 동일한 행동을 했을 때에는 공정한 행위가 아니였다라고 이중적 기준을 적용하고 있음이 드러나야만 한다. 따라서, "A:쉬운 임무를 선택함에 있어 공정하게 행동했다라고 말하는 자원자들 중 최소한 한명은 다른 사람이 그런 행동을 했었을 때에는 공정하지 않다라고 말했을 것이다"가 본문 결론이 맞다면 must be true여야만 한다.

3. Questionable Assumption = Assumption

불합리한 Assumption으로 해석이 되면서 Weaken처럼 혼동될 수 있으나 문제의 답은 Assumption을 찾는 문제이다. 다만, 본문의 연결고리가 되는 Assumption이 출제자 판단에 Questionable하게 느껴진다는 의미일 뿐이다.

4. Cannot —— Unless = Negation Test

Sample Question

Although the 10% tax credit was enacted to promote spending on research and development, outlays for research and development by Korean businesses increased only 5% in 2024. This figure actually continued a downward trend since 2020. It can be concluded that the 10% tax credit had no effect of stimulating spending on research and development.

The conclusion of the argument above cannot be true unless which of the following is true?

(A) Korean businesses, sensitive to their profit, tried to reduce their expenditure in 2024.
(B) Even without the 10% tax credit, spending for research and development by Korean businesses in 2024 would not have been substantially lower than it was.
(C) Generally, tax credits for specific investments are effective in inducing businesses to make those investments.
(D) Many politicians were opposed to introducing the 10% tax credit, predicting that businesses would not invest even with that credit.
(E) Business spending on research and development is usually directly proportional to business profits.

문제 의미의 해석:

"다음 중 무엇이 사실이 아니라면 본문 주장의 결론이 사실일 수 없겠는가?"

⇒ 답지 부정이 본문 결론 부정으로 연결되는 내용을 찾아야 하는 문제이다. 즉, assumption 답지 판단의 검증 방법인 Negation Test를 활용해서 문제를 풀어야 함을 알 수 있다.

Reasoning Summary:

R&D 지출을 늘리고자 10% 조세 감면이 입법 제정되었음에도 불구하고 2024년 한국 기업들의 R&D 지출이 고작 5% 증가하였음을 전제로, 10% 조세 감면이 R&D지출을 진작시키는 데 효과가 없었다라고 결론을 내리고 있다.

답지분석:

(A) 본문 결론이 맞다라고 가정되어도 답지 A"한국 기업들은 이익에 민감하여 2024년 지출을 줄이려고 노력하였다"는 can be true일뿐이므로 unnecessary하다.

(B) 정답
답지 B가 negate된다면, "10% 조세감면이 없었다면, 2024년 한국 기업들의 R&D지출은 실제 지출규모보다 훨씬 저조했었을 것이다"가 되는 바, 이럴 경우 비록 2024년 한국 기업들의 R&D 지출이 5%밖에 늘지 않았지만, 그 5%증가 부분에 10% 조세 감면의 영향이 있었을 것으로 판단되어 본문 결론이 사실일 수 없게 된다. 따라서 답지 B는 반드시 필요한 assumption이다.

(C) "일반적으로 조세 감면이 투자 증대에 효과적이다"라는 전제는 본문 결론을 위해 꼭 필요한 전제가 아니다.

(D) 정치인들의 반대 여부는 본문 논리와 무관한다.

(E) R&D지출과 기입이익의 비례 관계 성립 여부는 본문 논리와 무관하다.

EXERCISE

E

Q1 : Since last August when credit crisis began in US and Britain, London Interbank–Offered Rate(LIBOR) that banks charge each other for anything up to three–month loans has remained stubbornly high. During this period, the overnight loan rate has been consistently lower than LIBOR. But, while the overnight loan rate has risen, the gap between LIBOR and the overnight loan rate has widened. Clearly, therefore, several steps the Bank of England took to restore confidence in the banking system made no effects at all.

(A) The gap between LIBOR and the overnight loan is the most helpful in evaluating the effectiveness of measures the Bank of England initiated.

(B) Many economists have criticized the Bank of England for tardy responses to the grave financial crisis.

(C) The Bank of England did not expect credit crisis to spread to other countries in Europe.

(D) The trend of LIBOR is the only way to evaluate the effectiveness of steps the Bank of England took to stabilize capital market.

(E) Even without those steps the Bank of England has taken, the gap between LIBOR and the overnight loan rate would not be much greater.

Q2 : Unlike common people, many famous musicians are well developed in the absolute musical note. Among them, however, those who had started studying music before the age of 6 are generally far more proficient in the absolute musical note than those who started in later days. So, obviously, by beginning to study music before the age of 6, can one greatly enhance his or her sense of musical note.

Which of the following is a questionable assumption on which the argument depends?

(A) No musicians who had started studying music before the age of 6 are less developed in the absolute musical note than those who had started after the age of 6.

(B) Most of the musicians who begin to study music as children volunteer to do so.

(C) Those who are naturally gifted for the absolute musical note are not far more willing to start studying music before they are 6 years old than others.

(D) Studying music before the age of 6 can prevent children from playing outdoors, inhibiting physical growth.

(E) Many children don't like to play music.

EXERCISE 해설 & 정답

1 본문 해설 :

지난 8월 영국과 미국에서 신용위기가 시작된 이래로 은행들간 3개월까지의 대출물에 대해 부과하는 금리인 LIBOR금리가 높은 상태로 유지되어왔다. 이 기간 동안 하루짜리 대출물 금리는 LIBOR금리보다는 지속적으로 낮았다. 그러나, 하루짜리 대출물 금리가 상승한 반면 LIBOR금리와 하루짜리 대출물 금리의 격차는 더욱 커져 왔다. 따라서, 명백하게도 은행시스템의 확신을 복원하기 위해 영란은행이 취했던 여러 조치들은 아무런 효과를 거두지 못했다.

Reasoning Summary:

하루짜리 대출물 금리 상승과 LIBOR금리의 더 큰 폭의 상승을 근거로 영란은행 조치들의 무효성을 추정하고 있음

(A) LIBOR금리와 하루짜리 대출물 금리의 격차가 영란은행 조치 실효성을 평가하는데 가장 크게 도움을 줄 때만 본문의 논리가 가능한 것은 아니므로 답지 A는 논리를 위해 꼭 필요한 전제는 아님. 이런 답지에서는 "the most helpful"이라는 최상급 표현이 본문의 논리를 위해 꼭 필요한지를 따져보아야 한다.

(B) 경제학자들의 비판여부는 본문 논리에서 꼭 필요한 전제가 아니다.

(C) 다른 국가로의 신용위기 확산 예상 여부는 본문과 무관하다.

(D) LIBOR금리 추세가 영란은행 조치 실효성 판단에 유일한 방법일 필요는 굳이 없음. 이런 답지에서는 "the only"가 꼭 필요한지를 따져보면서 답을 판단해야 한다.

(E) 정답

답지 E가 부정되면, "영란은행의 조치마저 없었더라면, LIBOR금리와 하루짜리 대출물 금리의 격차가 더욱 컸을 것이다"가 되면서 영란은행 조치가 나름대로 효과 있었다는 논리가 전개되어지면서 본문논리가 약화되어진다. 따라서, 답지 E는 본문 논리를 위해 없어서는 안될 전제임이 확인되어진다.

2 **본문 해설 :**

평범한 사람들과는 달리, 많은 유명한 음악가들은 절대 음감이 발달되어있다. 그런데 이런 음악가들 중에서도 일반적으로 6살 이전에 음악을 시작한 음악가들이 그 이후에 음악을 시작한 음악가들에 비해 절대음감이 훨씬 더 발달되어 있다. 따라서, 명백하게도, 6살 이전에 음악을 시작함으로써, 사람

Reasoning Summary:

평범한 사람들과는 달리, 많은 유명한 음악가들은 절대 음감이 발달되어있다. 그런데 이런 음악가들 중에서도 일반적으로 6살 이전에 음악을 시작한 음악가들이 그 이후에 음악을 시작한 음악가들에 비해 절대음감이 훨씬 더 발달되어 있다는 비교 사실관계를 근거로, 6살 이전에 음악을 시작함으로써

(A) 본문은 상대적인 비교 관계를 근거로 제시한 것이기 때문에, 간혹 6살 이전에 시작한 음악가들 중에서도 6살 이후에 시작한 음악가보다도 음감이 나쁜 음악가가 있을 수 있다고 보고 있다. 따라서, 답지 A는 꼭 필요한 전제가 아니다.

(B) 음악가들의 자발성 여부는 본문 논리에서 꼭 필요한 전제가 아니다.

(C) 정답

답지 C가 부정되면, "음감이 선천적으로 타고난 음악가가 다른 음악가들에 비해 6살 이전에 음악을 시작하려는 의지가 훨씬 강하다"가 되면서, 본문에서 제시되었던 "조기교육과 좋은 음감 간의 인과 관계가 역전"되어져 본문논리가 약화되어진다. 따라서, 답지 C는 본문 논리를 위해 없어서는 안될 전제임이 확인되어진다. 그런데 상식적으로 생각해보면, 답지 C의 내용보다는 C의 부정인 "음감이 선천적으로 타고난 음악가가 다른 음악가들에 비해 6살 이전에 음악을 시작하려는 의지가 훨씬 강하다"가 보다 합리적으로 느껴질 수도 있다. 이런 점을 고려하여 출제자가 questionable assumption이란 말을 사용하여 문제를 출제하였다.

(D) 육체적 발달 여부는 본문 논리에서 꼭 필요한 전제가 아니다.

(E) 아동들의 선오 문지는 본문 논리에서 꼭 필요한 전제가 아니다.

Chapter V.
Conclusion & Inference

1. Conclusion & Inference 핵심개념

1) 일단 모든 본문 내용을 참인 것으로 간주한다

Weaken, Strengthen, Assumption을 풀 때처럼 본문에서 결론을 찾아 분석할 필요가 없고 일단 모든 본문 내용을 참인 것으로 간주한다. 이 때 본문의 전부 혹은 일부로부터 논리적으로 추론이 될 수 있는 즉 본문이 참이라면 반드시 참이 되는 답지를 요구한다.

- An inference is something that must be true based on one sentence or a combination of sentences from the text.

2) 본문을 나열형으로 정리한 후, 정보를 조합하면서 답을 찾아가면 효과적이다. 이 과정에서 대개 3단 논법식 조합이나, paraphrase를 통한 답지 제시가 많다.

3) 본문과 답지의 관계는 본문이 답지를 지지하는 관계로 구성된다.

- The statements above, if true, support which of the following?
- Which of the following can be inferred from the passage above?
- Which of the following can be concluded from the statements above?

4) 정답유형

- 본문을 paraphrase하면서 사실상 동일한 내용을 말하거나, 본문의 정보를 3단 논법식으로 조합한 답지가 주로 출제된다.

- 해석에서 주의 깊게 볼 단어들: can, some=at least one, possible, sometimes

5) 오답유형

- 본문의 정보를 확대하거나 과장을 한다. 예를 들어 some을 most로 바꾼다든지 can을 must로 바꾼다.

- 제시문에 언급되지 않았으나, 상식적으로 그럴듯해 보이는 새로운 정보를 제시한다. 만약 새로운 정보가 본문의 범위를 벗어나면 오답이다.

- "P이면 Q이다"의 진술을 "Q이면 P이다"라는 식으로 바꾸어 진술하면 오답이다.

– 비교관계나 인과관계 서술은 본문에서 확실히 추론이 될 수 있는지 확인해야 한다.

– 해석에서 주의 깊게 볼 단어들 :

　must, most, all, any, every, certain, always, tend to, only, 비교급이나 최상급의 표현

6) 본문과 답지의 상관 관계 주의 표현

본문	답지	Inferred 여부
X can be Y	X can be Y	O
	X must be Y	X
X must be Y	X can be Y	O
	X must be Y	O

2. 본문의 Paraphrase와 3단 논법

답지가 본문의 내용범위 안에서 도출되어야 한다. 그러면서도, 답지의 내용이 언뜻 보면 본문과 달라보이게 만든다. 그러므로, 본문의 일부를 paraphrase하거나 본문 내용을 3단 논법으로 압축시키는 내용의 답지가 많이 출제된다.

(EX) 본문: A=B, B=C → 답지: A=C,　본문: A=B, B=C, C=D → 답지: A=D

Sample Question 해설 : OG2025 Q682　▼

문제 Type : conclusion

Reasoning Summary:

1) 운동이후 혈중 젖산 농도를 지속적으로 측정한 결과, 순산소를 들여마신 운동선수와 일반공기를 들여마신 운동선수들의 혈중 젖산 농도가 동일하였다.

2) 혈중젖산농도가 낮을수록, 근육의 산소 재흡수가 높아진다.

정답분석:

본문 1과 2를 조합하면, 운동이후 순산소를 들여마신 운동선수와 일반공기를 들여마신 운동선수들의 혈중 젖산 농도가 동일하므로, 근육의 산소 재흡수도 동일함을 알 수 있다. 따라서, 본문과 일치하는 내용은 "정답 A: 운동선수들의 산소 재흡수는 일반적인 공기 대신에 순산소를 마신다고 해서 증가하지는 않는다" 이다.

3. Must(Can)(Cannot) be True

1) Must be true=Certain: 수식/명제관계/경우의 수 도출 문제인 경우가 많다. 따라서, 본문에 대해 논리적 시사점을 얻어가기 보다는 본문을 수나 기호화하여 풀어서 정답을 풀어내야 되는 경우가 많다.

2) Can be true = Possible:

3) Cannot be true or Can be true: EXCEPT= Impossible

본문과는 모순임이 확실해야 답이 된다. 본문의 내용을 통해서 판단이 불가능한 답지는 오답임을 유의해야 한다.

4. 부분집단의 share 변화 ⇔ 부분집단증가율: 전체집단증가율

출제자는 Inference의 문제에서 본문과 동일한 내용이면서 얼핏 달라보이는 답지를 만들어내려고 노력한다. 그런 관점에서 상기 개념은 매우 유용하여 출제 빈도가 높다.

(1) 부분집단의 share 증가시에는 부분집단의 증가율이 전체집단의 증가율보다 크다.
　　(왜냐하면, 분수식에서 분자의 증가율이 분모의 증가율보다 크면 분수값은 커지기 때문이다)

(2) 부분집단의 share 감소시에는 부분집단의 증가율이 전체집단의 증가율보다 작다.
　　(왜냐하면, 분수식에서 분자의 증가율이 분모의 증가율보다 작으면 분수값은 작아지기 때문이다)

(3) 부분집단의 증가율과 전체집단의 증가율이 동일하면 부분집단이 차지하는 share는 동일하게 유지된다.
　　(왜냐하면, 분수식에서 분자의 증가율이 분모의 증가율과 동일하면 분수값은 변화가 없기 때문이다)

(4) 본문의 내용 중 인구 증가율이 나오면 본문 내용을 "인구 대비 각 구성요소 즉 per capita (인구를 모집단으로 간주)"라는 개념으로 정리해본다.

> Updated statistic.s show that many Koreans are beginning to enjoy wine consumption. Against the previous year, the total consumption of wine in Koreas increased by 38.5% last year, while the total consumption of soju increased by only 0.4%. During the same period, the population of Korea increased by 1%.

EXERCISE

E

Q1 : Baking might lift the depression of people, because carbohydrates, both sugars and starches, boost the brain's levels of serotonin, a neurotransmitter that improves the mood. In this respect, carbohydrates act on the brain just as some antidepressants do. Thus, eating cookies may provide an effective form of self-prescribed medication for depressed people.

Which one of the following can be properly inferred from the passage?

(A) Depression is one of the most easily treated disease.

(B) Anyone should eat cookies for their health.

(C) People eating cookies are less likely to be depressed than others.

(D) Some antidepressants act by changing the brain's level of serotonin.

(E) Raising the level of neurotransmitter in the brain effectively relieves depression.

Q2 : According to a guidebook published by Seoul, more tourists stay in hotels in Seoul than stay in the neighboring city of Incheon. A brochure from the largest hotel in Incheon claims that more tourists stay in that hotel than stay in the Plaza Hotel in Seoul.

If the claims mentioned above are all true, each of the following can be true: EXCEPT.

(A) more tourists stay in hotel accommodations in Incheon than stay in the Plaza Hotel

(B) the Plaza Hotel is the only hotel in Seoul

(C) there are several hotels in Incheon that are larger than the Plaza Hotel

(D) some of the tourists who have stayed in hotels in Incehon have also stayed in the Plaza Hotel

(E) some hotels in Incheon have fewer tourist guests each year than the Plaza Hotel has.

Q3 : Updated statistics show that many Koreans are beginning to enjoy wine consumption. Against the previous year, the total consumption of wine in Koreas increased by 38.5% last year, while the total consumption of soju increased by only 0.4%. During the same period, the population of Korea increased by 1%.

If the statements above are true, which of the following must also be true on the basis of them?

(A) Last year, many soju producers went bankrupt.

(B) Wine became popular in Korea because many young people liked to follow Western culture.

(C) Last year, Koreans consumed about 38 times more wine than soju.

(D) Most Koreans now prefer to consume wine rather than drink soju.

(E) Per capita consumption of wine was greater in last year than in the previous year.

1 **본문 해설 :**

설탕과 녹말의 주성분인 탄수화물은 사람의 기분을 개선시키는 신경전달물질인 세로토닌 수치를 증가시키기 때문에 과자를 굽는 것은 사람들의 우울증을 제거할지도 모른다. 이런 점에서 탄수화물이 뇌에 끼치는 작용은 일부 항우울제와 같은 방식이다. 따라서, 쿠키를 먹는 것은 우울한 사람들에 대한 효과적인 자가 처방 진료일지도 모른다.

Reasoning Summary:

일부 항우울제의 작용원리처럼 과자를 구워먹음으로써 탄수화물을 섭취하면 뇌의 세로토닌 분비를 증가시켜 우울한 기분을 개선시킬 수 있다.

(A) "the most easily"를 주의 깊게 보면 답지 A는 본문에서 확인되지 않는 내용임을 알 수 있다.

(B) 쿠키를 먹는 것이 모든 사람들의 건강에 도움될지는 본문에서 판단할 수 없다.

(C) 쿠키먹는 사람들이 다른 사람들보다 덜 우울한지는 본문에서 판단할 수 없다.

(D) 정답

　　본문에서 "일부 항우울제의 작용원리처럼 과자를 구워먹음으로써 탄수화물을 섭취하면 뇌의 세로토닌 분비를 증가시켜 우울한 기분을 개선시킬 수 있다"라고 했으므로 답지 "D:적어도 하나의 항우울제는 뇌의 세로토닌 수치를 변화시켜 작용한다"는 본문과 정확히 일치한다.

(E) 세로토닌을 전체 신경전달물질로 확대 해석할 수 없으므로 E는 본문에서 확인할 수 없다.

2 본문 해설 :

Reasoning Summary:

1) 관광객 전체 수는 Seoul Hotels 〉Incheon Hotels

2) 특정호텔의 관광객 수 : the Plaza Hotel in Seoul 〈 the largest hotel in Incheon

일 때, 두 가지 사실과 모순일 수밖에 없는 내용을 고르는 문제이다.

두 가지가 모두 사실이라면, 수학적으로 Seoul에는 Plaza Hotel말고 다른 호텔이 있어야만 된다. 따라서, 이 내용과 모순인 것을 고르면 되므로 정답은 "B: Plaza Hotel이 Seoul에 있는 유일한 호텔이다."가 되어진다.

3 본문 해설 :

갱신된 통계 자료들은 많은 한국인들이 와인섭취를 즐기기 시작하고 있음을 보여준다.이전년도와 비교했을 때, 한국에서 와인섭취는 38.5%만큼 증가하였다. 반면 소주의 섭취는 오직 0.4%만 늘었다. 동기간, 한국 인구는 1% 증가하였다.

Reasoning Summary:

"와인섭취증가율 〉 인구증가율"이므로 "와인섭취/인구"의 값은 재작년에 비해 작년도 값이 커진다. 즉, 1인당 와인섭취가 재작년에 비해 작년도가 늘어났다는 것을 알 수 있게 된다. 따라서, 정답은 E가 된다.

Chapter VI.
Explain(모순해소)

1. Explain 핵심개념

1) 본문에서는 주로 결론 없이 두 개의 모순적인 사실을 보여준다.

2) 본문의 내용은 참이라고 간주하면서 본문에서 부자연스럽게 연결된 FACT간의 관계를 보다 자연스럽게 이어줄 수 있는 답지를 골라야 한다. 문제에서는 explain, resolve, reconcile 등의 단어들을 사용한다.

3) 답지 선택의 유의 사항

   – 두 개의 모순적 상황가운데 어느 하나만을 설명한다면 정답이 아니다. 반드시 모순처럼 보이는 두 가지 상황을 함께 설명할 수 있어야 한다. 본문 내용 중 surprisingly, paradoxically, perplexingly 등의 단어들로 모순관계를 표시하는 경우가 많다.

   – 답지는 전혀 새로운 정보를 포함하고 있더라도 true로 간주해야 한다.

   – 모순점에 대해 완벽한 설명까지는 아니어도 이해에 도움이 되면(more natural) 정답이다.

   – 본문에서, "despite, although, even though" 등의 boundary 설정에 유의해야 한다. 이 내용이 정/오답을 가리는 데 결정적인 단서로 작용하는 경우가 종종 있다.

4) Explain문제를 풀 때에도 T-Chart활용이 유용하다.

T-Chart 정리:

Targeting(모순점)	
기타사실	more natural

Sample Question 해설 #1: OG2025 Q743 ▼

문제 Type : explain(모순해소)

Reasoning Summary:

조류가 천천히 흐르는 물에서 잘 자라기 때문에, 일반적으로 비가 덜 오면 per unit of water당 조류의 양이 늘어나는데, 극한의 가뭄 이후에는 오히려, 매우 천천히 흐르는 강물 속에서조차도 조류의 양이 적었다는 모순점을 이해시켜야 함

정답분석

정답 D

Australia 강물은 극한의 가뭄 시기에 짧은 기간 동안 완전히 바싹 마른다"가 사실이라면, 극한의 가뭄 이후에 강물 속 모든 조류가 사라져버렸다가 다시 자리잡아야 하는 바, 천천히 흐르는 강물이더라도 조류가 적어졌다는 점이 more natural해진다.

EXERCISE

Q1 : On June 17th official figures revealed that inflation in the year to May was even higher than the City had predicted. Consumer prices rose by 3.3%, compared with the consensus forecast of 3.2% and up from 3.0% in April. Yet contrary to the expectation of financiers who predicted the Bank of England to raise interest rate for curbing inflationary pressure, it decided to keep the base rate at 5.0%.

Which of the following, if true, best explains the apparently conflicting decision of the Bank of England?

(A) Higher food and energy costs accounted for almost all the increase in consumer-price inflation.

(B) Inflationary expectations induced many workers to prompt higher wage demands which could spiral into higher inflation.

(C) Many City traders thought that the governor of the Bank of England would signal the need for higher interest rates.

(D) One member of the rate-setting meeting plumped for a cut to 4.75%.

(E) Rising energy prices have caused consumers to reduce their demand for other commodities, including properties, whose prices are beginning to drop significantly.

EXERCISE 해설 & 정답

A

1 본문 해설 :

6월 17일 공식적인 수치들은 5월까지의 연간 물가상승이 금융계 예상보다도 높았다는 것을 보여주었다. 소비자물가 3.3%만큼 상승하였는데 이 수치는 4월 3%나 시장 예상치였던 3.2%를 상회하는 수치였다. 그러나, 영란은행이 인플레이션 압력을 덜어내기 위해 금리를 인상시킬 것으로 예상했던 금융가들의 기대와는 달리 영란은행은 정책금리를 5%로 유지하기로 결정했다.

Reasoning Summary:

인플레이션 압력을 덜기 위해 정책금리를 인상하리라는 예상과 달리 영란은행은 금리를 유지하기로 결정했다는 언뜻 보면 납득하기 힘든 영란은행의 결정을 설명하라는 문제임

답지분석

(A) 소비자 물가 상승의 원인 규명은 영란은행 금리 결정의 설명과는 무관하다.

(B) 인플레이션 기대 심리가 노동자들의 보다 높은 임금 요구를 촉발시켰고 이게 다시 보다 높은 인플레이션으로 연결될 수 있다라고 한다면 영란은행의 금리 유지 결정은 더욱 설명하기 어려워진다.

(C) 당초 금융가의 생각은 영란은행 금리 결정 설명과는 무관하다.

(D) 통화정책모임의 한 구성원의 주장은 문제 요구 설명과는 무관하다.

(E) 정답

"에너지 가격의 상승 때문에 소비자들은 부동산과 같은 다른 상품들에 대한 수요를 줄이게 되었고 이런 제품들의 가격이 현저하게 떨어지기 시작하고 있다"가 사실이라면, 물가하락 요인이 나타나기 시작하면서 인플레이션 압력이 덜어지는 측면이 있다는 의미이므로 지금까지의 물가상승에도 불구하고 영란은행의 금리유지 결정이 보다 자연스럽게 이해될 수 있다. 따라서, E가 정답이다.

Chapter VII.
Boldic

1. Boldic 핵심개념

1) 문제 성격의 이해

문제의 의미를 "**Boldic's role for the main conclusion**"이라고 이해한다. 즉, 본문의 결론에 대해 Boldic의 역할을 묻는 문제이다. 따라서, 맨 먼저 본문 내용 중 Boldic역할의 기준이 되는 결론부터 찾아내야 하므로 다음과 같은 점을 주의하면서 본문을 정리해나간다.

– 본문을 긍정적인 시각에서 바라본다.
– 중간에 흐름을 끊지 않고 끝까지 읽으면서 맥락을 파악한다.
– However(But)등의 접속사나 내용상의 반전에 유의한다.
– 본문문장 중 conclusion sentence를 명확하게 정한다.

2) 답지의 판별

– 일정한 framework을 염두에 두면서 Boldic 부분이 Conclusion에 기여하는 형태적인 역할을 정리한다. 즉, 아래 기준을 염두에 두고 Boldic역할에 대해 주관식처럼 정리를 한 후 답지 해석과 비교해나간다.

(A) 순접·역접의 구분 : Boldic부분이 본문 주장의 결론과 일치되는 방향에서 역할을 하는 순접 관계인지 아니면, 결론과 반대되는 방향에서 역할을 하는 역접 관계를 파악하여 답지에서 나오는 맥락이 본문 Boldic의 역할과 일치하는 지를 따져 보아야 한다.

(B) 전제·결론의 구분 : Boldic부분이 결론을 뒷받침하는 전제의 성격인지 아니면, Boldic자체가 결론의 역할인지를 구분함으로써 답지에서 Boldic의 역할을 묘사하는 단어들이 Boldic의 실제 역할과 일치하는 지를 따져 볼 수 있다.

이를 표로 간단히 정리한 아래 framework을 항상 기억한다.

	전 제	결 론
순접	(i) 사실전제: fact, finding, evidence (주의:사실전제부분을 답지에서 judgment나 claim으로 묘사한다면 그 답지는 오답이다) (ii) 추적전제= 소결론 : assumption, evidence, judgment,	(Main) conclusion, judgment (주의: main conclusion 부분을 답지에서 evidence로 묘사한다면 그 답지는 오답이다)

<table>
<tr><td></td><td colspan="2">intermediate conclusion,
subsidiary conclusion,
secondary conclusion</td></tr>
<tr><td>역접</td><td>상동</td><td>상동</td></tr>
</table>

※ 전제, 결론에서 자주 사용되는 어휘들의 정리는 순접/역접 관계에 공통적으로 적용되므로 "상동"으로 표시하였다.

3) 답지 해석의 정확성을 높여야 한다.

(1) 빈출 단어 표현 정리

assumption	assumption문제를 풀 때보다 포괄적인 용어로 쓰이며, 추측 전제의 성격을 지칭하는 용어로 쓰인다.
claim	추측 성격이 들어간 볼딕에 적용 가능하며, 전제,결론 가리지 않고 지칭할 수 있다.
consideration	주로 전제 성격을 지칭하는 말로서, 의사 결정 이전에 고려해야 될 사항이라고 이해하면 된다. 사실-추측 가리지 않고 사용 가능하다. (things to be considered before making decisions)
context	background라고 이해한다. 즉, 논리 전개를 위한 배경 설정의 역할을 지칭한다.
defend	직역적인 "방어하다"라는 의미보다는 "support"라는 의미로 해석하는 게 보다 명확하다.
drawback	"결점"의 의미로 해석한다.
evidence	무언가를 지지하는 기능이 있을 때 사용하는 말로서, 사실-추측 가리지 않는다. 다만, main conclusion의 경우 무언가를 지지하는 기능이 없으므로 evidence라는 단어와 어울리지 않는다.
judgment	볼딕 표현이 추측의 성격이 들어간 경우 전제,결론 가리지 않고 지칭할 수 있다.
position	conclusion이라고 바꾸어 생각하면 된다. 대결론-소결론 두 가지 성격에 적용 가능하다.

(2) 지칭 대상 유의

a conclusion	수식구 없이 쓰이는 a conclusion은 any conclusion의 의미이다. 따라서, 본문 속 모든 conclusion이 지칭대상이 될 수 있으므로, 답지 문맥 해석을 먼저 실시한 후 그 해석에 맞는 conclusion을 대입한다.
the conclusion	수식구 없이 쓰이는 the conclusion은 the author's conclusion을 의미한다. 즉, 본문에서 작가가 정한 그 결론을 지칭하는 말로 이해한다.
that position	That position, that argument, that conclusion 등은 동일 답지 내에서 지칭대상을 끌고 오는 표현이다.
alternative strategy	"동일 답지 내에서 선행해서 나왔던 strategy와 다른 strategy"라는 의미로 해석한다.

(3) 수식 관계 해석

관계대명사 삽입절 구조	The first is a pattern of cause and effect that the consumer advocate argues will be repeated in the case at issue ("관계대명사 S V V1" 구조에서 S V는 삽입절이다)
전치사 수식구	in the case at issue:논란이 되고 있는 그 경우에서" 등의 전치사 수식구를 빠뜨리지 말고 해석해야 한다.
"명사+전치사+관계대명사" 구조시 선행사 파악 유의	The first presents a goal, strategies for achieving which are being evaluated in the argument ("strategies for achieving which"가 한 묶음이므로 which의 선행사는 그 앞에 있는 a goal이 된다.
"that+명사" 지칭대상	The first is a position that the reasoning contends is inadequately supported by the evidence; the second is evidence that has been used to support that position. 첫번째 볼딕은 결론인데, 본문의 추론이 주장하기를 이 결론은 증거에 의해 적절하게 뒷받침되지 않는다. 두번째 볼딕은 바로 그 결론(즉, that position의 지칭대상은 동일 답지 내에 있는 첫번째 볼딕의 position을 지칭한다)을 뒷받침하는데 활용되어온 증거이다.

Sample Question 해설 : OG2025 Q764 ▼

본문 해설 :

자동차보험이 자동차 사고시 겪어지는 편타성 상해에 대한 보상까지를 포함하는 나라들에서는 그러한 편타성 상해를 입었다라고 보고하는 빈도가 그런 상해에 대해 보상 처리를 하지 않는 나라들에 비해 2배 높게 나타난다. 현재, 편타성 상해여부에 대한 객관적 검사가 없으므로, 편타성 상해에 대한 허위보고를 쉽게 적발해낼 수 없다는 게 사실이다. 그럼에도 불구하고, 이렇게 허위보고를 쉽게 적발할 수 없다는 사실들이 편타성 상해의 보고 비율이 높은 나라들의 경우 보고된 편타성 상해 중 절반은 허위다라는 일부 논평가들에 의해 도출된 결론을 정당화시키지는 않는다. 명백하게도, 자동차 보험에서 편타성 상해에 대한 보상을 포함하지 않는 나라들에서는, 사람들은 종종 실제로 편타성 상해를 입었었어도 그런 상해를 보고할만한 동기 유발이 없기 때문이다.

Reasoning Summary:

본문에서 결론은 "그럼에도 불구하고, 이렇게 허위보고를 쉽게 적발할 수 없다는 사실들이 편타성 상해의 보고 비율이 높은 나라들의 경우 보고된 편타성 상해 중 절반은 허위다라는 일부 논평가들에 의해 도출된 결론을 정당화시키지는 않는다"라는 추정이다.

첫번째 Boldic은 "자동차보험이 자동차 사고시 겪어지는 편타성 상해에 대한 보상까지를 포함하는 나라들에서는 그러한 편타성 상해를 입었다라고 보고하는 빈도가 그런 상해에 대해 보상 처리를 하지 않는 나라들에 비해 2배 높게 나타난다"라는 사실을 제시하면서, 이 사실에 대한 일부 논평가들의 해석 및 그에 대한 작가의 반박으로 연결되고 있다.

두 번째 Boldic은 논평가 해석에 대한 작가의 반박을 뒷받침하는 추정전제이다.

답지분석:

(A) 첫번째 Boldic의 내용에 대해 본문에서 논란을 제기한 바 없으므로 답지 A번은 본문의 내용과 불일치한다.

(B) 두번째 볼딕은 작가 결론의 전제이지 결론 역할이 아니다.

(C) 두번째 볼딕은 작가 결론의 전제이지 결론 역할이 아니다.

(D) 정답

첫번째 Boldic의 사실에 대한 일부 논평가들의 해석 및 그에 대한 작가의 반박으로 연결되고 있고, 두번째 Boldic은 논평가 해석에 대한 작가의 반박을 뒷받침하는 추정전제이므로, 답지 "D: 첫번째 볼딕은 발견이고 그 발견에 대한 시사점들이 주장 내에서 논란이 되고 있다.; 두 번째 볼딕은 그 발견으로부터 어떤 시사점들을 도출하는 거에 대해 반대 주장을 하기 위해 제시된 주장이다.

(E) 첫번째 Boldic의 발견에 대한 정확성이 평가되고 있는 것이 아니므로 답지 E는 본문의 내용과 불일치한다.

EXERCISE

E

Q1 : Editorial: On Thursday, **South Korea agreed to resume the import of U.S. beef, removing one hurdle to ratification of the FTA by U.S. Congress**. Not surprisingly, many Korean journalists predict that U.S. Congress will shortly approve the free trade agreement with Korea. However, U.S. legislators still voice opposition to the trade deal, demanding South Korea reconvene auto sector negotiations to guarantee wider opening of the Korean market to U.S. cars. Therefore, it is reasonable to think that **KORUS FTA may not come into force in the near future.**

In the argument above, the two boldface portions play which of the following roles?

(A) The first supports the position that the argument challenges; the second is that position.

(B) The first is the judgment leading to a prediction; the second is the evidence consistent with that prediction.

(C) The first is the evidence for the conclusion of the argument; the second is the intermediate conclusion of the argument.

(D) The first provides a context for the prediction that the argument challenges; the second is the judgment the argument gave on that prediction.

(E) The first provides a context for the prediction that the argument challenges; the second provides evidence for the conclusion of the argument.

EXERCISE 해설 & 정답 A

1 본문 해설 :

사설: 목요일에 **한국은 미국 쇠고기 수입 재개에 동의했고 이에 따라 미국의회의 FTA비준에 있어 한 가지 걸림돌을 제거했다.** 놀랍지 않게도, 많은 한국 저널리스트들은 미국 의회가 조만간 한국과의 FTA를 승인할 것이라고 예상한다. 그러나, 미국 의원들은 한국이 자동차 시장의 미국차에 대한 개방 폭을 넓힐 것을 보장해주도록 자동차 부문에 대한 협상을 한국정부가 재고하도록 요구하면서 여전히 FTA에 대한 반대의견을 표시하고 있다. 따라서, **한미 FTA는 조만간 효력을 발휘하기는 힘들 것이다** 라고 생각하는 게 합리적이다.

Reasoning Summary:

본문에서 결론은 "한미 FTA는 조만간 효력을 발휘하기는 힘들 것이다"라는 두번째 볼딕이다. 이에 대해 첫번째 볼딕은 작가의 결론과 반대되는 결론을 위한 근거로 제시되어 있다. 따라서, 답지 "D: 첫번째 볼딕은 본문 주장이 반박하는 예상을 위한 맥락을 제공한다; 두번째 볼딕은 그 예상에 대한 본문 주장이 제시하는 판단이다"가 정답이다.

답지분석:

(A) 두번째 Boldic의 that position이 첫번째 Boldic의 설명에서 언급된 "본문 주장이 반박하는 position"을 받게 되어 본문과 불일치한다.

(B) 첫번째 Boldic은 fact로 제시된 내용인데 이를 답지에서 judgment로 묘사했으므로 오답이다.

(C) 첫번째 Boldic을 본문주장과 순접관계로 묘사했으므로 본문과 불일치한다.

(D) 정답

"첫번째 볼딕은 본문 주장이 반박하는 예상을 위한 맥락을 제공한다; 두번째 볼딕은 그 예상에 대한 본문 주장이 제시하는 판단이다": 본문의 내용과 정확히 일치한다.

(E) 두번째 Boldic은 main conclusion이므로 evidence라는 표현으로 묘사될 수 없다.

Chapter VIII.
Completion

1. Completion 핵심개념

1) 다른 CR문제는 문제를 통해 답의 방향성을 제시하는 반면, completion문제에서는 여러분이 빈칸의 역할을 차분하게 규명함으로써 그 답의 방향성을 파악해야 한다.

2) 빈칸의 역할은 종종 Conclusion이나 Weaken & Strengthen 등의 역할로 귀결되곤 한다.

Sample Question 해설 #1: OG2025 Q788 ▼

문제 Type : completion

Reasoning Summary:

천식이 다른 스포츠보다 수영선수들에게 보다 흔하고, 수영장 물 소독에 쓰이는 chlorine이 폐에 좋지 않은 것으로 알려져 있기는 하지만, 수영 선수들 사이에 보다 흔한 천식의 원인이 chlorine 노출때문이라고 단정짓지는 말아야 하는 이유가 빈칸의 역할이다.

정답분석

정답:"D

몇 년전까지, 의사들은 수영동작이 천식 증상을 완화시킬 것으로 믿으면서, 천식을 가진 아이들에게 수영을 추천했다"가 빈칸에 들어오면, 본문의 사실이 "천식을 가진 아이들이 수영을 하게 되었다"로 설명되면서, 수엉장 물 속의 chlorine 노출 때문에 천식이 생겼을 것이라는 추정은 약화된다.

EXERCISE

E

Q1 : Which of the following best completes the passage below?

For many years, it was taken for granted that there is a strong relationship between house prices and consumer spending. However, some researchers cast doubt on this view. Although the apparent breakdown in the relationship in the last year, when consumers did not respond to a surge in house prices by spending more, seemed to support them, it is premature to accept their view because

(A) the falling house prices enable businesses to spend more wages for their employees by lowering cumbersome rents for offices.

(B) there are more renters than owners of houses

(C) the long bear stock market of last year greatly influenced consumers to curb their spending

(D) this year, house prices continue to plunge

(E) many economists don't agree that the housing slump will hurt the economy by slashing the demand for consumer goods.

1 본문 해설 :

여러 해 동안, 주택가격과 소비자 지출 사이에는 강력한 상관관계가 있다는 점이 당연시 되었다. 그러나, 일부 연구자들은 이런 견해에 대해 의구심을 제기한다. 작년도의 경우 주택가격 상승에 대해 지출을 늘리는 식으로 소비자들이 반응하지 않았고 이런 점은 주택가격과 소비자 지출 사이의 상관관계가 단절된 것처럼 보이면서 의구심을 제기하는 일부 연구자들의 의견을 뒷받침하는 것처럼 보이기는 하지만, 그런 연구자들의 견해를 받아들이는 것은 불합리하다. 왜냐하면, ------------------.

Reasoning Summary:

작년도의 경우 주택가격 상승에 대해 지출을 늘리는 식으로 소비자들이 반응하지 않았으므로 언뜻 보면 주택가격과 소비자 지출 사이의 상관관계에 대해 의구심을 제기하는 일부 연구자들의 의견을 뒷받침하는 것처럼 보이기는 하지만, 그런 연구자들의 의견을 받아들일 수만은 없는 이유를 찾아와야 한다. "C:작년도에 오랜 기간 동안 주식시장이 약세를 보이면서 소비자들의 지출을 줄이도록 작용했다"가 빈칸에 들어오면 작년도 주택가격 상승에도 불구하고 소비자 지출이 늘지 않은 점이 주식시장 약세로 설명이 되기 때문에 일부 연구자들의 견해를 받아들일 수만은 없게 된다. 따라서, C가 정답이다.

Chapter IX.
Logic Types

1. 기타 오류 Type

1) 순환논증

결론이 전제를 반복하는 불합리한 논리

> **Example**
>
> TV시청은 아동들의 정서발달에 방해가 된다. 왜냐하면, 아동들의 정서발달에 방해가 되는 것이 TV시청이기 때문이다.

2) 권위에 호소하는 오류

주장을 하는 사람의 권위를 논리의 근거로 삼는 불합리한 논리

> **Example**
>
> 세계적으로 유명한 동물복제 학자 황박사는 A라는 향수를 B의 향수보다 좋은 것으로 평가했다. 따라서, 향수 A가 향수 B보다 좋은 제품임에 틀림없다.

3) 사람을 탓하는 오류

주장이나 이론에 대해 논증하지 않고 사람의 인간성, 성격 등을 반론의 근거로 삼는 불합리한 논리

> **Example**
>
> FTA에 대한 반론을 펴는 A씨의 주장은 전혀 근거 없다. 왜냐하면 A씨는 무척 게으른 사람이기 때문이다.

2. 2인 사이의 대화

2인 사이의 대화는 대부분 두 사람간의 견해가 엇갈리는 경우가 많다. 이런 경우에는 다음과 같은 두 가지 type의 문제가 종종 출제된다.

1) 논란의 초점을 묻는 문제(at issue)

2) 반론의 전개 방법을 묻는 문제

반론이 진행되는 과정에서 다음과 같은 세가지 범주 중 하나에 포함되는 경우가 많다.

– 동문서답형: 상대방의 논리와 초점이 벗어난 논거를 제기하면서 반대하는 경우로서 사실상 반론의 효력이 없게 된다.

Example

> A: 심각한 경기침체에 직면하여 한국은행은 지난 목요일 정책금리를 전격적으로 1% 인하하였다. 이에 따라, 정기 예금의 실질 수익률은 더욱 낮아질 것이다. 따라서, 정기예금의 증가추세가 둔화될 것이다.
>
> B: 전혀 그렇지 않다. 사실, 한국은행은 경기침체 극복을 위해 최선을 다하고 있다.

– 상대방의 전제 진실성부터 의문을 제기함으로써 논리를 반박하는 경우

Example

> A: 심각한 경기침체에 직면하여 한국은행은 지난 목요일 정책금리를 전격적으로 1% 인하하였다. 이에 따라, 정기 예금의 실질 수익률은 더욱 낮아질 것이다. 따라서, 정기예금의 증가추세가 둔화될 것이다.
>
> B: 전혀 그렇지 않다. 최근 유가 급락으로 인해 물가 하락 폭이 더욱 커지고 있으므로 금리인하에도 불구하고 정기예금의 실질 수익률은 낮아지지 않을 것이다.

– 상대방의 전제 진실성은 인정을 하면서도 다른 논점을 제기함으로써 전제로부터 결론까지의 연결관계
  를 약화시키는 경우

Example

A: 심각한 경기침체에 직면하여 한국은행은 지난 목요일 정책금리를 전격적으로 1% 인하하였다. 이에 따라, 정기 예금의 실질 수익률은 더욱 낮아질 것이다. 따라서, 정기예금의 증가추세가 둔화될 것이다.

B: 전혀 그렇지 않다. 정기 예금을 제외한 다른 대부분 투자 수단의 실질 수익률은 마이너스 수익률을 보여주고 있다.

Chapter X.
CR (테마정리)

Theme 1 : Generalization

전제와 결론의 연결 과정에서 대상의 확대가 이루어지면 그 전제가 결론의 대상에 대해 representative한지 확인해본다.

Theme 2 : Analogy

Analogy Fallacy : 두 시점의 차이점 부각을 통해 Weaken이 가능하다.

Theme 3 : 수나 양 ≠ 비율

Theme 4 : sales ≠ profit, sales-cost=profit

Theme 5 : Report or Diagnosis 변화 ≠ Incidence 변화

Theme 6 : 시점 ≠ 기간

Theme 7 : trend ≠ level

W: The rapid rise in the rate of unemployment is a serious economic problem; it will undoubtedly cost the majority party votes in the coming election.

Z: I disagree. Statistics for the past 40 years show that there is no significant relationship between the prevailing level of unemployment and political gains or losses by the party that happens to be in the majority at election times.

Theme 8 : decrease of increase rate ≠ decrease

Theme 9 : wholesale price증/감 ≠ retail price증/감

Theme 10 : CR terminology

in the rate of unemployment 다음과 같은 용어를 논리적으로 정리하면, 논리의 scope설정에 유용하다.

Many=more than one	Some=at least one
Most=more than half	Improve=better than now

PART IV
Reading Comprehension(RC)

Reading Comprehension

Chapter I.
Passage Breaking

1. Active Reading for Passage Breaking:

전형적인 GMAT 독해 지문의 구성을 이해하고 지문을 읽어나가면, 글의 흐름을 예측할 수 있고 주제를 확신 있게 가려낼 수 있다. 본문에서 주제와 부수적인 이야기들을 구분해내지 못하면 gmat독해에서는 문제를 제대로 풀 수가 없는 바, 이 점은 TOEFL 독해와 확연히 구분되는 점이다. GMAT 독해 지문의 구성을 아래 표와 같이 흐름적 구성과 내용적 구성으로 나눌 수 있는 바, 이를 일단 숙지한다.

흐름적 구성	Diversion → Transition(Key Twist) → Main Topic	
내용적 구성	전조	주제
	문제점 제시(Problem)	해결책(Solution) 제시 및 평가
	질문(Question)	답변(Answer)
	과거(Conventional)이론	최근(Recent) 경향
	뜻밖(Unexpected)의 현상	원인분석(Cause Analysis)

1) 흐름적 구성을 통한 글의 분석

지문을 나열식으로 읽지 말고 주도적으로 챙길 내용을 챙기고, 가볍게 볼 내용은 가볍게 보는 식으로 경중을 구분하면서 읽는다.

역할	Signal
Diversion	throughout ~~~, conventional(ly)=traditional(ly), until recently, until now for a long time, for many years, for a while, for a few centuries, once(adverb: "not now"의 느낌을 강하게 받는다)
Transition	however, but, yet, nevertheless, nonetheless, on the other hand, in contrast, conversely, still new, recent today, now, recently

Main Topic
(동사,형용사,부사 등을
통해 분위기 및 주제를
암시한다)

- Positive-nuanced Expressions:

adequate, attractive, brilliant, compelling, convincing, fortunately, fruitful, illuminating, ingenious, legitimate, plausible, seminal, splendid, useful 등

- Negative-nuanced Expressions:

arbitrary, argumentative, condescending, dangerous, myth, naive, outdated, overly, overstate, patronizing, pedantic, problematic, questionable, rhetoric, skeptical, too, unfortunately 등

(1) Diversion을 전략적인 관점에서 접근한다.

대개 과거 시점 부사구의 이야기는 Diversion의 성격이 강하다. 즉, 초반부에 특정 과거 시점의 이야기를 꺼내는 지문의 경우 뒷 부분에서 최근 이야기로 글의 흐름을 반전시키는 경우를 종종 보게 된다. 따라서, 과거 시점 부사구가 글의 초반부에 나오면 그 문장의 내용을 기초로 뒤에 반전될 내용에 대해 미리 예측해나갈 수 있어야 한다.

반면, 출제자는 이 부분에 의도적으로 자세한 mechanism이나 현상에 대한 묘사 등을 추가함으로써, 앞으로 전개 될 주제에 대한 예측을 가로막는 바, 이런 mechanism이나 description 등을 가볍게 보고, 글의 맥을 잡는 데 초점 맞추어야 한다.

(1-1) Signal Review

throughout ~~~, conventional(ly)=traditional(ly), until recently, until now
for a long time, for many years, for a while, for a few centuries,
once(adverb: "not now"의 느낌을 강하게 받는다)

(1-2) EXAMPLE

> The conventional wisdom is that, for better or worse, trade unionism is in irreversible long-term decline, at least in the world's leading economies. In America, for example, only 12.5% of the workforce belongs to a union, and a mere 7.8% of private-sector workers, down from one-third in 1960. Most forecasts predict that this trend will continue, perhaps until unionism is confined to museums and history books. But Sara Horowitz is determined to prove them wrong.

해석 : 전통적인 지혜에 따르면, 좋든 싫든 노조는 적어도 선진 경제권에서는 장기적 쇠퇴국면이라는 게 거스를 수 없는 대세이다. 예를 들면, 미국에서는 노조 가입률이 12.5%에 지나지 않고, 민간 부문에서는 7.8%밖에 되지 않는데 이 비율은 1960년의 노조 가입률이 1/3이었다는 것과 비교하면 엄청나게 낮아진 비율이다. 대부분의 예측들은 이런 추세가 지속되어 마침내 노조가 박물관에서나 역사책의 뒤안길로 사라져갈 수도 있다라고 말한다. 그러나, Sara Horowitz는 그런 예측이 잘못되었다는 것을 입증하려 한다

바람직하지 못한 독해

전통적인 지혜에 따르면, 좋든 싫든 노조는 적어도 선진 경제권에서는 장기적 쇠퇴국면이라는 게 거스를 수 없는 대세이다.

➡ 독해의 초점을 topic으로 제시된 노조에만 맞추면서 "그렇지, 요즘 노조는 전세계적으로 맥을 못추고 있다"라는 상식을 동원하여 "그렇겠구나, 노조는 장기적 쇠퇴 국면일 수밖에 없겠구나"라고 분석한다. 그런 분석 속에서 해석하면 마지막 문장 "그러나, Sara Horowitz는 그런 예측이 잘못되었다는 것을 입증하려 한다"라는 부분에서 당황하게 되고 글의 초점이 혼동스러워진다.

바람직한 독해

전통적인 시혜에 따르면, 좋든 싫든 노주는 적어도 선진 경제권에서는 장기적 쇠퇴국면이라는 게 거스를 수 없는 대세이다.

➡ 독해의 초점을 conventional라는 형용사에 맞추면서 분위기를 파악한다. 즉, "뒤에서 말이 바뀌어질 수 있겠구나"라고 반전의 흐름을 예측한다. 그러면, 마지막 문장 "그러나, Sara Horowitz는 그런 예측이 잘못되었다는 깃을 입증하려 한다"라는 부뷰에서 글의 흐름이 선명해지면서 읽는 속도에 탄력을 받게 된다.

(2) Transition에서 정신 번쩍 차리기:

▶ 역접 접속사(접속부사) 및 최근 시점을 의미하는 형용사나 부사(구) 등의 Key Twist서 글의 전환점 (Transition)에 대한 힌트를 얻고, 그 부분에서 강하게 집중한다.

▶ 문장의 연결에서와 마찬가지로 문단의 연결 과정에서도 역접 접속사나 접속부사를 사용하여 말의 초점을 바꾸는 경우가 많으므로, 역접 표현이 나오면 의도적으로 집중하면서 그 문장을 보아야 한다.

▶ 글쓴이는 대부분 최근 시점에 언급된 내용에 관심을 집중하는 경우가 많으므로, 여러분도 최근 시점을 나타내는 부사나 부사구가 나오면 더욱 집중력을 높여야 한다. 그런데, 대부분 독해 지문에서는 최근 시점을 알리는 부사(구)와 역접표현이 더불어 나오는 경우를 종종 보게 된다.

(2-1) Signal Review

however, but, yet,
nevertheless, nonetheless, on the other hand, in contrast, conversely, still
new, recent
today, now, recently

(2-2) Pattern Drilling (해석 연습 : 집중해야 될 signal에 표시를 하면서 해석해본다)

1. The idea of analysing or synthesising small quantities of chemicals in a chip-sized apparatus is not new, but labs on chips have **conventionally** relied on systems of tiny pipes etched into them to move the chemicals around. That limits what they can be used for, since you need different combinations of pipes to bring chemicals together in the right order for different sorts of reactions to take place. **A new technology** of utilizing digital fluidics dispenses with the pipework.

2. The severity of the recession spared Mr Obama, **at first**, from confronting the deficit. Indeed, with the economy spiralling downward and the Federal Reserve's monetary ammunition all but spent, he rightly chose to boost the deficit in the short term through hefty fiscal stimulus. But the recession has inflicted horrific damage on the government's accounts; **Now**, Ohama has to reckon with the deficit.

(3) Main Topic 움켜잡기:

▶ 글쓴이의 nuance를 드러내는 "동사/형용사/부사"를 통해 글의 흐름을 적극적으로 예측해가는 습관을 길러야 한다.

▶ 특정 이슈에 대한 작가의 태도는 명사보다는 동사/형용사/부사를 통해 드러난다. 특히, 의견이나 가설이 2개 이상으로 대립될 때에는 작가가 중립적으로 비교/대조하는 성격인지 아니면 한쪽 편을 드는 것인지 구분하는 게 글의 주제 및 문제 파악에 중요한 역할을 하는데, 이런 작가의 태도를 파악하는 데 있어 nuance가 풍겨나오는 동사/형용사/부사를 통해 강한 힌트를 얻을 수 있다.

(3-1) Signal Review

Positive-nuanced Expressions:
adequate, attractive, brilliant, compelling, convincing, fortunately, fruitful, illuminating, ingenious, legitimate, plausible, seminal, splendid, useful 등

Negative-nuanced Expressions:
arbitrary, argumentative, condescending, dangerous, myth, naïve, outdated, overly, overstate, patronizing, pedantic, problematic, questionable, rhetoric, skeptical, too, unfortunately 등

(3-2) Pattern Drilling (해석 연습 : 집중해야 될 signal에 표시를 하면서 해석해본다)

1. **Unfortunately**, Eisenstein's unfinished study does not develop these ideas in sufficient depth or detail, offering tantalizing hints rather than an exhaustive analysis.

2. Some geophysicists believe that tektites are thrown up from the impact of huge meteorites hitting the Earth. A **more plausible** theory is that tektites are produced by the impact of meteorites on the Moon.

3. These researchers, influenced by Robert Heilbroner's now **outdated** development theory, tend to view nontechnological development as an obstacle to progress.

2. Efficient Reading(Big Picture Reading)

1) 완벽한 지식 습득의 욕심을 버리고 집중할 내용과 가볍게 볼 내용을 구분해간다:

RC 지문을 보는 목적은 문제를 잘 푸는 데 있음을 염두에 두면서, 중요한 내용과 그렇지 않은 내용을 철저하게 구분하여 접근한다.

▶ 문단별 초반부 흐름에 집중한다.

▶ 글쓴이의 태도가 담기는 형용사/부사에 집중한다.

▶ Key twist 부분에 집중한다.

▶ 반면, 구체적인 mechanism description은 가볍게 읽어가면서 문제 나올 경우 다시 되돌아올 생각으로 바라본다.

▶ 지문 전체적으로 보았을 때에는 초반부 transition까지는 정독 위주로 속도를 떨어뜨리면서 읽어나가다가, 글의 윤곽이 잡힌 후에는 약간 빠른 리듬으로 읽어나가면서 문제 나올 수 있는 부분들을

---

2) 문장과 문단의 function을 인식해가면서 읽어나간다:

GMAT 독해는 문답의 내용이 Rhetorical한 경우가 많다. 따라서, 문제에 나온 Reference 문장의 전후 문맥에 대한 파악이 선행되지 않으면 문답 해석의 오류가 발생하기 쉽다.

▶ 내용적 측면에서 글의 유형화
(1) 인과관계 분석
(2) 찬반 대립
(3) 중립적인 비교·대조 서술
(4) 구체적인 과정 서술

▶ 글쓴이 판단적 측면에서 글의 유형화
(1) 가설이나 이론(Hypotheses and Theories) 제시
(2) 작가의 찬반 의견 제시

---

3) Signal 확인

문장과 문장의 연결 관계를 알리는 signal들이 접속사, 접속부사, 전치사구의 형태로 종종 표현된다. 이런 signal들을 눈여겨 봄으로써 다음 문장의 내용을 적극적으로 예측하는 습관을 기른다.

관계	Signal
역접	however, but, yet, nevertheless, nonetheless, on the other hand, in contrast, conversely, still although, even though, while, whereas, all the same despite, in spite of, unlike, as opposed to, in contrast to
역접성격의 surprise signal	actually, in reality, in fact, indeed surprising(ly), paradoxical(ly), perplexing(ly), ironic(ally)
상관 어구	Granted=It is true that=Admittedly ~. But(However) ---------- Originally=Initially=At first ~. But(However) ------------ In theory ------. In practice ---------.
인과관계	because, since, for, as, in that, due to, because of so, therefore, hence, as a result, consequently, thus, as a consequence
예시	for example, for instance, in particular so ~ that

4) 문제예측

단순한 정보 기술의 내용보다는 어떤 이슈에 대한 이유 설명이나, 판단제시 부분에서 문제가 자주 출제된다. 이런 출제 가능성이 있는 본문내용을 예측하면서 독해를 해나간다. 문제에서 자주 다루어지는 내용들을 아래 표로 정리하였다. 다만, 순간적으로 모든 내용을 암기해야만 하는 것은 아니고, 그런 내용에 대해 집중력을 높여 실제 문제 출제시 관련 본문 내용을 빨리 찾아가 문제를 풀 수 있도록 준비를 하자.

---

(1) 인명, 숫자, 열거 : 이런 부분들은 글의 전개 과정에서 특정 목적을 가지고 언급되는 경우가 많다. 따라서, 이런 부분들이 언급되어진 목적을 파악해 놓아야 한다.

(2) 원인관계 분석이나 특정 주장에 대한 약화나 강화, Assumption의 내용들 : GRE, GMAT, LSAT RC문제 중 많은 문제들이 추론 능력 점검의 목적을 지닌다. 따라서, 비판적 추론 능력의 점검 사항이 될 수 있는 내용들은 문제로서 예측해 놓아야 한다.

(3) 예시의 기능 : "For example"성격이 나오면 구체적 내용보다도 그 예가 지문에서 하고 있는 기능에 초점을 맞춘다.

(4) Comparison & Contrast(Like, Unlike) : 비교/대조되었던 내용을 문제로 확인하는 경우가 종종 있으니, 외우려 하기보다는 Reference를 기억해 두었다가 빨리 찾아서 문제를 풀 수 있도록 집중력을 가지자. 특히, 대조되는 특징에 대해 문제에서 자주 묻는다.

(5) 가정법: 직설법적으로 이해할 때에는 반대 의미가 된다는 점을 인식해야 한다.

(6) "---"(단어의 재해석): GRE,GMAT,LSAT 독해 지문에서 특정 단어에 Quotation mark가 붙어 있는 경우 그 단어가 본문에서 중의적으로 쓰였을 가능성이 크며 그 문맥상 의미를 정확히 파악했는지를 문제를 통해 묻는 경우가 많다

(7) 마지막 첨언과 주제의 구분(Additional Comment) : 글의 끝부분에서 주제와는 약간 구분되는 첨언이 들어가는 경우 이 첨언과 주제를 혼동하고 있는 지 혹은 그 첨언의 목적이 무엇인지를 문제를 통해 확인한다. 이런 관점에서 글의 마지막 부분에서 "however(but) ----"의 흐름이 전개되는 경우 이 흐름이 글의 전반적 내용을 다시 한번 반전시키는 것인지 아니면, 주제는 주제대로 놓아두고 마지막 한마디 첨언 역할을 하는 것인지를 잘 구분해야 한다.

3. Active & Efficient Reading 실전 적용 절차 정리

앞에서 정리하였던 내용을 실제 지문에 적용하기 위해, 다음과 같은 4가지 step을 밟아나간다

STEP1. Signal 확인
STEP2. Skimming
STEP3. 주제에 대한 확신 갖기
STEP4. 문제예측

1) Step 1. Signal 총정리

GMAT독해 중 대부분의 long passage는 Diversion → Transition → Main Topic의 과정을 거쳐간다. 따라서, 작가 논리의 방향을 예측할 수 있는 signal(대부분 동사,형용사,부사 등으로 표현)들을 통해 글의 방향성을 예측하면서 흐름을 타는 듯하게 해나가야 한다. 아래에서 이런 작가 논리의 방향을 예측할 수 있는 대표적 표현들을 예시하였다.

(1) Diversion : 반전예고

다음과 같은 표현이 오면 글의 흐름이 반전될 것이 예상된다.
따라서, 지금까지의 내용을 토대로 반전의 내용을 예측해본다.

throughout -----, conventionally, traditionally
until recently, for ------- years---,for sometimes, once(ad)
have long thought(believed) that, was thought(believed) to, seemed to V
but(however)----

(2) Transition : 역접 표현

GMAT독해는 정보전달의 목적이기 보다는 argument 대립의 글이 많다. 따라서, However등의 역접 표현들이 많이 사용된다. 이는 글의 맥락을 잡는 길잡이 역할을 하는 접속사이므로 유념해서 보아야 한다.

Admittedly -----. But(However),
Granted ------. But(However),
It is true that ----------. But(However), it is also true that
Originally=Initially=At first -----. But(However) ----.
However, Still, Nonetheless, Nevertheless, On the other hand
Now, Today

(3) Main Topic과 더불어 나오는 동사·형용사·부사 등의 어감 확인

명사로 제시되는 Topic의 자세한 내용을 파악하기 이전에 작가의 Nuance를 드러내는 형용사·부사 등을 유의하면서 글의 분위기를 positive·negative·neutral로 나누어가면서 분석한다.

Positive-nuanced Expressions:
brilliant, compelling, convincing, fortunately, fruitful, illuminating, ingenious, legitimate, plausible, seminal, splendid 등

Negative-nuanced Expressions:
arbitrary, argumentative, condescending, myth, naive, overly, patronizing, pedantic, problematic, questionable, rhetoric, skeptical, too, unfortunately 등

Sample Long Passage(Signal 확인)

It has long been thought that small firms do not greatly contribute to a Korean economy that should overtake other countries, leading the government's policies to favor large-sized companies over small ones. Large firms were supposed to be superior in a lot of aspects including productivity, technological progress, and job security and compensation.

Recently, however, researchers observe small firms in many industries performing better than their larger counterparts. Indeed, in the steel industry, examples abound of new firms entering the market in the form of "mini-mills," and the employment of these small firms expanded, whereas large companies have reduced their businesses. True, it cannot conclusively be argued that smaller firms are as efficient as large firms. However, it is obvious that small size is not an intrinsic stumbling block. Not surprisingly, a different view on small firms has emerged that small firms perform significant roles in a lot of industries. For instance, small firms often trigger technological changes by trying various innovative activities. Moreover, small firms bring about market upheaval that leads to new dimensions of competition, and they also foster competition through newly created niches in an international background. Finally, the share of small firms in generating new jobs is significant.

Yet, evidence and researches on which empirical knowledge about the relative roles of large and small firms is based are fragmentary and not sufficient enough to answer major questions concerning the role of small firms across various industries and nations. Moreover, the question of what criteria should be used for distinguishing between small firms and large ones is not clearly resolved.

[해설]

1. It has long been thought that : 과거시점 부사구이므로 이 부분은 주제 도입 이전임을 알 수 있다. 너무 자세한 내용에 빠져들지 말고 뒤에 나올 내용에 대한 예측에 초점을 맞춘다.

2. Recently, however, : 글이 본격적으로 transition이 되면서 주제도입에 들어왔음을 느껴야 한다.

3. Yet, : 글의 끝부분에서 나오는 역접표현은 글을 또다시 transition하기 보다는 앞 내용에 대해 단서적인 첨언을 소개하는 경우가 종종 있다. 따라서, 해석을 하면서 앞 내용의 주제를 또다시 전환시키는 것인지 첨언이지를 명확히 구분하여 주제에 대한 확신 및 이를 통한 문제 대비에 나서야 한다.

2) Step 2. Skimming

(1) Short Passage Skimming

▶ 한 문단 내지 두 문단 구성을 하면 전체 지문 길이가 50줄이 넘지 않는 지문을 **Short Passage**라고 볼 수 있다. 지문의 길이가 짧아서 **Step 1. Signal** 인식과 **Step 2. Skimming** 과정이 동시에 이루어지게 된다.

▶ 지문 전체의 주제에 대한 확신과 주제를 기준으로 했을 때 본문 전체 구성을 이해하고 문제를 풀어나가야 한다.

▶ 문제에서 본문의 아주 자세한 부분까지 물어보는 경우가 많아서 엄청난 집중력을 가지고 문제 이슈가 될만한 사항을 기억하는 게 중요하다.

▶ 대표적인 문제 이슈인 인명,숫자,비유를 드는 예,비교·대조,첨언 등의 부분이 보이면, 본문 중 어느 부분이었는 지를 기억해 놓고 필요할 경우 암호처럼 Note-taking해놓는 것도 좋은 전략이다.

(EX)

본문 : Einstein challenges the previous theory

　　　Note : "E—p.t.(X)"

▶ 단, 문제 이슈가 되는 Specific한 내용만을 간결하게 Note-taking해야 하는 것이지 본문을 요약하는 식으로 note-taking하다가는 시간만 허비할 수 있다. 한 지문에 적절한 Note-taking의 길이는 5줄 이내여야 한다.

Sample Short Passage(Signal 확인)

A lot of ethologists are interested in comparing human cultural behavior with genetically programmed animal behavior, such as monkeys and children. **Admittedly**, humans are animals in that they have much in common with other animals. Indeed, some characteristics of human behavior may seem analogous to those of other animals. Such analogies, **however**, have the potential of misleading us if the context of a particular bit of behavior is not taken into account. For example, one researcher compares the presentation of a branch by a black bird with gift-giving in people. But the black bird's behavior simply inhibits attack and is equal to other placating rituals of many other species. Human gift-giving, in contrast, is greatly different in form and purpose from culture to culture, and within the same culture it is carried out in various contexts. All important elements in this human behavior derive from its social context. Thus, ethologists cannot accomplish anything until they study humans as cultural beings.

"Admittedly" ----와 "however"의 대응 구조를 통해 인간도 동물들이긴 하지만, 인간 행동의 경우 그 행동이 이루어지는 맥락을 고려하지 않고서는 제대로 된 해석을 할 수 없다는 점을 예를 들어가면서 설명하고 있다.

(2) Long Passage Skimming

▶ 글의 전체적인 구조를 파악하면서, 지문을 요약할 수 있도록 Active Reading skill을 발휘해야 한다. 이런 면에서 Short Passage에 비해 첫 문단에서 글의 방향을 예측하는 노력이 훨씬 중요 해진다. 앞에서 정리하였던 자주 출제되는 첫문단 서술 형태와 그에 따른 주제의 방향성 예측표 를 다시 한번 복습한다.

▶ 지문 전체의 주제에 대한 확신과 주제를 기준으로 했을 때 본문 전체 구성을 이해하고 문제를 풀 어나가야 한다.

▶ 본문 전체 내용이 다 문제로 활용될 수는 없다. 본문 중에서 자주 출제되는 문제 이슈들―인명,숫 자,비유를 드는 예,비교·대조,첨언―을 간추려내는 노력을 기울여 한다.

▶ 문제 이슈들에 대해서는 Short Passage와 마찬가지로 Note-taking 전략을 활용하는 것도 좋 은 방법이다. 다만, 이 때에도 한 지문에 적절한 Note-taking의 길이는 5줄 이내여야 한다.

Sample Long Passage(Skimming)

It has long been thought that small firms do not greatly contribute to a Korean economy that should overtake other countries, leading the government's policies to favor large-sized companies over small ones. Large firms were supposed to be superior in a lot of aspects including productivity, technological progress, and job security and compensation.

Recently, however, researchers observe small firms in many industries performing better than their larger counterparts. Indeed, in the steel industry, examples abound of new firms entering the market in the form of "mini-mills," and the employment of these small firms expanded, whereas large companies have reduced their businesses. True, it cannot conclusively be argued that smaller firms are as efficient as large firms. However, it is obvious that small size is not an intrinsic stumbling block. Not surprisingly, a different view on small firms has emerged that small firms perform significant roles in a lot of industries. For instance, small firms often trigger technological changes by trying various innovative activities. Moreover, small firms bring about market upheaval that leads to new dimensions of competition, and they also foster competition through newly created niches in an international background. Finally, the share of small firms in generating new jobs is significant.

Yet, evidence and researches on which empirical knowledge about the relative roles of large and small firms is based are fragmentary and not sufficient enough to answer major questions concerning the role of small firms across various industries and nations. Moreover, the question of what criteria should be used for distinguishing between small firms and large ones is not clearly resolved.

Skimming

도입 및 전개부 : 두번째 문단의 However로 넘어오는 오랫동안 생각해온 바와 달리 소규모 회사들의 역할이 중요하다는 점을 시사하는 최근의 관찰 사례를 지적하고 있다.

결말부 : 마지막 문단의 Yet를 통해 소규모 회사의 역할을 확실하게 뒷받침할 수 있는 실증적 증거의 토대가 약하다는 점과 소규모 회사에 대한 정의가 분명하지 않다는 점을 지적함으로써 소규모 회사들의 공헌이 대기업보다 일관되게 크다라고 난정직으로 말하기는 어렵다는 첨언적인 단서를 지적하면서 글을 마무리하고 있다.

3) Step 3 : 주제에 대한 확신갖기

▶ 문단별 결론의 흐름을 잡아나가면, 주제에 대한 확신을 높여갈 수 있다.

　　자주 나오는 지문 흐름 유형의 예
　　초반 도입부
　　질문 제시　　　　　　　　　 ------〉
　　과거의 이론이나 연구방법 제시　 ------ 〉
　　뜻밖의 관찰이나 현상소개　　 ------〉
　　질문에 대한 답변
　　최근에 소개된 다른 이론, 연구방법
　　그런 관찰이나 현상의 원인 분석

▶ 주제 : 글쓴이가 본문을 통해 전달하고 싶은 핵심 내용이다. 즉, 본문 전체를 요약하는 핵심 메시지라고 보면 된다. 이는 특정 주장이 될 수도 있고, 전체 사실을 요약하는 정보가 될 수도 있다.

▶ 주제를 통한 글의 목적 분석 : GRE,GMAT,LSAT 독해 문제에서 글의 목적을 자주 물어보곤 한다. 주제가 전체 내용의 요약이라고 한다면, 이를 좀더 넓은 의미로 추상화시켜 표현하는 것이 글이 목적이라고 보면 된다.

▶ 전제 : 주제를 꺼내오는 배경 정보나 주제를 뒷받침하는 증거

▶ 주제에 따른 시사점 : 주제를 전달한 후 이를 토대로 시사점을 제시하는 경우가 있다. 이는 항상 본문에서 제시되는 건 아니지만 시사점까지 제시된 경우 대부분 이러한 시사점을 문제에서 활용하는 경우가 많기 때문에 주의기울여야 한다.

Sample Short Passage (주제에 대한 확신 갖기)

A lot of ethologists are interested in comparing human cultural behavior with genetically programmed animal behavior, such as monkeys and children. Admittedly, humans are animals in that they have much in common with other animals. Indeed, some characteristics of human behavior may seem analogous to those of other animals. Such analogies, however, have the potential of misleading us if the context of a particular bit of behavior is not taken into account. For example, one researcher compares the presentation of a branch by a black bird with gift-giving in people. But the black bird's behavior simply inhibits attack and is equal to other placating rituals of many other species. Human gift-giving, in contrast, is greatly different in form and purpose from culture to culture, and within the same culture it is carried out in various contexts. All important elements in this human behavior derive from its social context. Thus, ethologists cannot accomplish anything until they study humans as cultural beings.

"Admittedly" ----와 "however"의 대응 구조를 확인하였으므로, however 뒤쪽에 글의초점을 맞춘다.

따라서, "인간 행동의 경우 그 행동이 이루어지는 맥락을 고려하지 않고서는 제대로 된 해석을 할 수 없다" 는 주장이 글의 주제임을 확신한다.

Sample Short Passage2 (주제에 대한 확신 갖기)

It has long been thought that small firms do not greatly contribute to a Korean economy that should overtake other countries, leading the government's policies to favor large-sized companies over small ones. Large firms were supposed to be superior in a lot of aspects including productivity, technological progress, and job security and compensation.

Recently, however, researchers observe small firms in many industries performing better than their larger counterparts. Indeed, in the steel industry, examples abound of new firms entering the market in the form of "mini-mills," and the employment of these small firms expanded, whereas large companies have reduced their businesses. True, it cannot conclusively be argued that smaller firms are as efficient as large firms. However, it is obvious that small size is not an intrinsic stumbling block. Not surprisingly, a different view on small firms has emerged that small firms perform significant roles in a lot of industries. For instance, small firms often trigger technological changes by trying various innovative activities. Moreover, small firms bring about market upheaval that leads to new dimensions of competition, and they also foster competition through newly created niches in an international background. Finally, the share of small firms in generating new jobs is significant.

Yet, evidence and researches on which empirical knowledge about the relative roles of large and small firms is based are fragmentary and not sufficient enough to answer major questions concerning the role of small firms across various industries and nations. Moreover, the question of what criteria should be used for distinguishing between small firms and large ones is not clearly resolved.

1. "It has long been thought → Recently, however,"의 흐름을 통해 지문의 주제는 "오랫동안 생각해온 바와 달리 소규모 회사들의 역할이 중요하다"는 견해를 제시하는 데 있음을 확신할 수 있다.

2. 주제에 대한 확신을 통해 1) main idea 2) primary purpose 3) organization 등의 general question에 대비한다.

4) Step 4 : Specific Question 예측

단순한 정보 기술의 내용보다는 어떤 이슈에 대한 이유 설명이나, 판단 제시 부분에서 문제가 자주 출제된다. 이런 출제 가능성이 있는 본문 내용을 예측하면서 독해를 해나간다. 문제에서 자주 다루어지는 내용들을 아래 표로 정리하였다. 다만, 순간적으로 모든 내용을 암기해야만 하는 것은 아니고, 그런 내용에 대해 집중력을 높여 실제 문제 출제시 관련 본문 내용을 빨리 찾아가 문제를 풀 수 있도록 준비를 한다.

(1) 인명, 숫자, 열거 : 이런 부분들은 글의 전개 과정에서 특정 목적을 가지고 언급되는 경우가 많다. 따라서, 이런 부분들이 언급된 목적을 파악해 놓아야 한다.

(2) 원인관계 분석이나 특정 주장에 대한 약화나 강화, Assumption의 내용들 : GRE, GMAT, LSAT RC문제 중 많은 문제들이 추론 능력 점검의 목적을 지닌다. 따라서, 비판적 추론 능력의 점검 사항이 될 수 있는 내용들은 문제로서 예측해 놓아야 한다.

(3) 예시의 기능 : "For example"성격이 나오면 구체적 내용보다도 그 예가 지문에서 하고 있는 기능에 초점을 맞춘다.

(4) Comparison & Contrast(Like, Unlike) : 비교·대조되었던 내용을 문제로 확인하는 경우가 종종 있으니, 외우려 하기보다는 Reference를 기억해 두었다가 빨리 찾아서 문제를 풀 수 있도록 집중력을 가지자. 특히, 대조되는 특징에 대해 문제에서 자주 묻는다.

(5) 가정법: 직설법적으로 이해할 때에는 반대 의미가 된다는 점을 인식해야 한다.

(6) "---"(단어의 재해석): GRE,GMAT,LSAT 독해 지문에서 특정 단어에 Quotation mark가 붙어 있는 경우 그 단어가 본문에서 중의적으로 쓰였을 가능성이 크며 그 문맥상 의미를 정확히 파악했는지를 문제를 통해 묻는 경우가 많다

(7) 마지막 첨언과 주제의 구분(Additional Comment) : 글의 끝부분에서 주제와는 약간 구분되는 첨언이 들어가는 경우 이 첨언과 주제를 혼동하고 있는 지 혹은 그 첨언의 목적이 무엇인지를 문제를 통해 확인한다. 이런 관점에서 글의 마지막 부분에서 "however(but) ----"의 흐름이 전개되는 경우 이 흐름이 글의 전반적 내용을 다시 한번 반전시키는 것인지 아니면, 주제는 주제대로 놓아두고 마지막 한마디 첨언 역할을 하는 것인지를 잘 구분해야 한다.

4. Question Analysis

문제를 풀 때에는 문제의 요구 사항에 맞는 답을 찾도록 노력해야 한다

GMAT RC는 독해 문제의 수준이 한국어 대입 수능 이상의 국어 문제 수준이다. 즉, 답지의 내용이 본문과 일치하는지 여부를 가리는 수준이 아니라 문제에서 요구하는 바를 정확하게 파악하여 그에 맞는 답지를 찾아낼 것을 요구한다. 따라서 문제를 풀 때에 단순히 본문에 그런 내용이 있어는지가 아니라 문제의 요구 사항을 정확히 분석하여 그에 맞는 답지를 찾아야만 한다. 이와 관련한 주의 사항을 아래와 같이 요약 정리한다.

1) General Questions

(1) Main Idea or Primary Purpose

주제를 묻는 문제이므로 본문과 일치한다고 해도 지엽적인 내용은 답이 될 수 없다.

▶ 전형적인 오답 pattern
(1) true but too specific
(2) extreme words 주의
(3) half-right but half-wrong

▶정답은 전체 내용을 포괄하는 내용이어야 한다. 자주 나오는 단어들을 유형별로 분류하면 아래와 같다.

지지	반론	묘사,예시,설명	비교,대조	추정
strengthen	weaken	describe	compare	speculate
support	dispute	explain	contrast	presume
reinforce	challenge	delineate		postulate
buttress	undermine	depict		posit
bolster	discredit	exemplify		
endorse	refute	illustrate		
		elaborate		

(2) Organization of the passage : 전체 글의 구성을 묻는 문제

(3) Tone or Attitude of the passage(Key Terms)

aloof : remote in attitude
ambivalent : of two minds ; unable to decide
cautionary : conveying a warning
compassionate : sympathetic
condescension : patronizing behavior
cynical : distrustful of the motives of others
defensive : self-justifying
detachment : aloofness ; indifference
didactic : moralizing ; instructive
disdain : scorn ; contempt
disparaging : belittling ; disapproving
dispassionate : unbiased ; objective
esteem : respect
flippant : lacking proper seriousness
grudging : reluctant ; unwilling
hypocritical : insincere
indifference : lack of interest
ironic : contrary to what was expected
judicious : sensible ; showing good judgment ; prudent
naïve : unsophisticated
nostalgia : homesickness
objective : impartial ; neutral
optimistic : cheerfully confident
pedantic : excessively bookish
pessimistic : lacking confidence ; gloomy
prosaic : commonplace ; pedestrian ; ordinary
resigned : passively accepting the inevitable
sarcasm : stinging rebuke
satirical : exposing folly to ridicule
skeptical : doubtful
trite : stale ; clichéd
whimsical : capricious

2) Specific Questions

(1) 주의사항

- 직관에 의존하기 보다는 본문의 내용을 찾아가 답지와 비교하면서 풀어나가면서 본문과 정확히 일치하는 내용을 골라야 한다

- 정/오답 파악이 고민스러울 때에는 답지에 나오는 단어 하나 하나에 대해 본문과 일치 여부를 확인한다.

- 오답유형

  (1) 상식적으로 보았을 때 타당한 내용이더라도 제시문의 진술 자체에서 벗어나 논리적으로 유추된 진술은 정답이 될 수 없다

  (2) 지문의 내용을 과장시키는 내용에 주의해야 한다

  (3) 인과관계 확인(사실관계를 인과관계로 함부로 유추할 수는 없다

  (4) 비교관계 확인(본문의 비교근거가 있는지를 정확히 확인해야 함

  (5) 시제관계나 extreme words(all, any, every, only, 최상급, never 등)를 주의깊게 살핀다

(2) Specific Question Types

(2-1) in order to : reference 및 주체확인

- true but out of reference :전형적인 오답 pattern

- 본문 전체 속에서 작가의 의도를 물어보는 문제가 아니라 문제에서 지칭된 부분이 사용된 목적을 묻는 것임에 유의해야 한다

- 답지의 표현이 rhetorical하므로 특히 답지 해석을 잘 구분해야 한다.

지지	반론	묘사,예시,설명	비교,대조	추정
strengthen	weaken	describe	compare	speculate
support	dispute	explain	contrast	presume
reinforce	challenge	delineate		postulate
buttress	undermine	depict		posit
bolster	discredit	exemplify		
endorse	refute	illustrate		
		elaborate		

(2-2) inferred=concluded는 CR에서와 마찬가지로 본문과 일치되는 것을 찾아야 한다

- Key terms

conclusive : definitive

criterion : a standard used in judging something

excerpt : a selection from a longer work

implication : an indirect suggestion

imply : to suggest without stating explicitly

likelihood : probability

plausible : appearing reasonable

tentative : provisional

(2-3) 본문 내용 찾기(according to the passage, ————) : 문제에서 묻는 reference를 정확히 인식하고 그 문맥과 일치하는 내용을 고른다.

(2-4) Organization of the particular paragraph : 특정 문단 구성 및 기능을 묻는 문제

- Key terms

abstract : theoretical ; not concrete

analogy : similarity of functions or properties

antithesis : direct opposite

argumentative : presenting a logical argument

assertion : declaration

cite : to quote as an authority

concrete : real ; actual

evidence : data presented as proof

explanatory : serving to explain

expository : concerned with explaining ideas or principle

generalization : general idea or principle

incompatible : not able to exist in harmony ; discordant

indicative : suggestive

misconception : mistaken idea

abstract : theoretical ; not concrete

analogy : similarity of functions or properties

antithesis : direct opposite

argumentative : presenting a logical argument

assertion : declaration

cite : to quote as an authority

concrete : real ; actual

evidence : data presented as proof

explanatory : serving to explain

expository : concerned with explaining ideas or principle

generalization : general idea or principle

incompatible : not able to exist in harmony ; discordant

indicative : suggestive

misconception : mistaken idea

narrative : relating to telling a story

persuasive : intended to convince

phenomenon : observable fact or occurrence

preclude : to keep from happening

rhetorical : relating to the effective use of language

thesis : the central idea in a piece of writing

(2-5) logic questions
– CR과 비슷한 형태의 문제(Weaken/Strengthen/Assumption)도 종종 출제된다

(2-6) 글의 특정 부분에 대한 작가의 Tone이나 Attitude를 묻는 문제

5. Sample Passage 적용

1) Sample Short Passage (Specific Question 예측)

A lot of ethologists are interested in comparing human cultural behavior with genetically programmed animal behavior, such as comparison of children with monkeys. Admittedly, humans are animals in that they have much in common with other animals. Indeed, some characteristics of human behavior may seem analogous to those of other animals. Such analogies, however, have the potential of misleading us if the context of a particular bit of behavior is not taken into account. For example, one researcher compares the presentation of a branch by a black bird with gift-giving in people. But the black bird's behavior simply inhibits attack and is equal to other placating rituals of many other species. Human gift-giving, in contrast, is greatly different in form and purpose from culture to culture, and within the same culture it is carried out in various contexts. All important elements in this human behavior derive from its social context. Thus, ethologists cannot accomplish anything until they study humans as cultural beings.

1. **compare and contrast** : Admittedly, humans are animals in that they have much in common with other animals. Indeed, some characteristics of human behavior may seem analogous to those of other animals. Such analogies, however, have the potential of misleading us if the context of a particular bit of behavior is not taken into account.

2. **특정 주장에 대한 약화나 강화의 내용들** : But the black bird's behavior simply inhibits attack and is equal to other placating rituals of many other species. Human gift-giving, in contrast, is greatly different in form and purpose from culture to culture, and within the same culture it is carried out in various contexts.

3. **작가의 태도 전달** : All important elements in this human behavior derive from its social context. Thus, ethologists cannot accomplish anything until they study humans as cultural beings.

2) Sample Long Passage (Specific Question 예측)

It has long been thought that small firms do not greatly contribute to a Korean economy that should overtake other countries, leading the government's policies to favor large-sized companies over small ones. Large firms were supposed to be superior in a lot of aspects including productivity, technological progress, and job security and compensation.

Recently, however, researchers observe small firms in many industries performing better than their larger counterparts. Indeed, in the <u>steel industry</u>, examples abound of new firms entering the market in the form of "mini-mills," and the employment of these small firms expanded, whereas large companies have reduced their businesses. True, it cannot conclusively be argued that smaller firms are as efficient as large firms. However, it is obvious that small size is not an intrinsic stumbling block. Not surprisingly, a different view on small firms has emerged that small firms perform significant roles in a lot of industries. For instance, small firms often trigger technological changes by trying various innovative activities. Moreover, small firms bring about market upheaval that leads to new dimensions of competition, and they also foster competition through newly created niches in an international background. Finally, the share of small firms in generating new jobs is significant.

Yet, evidence and researches on which empirical knowledge about the relative roles of large and small firms is based are fragmentary and not sufficient enough to answer major questions concerning the role of small firms across various industries and nations. Moreover, the question of what criteria should be used for distinguishing between small firms and large ones is not clearly resolved.

1. 특정 주장에 대한 약화나 강화의 내용들 : Indeed, in the steel industry, examples abound of new firms entering the market in the form of "mini-mills," and the employment of these small firms expanded, whereas large companies have reduced their businesses

2. **작가의 태도 전달** : True, it cannot conclusively be argued that smaller firms are as efficient as large firms. However, it is obvious that small size is not an intrinsic stumbling block. Not surprisingly, a different view on small firms has emerged that small firms perform significant roles in a lot of industries.

3. **마지막 첨언과 주제의 구분(Additional Comment)** : Yet, evidence and researches on which empirical knowledge about the relative roles of large and small firms is based are fragmentary and not sufficient enough to answer major questions concerning the role of small firms across various industries and nations. Moreover, the question of what criteria should be used for distinguishing between small firms and large ones is not clearly resolved

*** Reading의 속도와 정확성을 동시에 높이자.

많은 한국의 GMATter들은 "정독이 중요한지 아니면 속독이 중요한지?"라는 딜레마에 빠지곤 한다. 결론부터 말하자면 정독과 속독은 병행되어야 한다. 즉, 수업 등을 통한 정독 능력을 갖춘 후 독해학습량을 늘려감으로써 속독이 가능해지는 것이다. 만약 정확한 독해 학습능력을 갖추지 않은 상태에서 무리하게 속도만 높이다보면 정답률이 현저하게 저하된다. 반대로 정독만 하면서 학습량을 늘려가지 않으면 독해 실력이 정체 상태를 보이게 된다.

GMAT독해에서 Accuracy와 Speed는 반비례관계가 아니고, 같이 비례해서 늘어간다. 다만, 이게 반비례관계처럼 느껴진다면 아직 문장과 지문에 대한 적응도가 높아지지 않은 상황이다. 이 때는 집중적이고 연속적으로 독해를 해나가야 한다. 때로는 피곤할 정도의 많은 지문을 연속적으로 독해연습을 해나가다

1) 매일 독해 지문을 3지문을 쉬지 말고 연속으로 풀자.

2) 수업과 더불어서 매주 self-study자료를 cafe.daum.lnet/eduken에 게시할 예정이니 게시된 자료를 반드시 풀어보자.

3) 시간되는 대로 끊임없이 cafe.daum.net/eduken을 방문하여 article자료를 끊임 없이 읽어나감으로써 독해능력과 화면 적응력을 동시에 키워나간다.

4) 일주일에 한두번 정도는 CR11문제, RC3지문 정도를 묶어서 쉬지 말고 푸는 훈련을 해나 간다. 이렇게 지칠 정도로 연습을 하면 자연스럽게 문제를 푸는 속도가 빨라지게 된다. 그리고 이렇게 연습해야만 속도가 빨라지면서 정답률도 같이 개선되는 효과를 거둘 수 있다.

5) 본인이 틀린 문제에 대한 의문을 정확히 해결하려 노력하면서 본인의 해석과 강의 중 말씀드리는 해석을 비교하면서 오류를 고쳐나간다

6) 수업시간 중 설명드리는 식의 지문에 대한 구조정리와 문제찾기 연습을 본인 혼자서 공부할 때에도 그대로 적용하려고 노력해본다

Chapter II.
Sample Passages 해설

1. Short Passage

▶ 짧은 지문은 속성상 본문의 Specific한 부분까지 문제로 출제된다.

▶ 문제-답지 해석에 있어 미세한 Qualifier(한정어구)들을 주의해서 해석한다.

Sample Passage #1 : OG2025 p424~p425(Q464~Q467) ▼

본문 해설 :

생태시스템의 기능에 대해 화폐가치를 부여해야 한다는 주장은 다음과 같다: 천연 자원 고갈에 대한 염려는 널리 퍼져 있으나, 이런 염려가, 보존에 대한 경제적 주장이 수반되지 않으면, 의미있는 천연자원 보존의 진전으로 옮겨지지 아니해왔다. 일부 비판론자들은 이런 교착 상태에 대해 환경 훼손의 경제적 이슈들을 다루지 않고 있는 환경론자들때문이라고 지적한다. 얼핏 보기에는 생태시스템의 보존이, 원시 해안과 같은 천연 자산을 리조트 호텔과 같은 가시적인 상업 자산으로 전환시킴으로써 얻어지게될 경제적 보상에 비해, 이익이 되지 않을 것처럼 보일 수 있다. 그러나, David Pearce에 따르면, 그런 착각은 생태시스템에 의해 제공되는 서비스들이 상품시장에서 거래되지 않고 있고, 따라서 쉽게 계량화될 수 있는 가치를 가지고 있지 않다는 사실에 기인한다.

이런 문제를 바로잡기 위해, 모든 생태시스템들이 경제적 가치가 있음-실로, 모든 생태적 서비스들이 경제적 서비스들임-을 보여주어야만 한다고 Pearce는 말한다. 예를 들어, 야생생물 보호지구를 방문하는 관광객들은 일자리와 소득을 만들어냄으로써, 국가경제에 도움을 준다; 천연 그대로의 수풀과 늪지는 배수를 조절하고, 정수 시스템으로서 작용함으로써, 수백만 달러 가치의 의 재산 및 해양 생태시스템 피해를 막아준다. Gretcher Daily의 관점에서는, 화폐가치부여라는 게 많은 환경론자늘에게는 인기기 없지만, 이 화폐가치부여야말로 경제적 고려가 인간 행동에 끼치는 지배적인 역할을 반영하는 것이고, 통용되는 화폐로 경제적 가치를 표현하는 것이 환경과 관련된 의사결정에 있어 필요한 정보를 제공하도록 도움을 주는 것이다.

464. 본문의 정보는 David Pearce가 생태시스템 기능에 대한 화폐가치 부여에 대해 다음 중 어떤 문장을 지지할 것이라고 시사하는가?

해설:본문 line14~26에 따르면, Pearce는 생태시스템 보존이 경제성이 없다는 착각이 생겨난 이유가 생태 시스템에 대한 화폐가치 부여가 이루어지지 않았기 때문인 바, 생태시스템에 대한 화폐가치 부여가 이루어지면, 생태시스템에 의해 제공되는 서비스의 경제성 인식이 될 것이라고 말하고 있다. 따라서, 정답은 "D:생태시스템에 대한 화폐가치 부여는 환경보존의 가치를 설득력 있게 나타내는 수단이 될 수 있다"이다.

465. line20에서 사용된 "생태적 서비스"의 예를 가장 명확하게 나타내는 것은 무엇인가?

해설:본문 맥락에서 "생태적 서비스"는 상업적 자원으로 전환되지 않은 천연자원이 제공하는 서비스를 의미하는 바 정답은 "C: 많은 국제 관광객을 끌어들이는 야생동물 보존 지역"이다.

466. 본문에 따르면, Daily는 생태시스템에 대한 화폐가치 부여는 다음 중 어떤 내용을 나타낸다고 보고 있는가?

해설:line26~32에서, Daily는 "생태시스템의 화폐가치 부여는 인간 행동을 결정짓는 데 있어서, 경제적 요소가 지배적인 역할을 한다는 사실을 반영한다" 라고 서술하였는 바, 정답은 "A: 사람들의 행동을 결정하는 데 있어서, 경제적 이해관계의 중용성"이다.

467. line8에서 언급된 환경론자들에 대해서 추론될 수 있는 바는 무엇인가?

해설:본문에서 환경론자들을 비판하는 사람들은 "환경론자들이 환경파괴가 가져오는 경제적 측면들을 제대로 다루지 못한다"라고 지적하는 바, "C:환경론자들은 때때로, 환경보존 목적을 추구하는 데 있어 한 특정 전략을 활용하지 못한다는 비판을 받아왔다"가 정답이다.

본문 해설 :

천연색소 무리인 카로티노이드는 많은 동물들에 의해 사용되는 화려한 신호들의 중요한 부분을 형성한다. 동물들은 카로티노이드를 만드는 식물과 조류로부터 카로티노이드를 직접 획득하거나 곤충을 먹음으로써 간접적으로 카로티노이드를 획득하고, 이러한 카로티노이드를 여러 조직 안에 저장한다. 여러 동물 종들에 대한 연구들은 짝짓기 대상을 선택할 때, 암컷들은 보다 밝은 카로티노이드 바탕 색깔을 지니는 수컷들은 선호함을 보여주어왔다. Owens와 Olson은, 만약 카로티노이드가 희소하거나 건강을 위해 필요로 되는 것이라면, 색깔에 의해 신호되어지는 카로티노이드의 존재가 짝짓기 대상 선택에 있어 중요할 것이라고 가설을 세웠다.

전통적인 견해에서는 카로티노이드는 희소하기 때문에 중요하다고 본다. 즉, 보다 건강한 수컷들이 열등한 수컷에 비해 보다 많은 색소를 위해 먹이를 찾을 수 있다고 해석한다. 물론 이런 견해가 사실일 수도 있겠으나, 점점 더 많은 증거들은 카로티노이드가 건강을 위해 필요하기 때문에 중요하다는 점을 보여준다. 즉, 카로티노이드가 면역시스템에 의해 건강 유지를 위해 중요한 독소제거 과정에 쓰인다는 것이다. 어찌보면, 수컷들은 많지 않은 카로티노이드를 면역방어 및 독소제거를 위해 사용하거나 혹은 암컷들을 유혹하는데 사용할지도 모른다. 질병 및 기생충에 보다 취약한 수컷들은 그들 자신의 면역시스템 강화를 위해 그들이 가진 카로티노이드를 사용할 수밖에 없을 것이다. 반면, 유전적으로 저항력이 강한 수컷들은 질병과 맞서 싸우는데, 카로티노이드를 덜 사용할 것이고, 화려한 색깔을 뽐내기 위해 색소를 사용함으로써 암컷들에게 이런 강점을 알릴 것이다.

514. 전통적인 견해에 따르면, 보다 밝은 카로티노이드 바탕 색깔은 한 개체가 ----------라는 점을 시사한다.

해설 : 본문에서, "전통적인 견해에서는 카로티노이드는 희소하기 때문에 중요하다고 본다. 즉, 보다 건강한 수컷들이 열등한 수컷에 비해 보다 많은 색소를 위해 먹이를 찾을 수 있다고 해석한다"라고 하였는 바, 보다 밝은 카로티노이드 바탕 색깔은 그 개체가 우수한 먹이 찾기 능력이 있음을 시사한다. 따라서, 정답은 D이다.

515. "카로티노이드가 건강을 위해 필요하기 때문에 중요하다"라는 생각은 밝은 색깔이 부족한 숫컷이 시사하는 바는 무엇인가?

해설: line 17~23에 따르면, "질병 및 기생충에 보다 취약한 수컷들은 그들 자신의 면역시스템 강화를 위해 그들이 가진 카로티노이드를 사용할 수밖에 없을 것이다"라고 서술하였으므로, 밝은 색깔이 부족한 숫컷은 질병에 대한 유전적 면역력이 낮음을 나타낸다고 볼 수 있으므로 정답은 C이다.

516. 본문에 따르면, 상대적으로 밝은 카로티노이드 바탕의 색깔이 수컷들에 대해 다음 중 어떤 특징을 나타내어주는 신호라고 불 수 있는가?

해설: 본문 세번째 문장에 따르면, "짝짓기 대상을 선택할 때, 암컷들은 보다 밝은 카로티노이드 바탕 색깔을 지니는 수컷들은 선호함을 보여주어왔다"라고 하였으므로, 밝은 카로티노이드 바탕 색깔은 짝짓기 대상으로서의 적합성을 보여줌을 알 수 있다. 따라서, 정답은 E이다

517. 본문은 동물들이 카로티노이드를 얻는 매개체인 곤충에 대해 다음 중 어떤 내용을 시사하는가?

해설: line3-6에서 "동물들은 카로티노이드를 만드는 식물과 조류로부터 카로티노이드를 직접 획득하거나 곤충을 먹음으로써 간접적으로 카로티노이드를 획득한다"라고 서술하였는 바, 이 곤충들이 직접 카로티노이드를 만들지는 않음을 알 수 있다. 따라서, "A:그 곤충들은 스스로 카로티노이드를 만들지 않는다"가 정답이다.

518. 본문에 나타난 정보는 수컷이 독소제거를 위해 사용한 카로티노이드에 대해 다음 중 무엇이 사실이라는 점을 시사하는가?

해설: 본문에서, 수컷들의 카로티노이드 사용에 대해 "either for immune defense and detoxification or for attracting females"라고 서술하였는 바, 카로티노이드 사용이 면역방어와 암컷을 유인하기 위한 뽐내기에 동시에 사용될 수 없음을 알 수 있다. 따라서, 정답은 C이다.

본문 해설 :

1980년대 중반, Linda Kerber는 미국혁명 이후 "공화주의적 모성"이라는 이데올로기 때문에 미국내 여성들의 교육기회가 늘어났다라고 주장했다. Kerber는 새 국가의 지도자들은 정치적으로 덕 있는 자식들을 길러내고자, 여성들이 교육되어지기를 원했다. 정치적으로 덕 있는 시민이 미국 공화주의 정부 형태 성공에 필수적인 것으로 여겨졌다; 정치적 덕은 교회나 학교 뿐만이 아니라 가족들에 의해서도 불어넣어지는데, 가족 내에서 어머니의 역할이 중요하다. 따라서, Kerber에 따르면, 모성이 공화주의 운명에 중추적인 요소가 되는 바, 여성 교육에 대한 전례없는 관심이 정당화되었다.

공화주의적 모성 이론 도입은 역사기술을 급격하게 바꾸어놓았다. Kerber연구 이전에는, 교육 역사가들은 여성과 소녀들에 대해 거의 언급하지 않았다; 다만, Thomas Woody의 1929년 연구가 눈에 띄는 예외이다. 교육기관에 대한 신문광고들을 조사하면서, Woody는 1750년경 소년들과 소녀들을 위한 교육 기회가 늘었다는 사실을 발견했다. 이런 관점의 변화를 보여준 예로서 "An Essay on Woman"이라는 작품을 지적하면서, Woody는 여성들을 위한 실용적 교육이 미국 혁명 이전부터 많은 이들의 지지를 받고 있었다라고 주장했다. 이런 Woody의 증거는 미국 혁명이, 여성교육에 대해 미국 여성 이전부터 나타난 지지 추세를 가속화시켰을지는 몰라도, 여성 교육에 대한 태도를 전향적으로 바꾸어 놓았다는 개념에 대해서는 반론을 가하는 셈이다. 역사가들이 Kerber의 "공화주의적 모성" 개념에 의지하다보니, 그 이전부터 여성 교육에 대한 지지 추세가 있었다는 점을 간과했을지도 모르는 바, 미국 혁명이 여성들의 삶을 어느 정도 변화시켰는지 결정하기가 어렵다.

519. 본문에 따르면, Kerber는 다음 중 무엇이 미국혁명 이후 미국에서 여성에 대한 교육 기회의 증가로 연결되었다라고 주장하는가?

해설: 첫 문단에 따르면, Kerber는 새로운 미국 정부가 성공하려면, 시민들에게 정치적 의식을 심어 주어야 하는데 이를 위하여 가족 내 어머니의 역할이 중요하므로, 여성들에 대한 교육에 대해 전례없는 관심을 가지게 되었다라고 주장하는 바, 정답은 "D:여성들이 새로운 미국 정부 성공에 기여하기 위해서는 여성들이 교육받을 필요가 있다는 믿음"이다.

520. 본문에 따르면, 교육역사 분야내에서 1929년 Wood의 연구는 ------이다. ?

해설: line 17~20에 따르면, Kerber연구 이전에는 교육 역사가들이 여성들 혹은 소녀들에 대한 언급을 거의 하지 않았던 반면, Wood의 1929년 연구가 예외적이라고 하였으므로 정답은 "E:Woody의 연구는 소녀들의 교육을 살펴보았다는 점에서 예외적이다"이다.

521. 본문은 "An Essay on Woman"과 관련하여 Woody가 다음 중 어떤 문장에 동의할 것이라고 시사하는가?

해설: line 21~25에 따르면, 1750여년경 소년 소녀들에 대한 교육 기회가 늘었다는 사실의 발견과 이런 변화를 "An Essay on Woman"이 반영하고 있다라고 서술하는 바, 정답은 "A:이 글은 1750년 이후 여성들이 교육을 받을 수 있는 새로운 기회 속에 반영된 여성 교육에 관한 태도를 나타내고 있다"이다.

522. 본문에서는, 미국 내 여성 교육 역사와 관련하여, Kerber의 연구와 Woody의 연구가 다음 중 어떤 점에서 의견을 달리한다라고 시사하고 있는가?

해설: 본문에서 Kerber는 미국 혁명 이후 미국 내 여성 교육에 대한 지지가 늘었다고 서술하는 반면, Woody는 미국 혁명 이전부터, 이미 여성 교육에 대한 지지가 늘었다라고 서술하고 있으므로 정답은 "B:미국 혁명 이전 소녀들의 교육기회에 대한 지지 정도"이다.

523. 본문 Kerber 주장에 따르면, 정치지도자들은 미국 혁명 이후 미국에 의해 채택된 정부가 성공하기 위해서 다음 중 무엇이 필요하다고 생각했는가?

해설: line 7~12에서, Kerber는 새 국가의 지도자들은 정치적으로 덕 있는 시민이 미국 공화주의 정부 형태 성공에 필수적인 것으로 여겼고, 정치적 덕은 교회나 학교 뿐만이 아니라 가족들에 의해서도 불어넣어지는데, 가족 내에서 어머니의 역할이 중요하다고 믿었다라고 주장하는 바, 정답은 "C:아이들에게 정치적 의식을 심어주는 주요 수단 중 하나로서 역할을 하는 가족"이다.

본문 해설 :

입자를 빛보다 빠른 속도록 보내려는 대부분 시도는 양자터널링이라고 불리우는 주목할만한 현상을 수반한데, 이 양자터널링에서는 입자들이 통과되기 어려워 보이는 고체 장벽을 통과하여 움직인다. 만약 당신이 공을 벽에 던진다면, 그 공이 벽을 관통하는 게 아니라 되튀어 돌아올 것으로 예상하게 마련이다. 그런데, 아원자 입자들이 바로 그런 공적을 수행한다. 양자이론은, 그런 아원자 소립자들이 고체 장벽을 관통해서 나아갈 가능성이 작기는 하지만, 뚜렷이 있다라고 말한다; 장벽의 두께가 두꺼워짐에 따라 그 가능성은 기하급수적으로 줄어든다.

이런 양자터널링의 극단적인 빠르기는 이미 1932년에 주목되었지만, 1955년 이후가 되어서야 Wigner와 Eisenbud가 터널링 입자들이 때때로 빛보다 빠르게 움직인다라고 가설을 제시하였다. 그들의 가설은, 한 입자가 장벽을 통과하는 소요시간이 장벽의 두께에 따라 늘어는데 이 소요시간이 최대 소요 시간에 이르고 나면 더 이상 늘어나지 않는다는 점을 시사하는 계산에 기초했다; 그 최대 소요 시간을 넘어서면, 장벽의 두께와 무관하게 장벽 통과 시간은 일정하게 유지된다.

이는, 일단 최대 장벽 통과 시간에 이르고 나면, 장벽 두께가 두꺼워짐에 따라 장벽 통과 속도가 무제한으로 늘어날 것이라는 점을 시사한다. 여러 최근 실험들은 터널링 입자들이 때때로 빛의 속도를 넘어선 속도에 도달한다는 이러한 가설을 뒷받침해왔다. 에를 들어 Ramond Chiao와 동료들이 수행한 실험 측정에 따르면, 광자는 빛속도의 1.7배에 이르는 속도로 광필터를 통과할 수 있다.

617. 본문의 작가가 터널 통과 시간과 장벽의 두께에 대한 계산을 언급한 목적은 무엇인가?

해설:line 14~21에서, Wigner와 Eisenbud가 터널링 입자들이 때때로 빛보다 빠르게 움직인다라고 가설의 토대가 되는 계산으로서, 터널 통과 시간과 상벽의 두께 관계를 언복하고 있으므로, 정답은 "E: Wigner와 Eisenbud의 가설에 대한 토대를 설명하기 위해서"이다.

618. 본문은 "만약 장벽 두께 증가에 따른 터널 통과 시간 증가에 최대값이 없다라고 한다면, ─────────────"라고 함축하고 있다.

해설:line 18~24에서, "한 입자가 장벽을 통과하는 소요시간이 장벽의 두께에 따라 늘어나는데 이 소요시간이 최대 소요 시간에 이르고 나면 더 이상 늘어나지 않는다는 점을 근거로, 장벽 두께가 두꺼워짐에 따라 장벽 통과 속도가 무제한으로 늘어날 수 있을 것"으로 서술하고 있다. 따라서, 만약 장벽 두께 증가에 따른 터널 통과 시간 증가에 최대값이 없다라고 한다면, 터널링 입자들의 속도가 무제한적으로 늘어나지는 않을 것이므로, 정답은 D이다.

619. 양자터널에 대한 가장 초창기 과학 연구와 관련하여 본문으로부터 추론될 수 있는 바는 무엇인가?

해설:line 12~16에서, "양자터널링의 극단적인 빠르기는 이미 1932년에 주목되었지만, 1955년 이후가 되어서야 Wigner와 Eisenbud가 터널링 입자들이 때때로 빛보다 빠르게 움직인다라고 가설을 제시하였다"라고 하였으므로, 1955년 이전에는 터널링 입자들의 속도가 빛보다 빠르리라고까지는 추측하지 않았음을 알 수 있다. 따라서, "C:가장 초창기 연구들은 터널링 입자들이 빛보다 빠르게 움직인다라고 추측하지는 않았다"가 정답이다.

2. Long Passage

▶ 긴 지문은 모든 Specific한 내용보다는 흐름의 맥을 잡도록 동사, 형용사, 부사, 접속사 등의 연결사에 초점을 맞추어야 한다.

▶ 지문의 흐름을 잡기 위해 문단마다의 결론을 인식하면서 글의 분위기와 흐름을 잡아나간다.

▶ 글쓴이의 태도가 positive·negative·neutral 중 어떤 입장인지를 끊임없이 점검하면서 읽어나간다.

▶ 문제-답지 해석에 있어 미세한 qualifier(한정어구)들을 주의해서 해석한다.

Sample Passage #1 : 본문해설:OG2025 p439~p441(Q501~Q508) ▼

본문 해설 :

Winters v. United States(1908)년 판결에서, 대법원은 the Fort Berthold 인디언 보호 구역을 관통해서 흐르거나, 그 근처에 있는 물의 사용 권한이, 인디언 보호 구역을 제정하였던 조약에 의거하여, 미국 인디언들에게 보유되어진다고 판결하였다. 상기 조약에서는 물권리를 언급하지는 않았지만, 법원은 연방정부가 인디언 보호 구역을 만들 당시 인디언들을 위해 물권리-사실 물이 없으면 그 인디언 보호 구역의 땅은 쓸모가 없었을 것임-를 지정함으로써, 미국 인디언들에게 공평하게 처우하려고 의도했다라고 판결을 내렸다. Winters 판례를 인용하면서, 훗날의 법원 결정들은 다음과 같은 조건을 갖출 경우 특정 목적을 위해 물권리를 지정할 수 있는 연방정부의 권리에 대해 유권해석을 내릴 수 있음이 확립되었다. 그 조건은 "(1) 대상이 되는 토지가 배타적인 연방 정부 관할 범위 내 영토범위 안에 있을 것 (2) 그 토지가 연방정부 공유지로부터 공식적인 절차를 거쳐 떼내어져-다시 말하면, 연방 정부 토지 용도법 하에서 사적 활용을 위해 이용될 수 있는 연방 정부 토지 비축분으로부터 떼내어져야 함-토지 사용 권한이 지정될 것 (3) 정황상 정부가 인디언 보호 구역을 제정할 당시 토지 뿐만 아니라 물도 권리 지정을 하려고 의도했음이 드러날 것"이다.

일부 미국 인디언 부족들은 또한, 미국이 주권을 획득하기 이전부터 전통적으로 일부 물줄기를 돌려서 사용했왔음을 근거로 법원을 통해 물권리를 확립하였다. 예를 들어, 미국이 1848년 New Mexico주에 대한 주권을 획득했을 당시 the Rio Grande Pueblos는 이미 존재해있었다. 1848년 Rio Grande Pueblos의 토지가 미국의 일부가 되기는 했지만, 그 Pueblos토지가 공식적으로 연방정부 공유지의 일부를 구성한 적은 결코 없었다; 어떤 경우에도, 조약이나 법령이나 행정명령을 통해 연방 정부 공유지로부터 Puelos토지를 미국 인디언 보호 구역으로서 떼어내어

지정한 적이 없었다. 그러나, 이러한 사실이 Winters doctrine의 적용을 통한 물권리 지정을 가로 막지는 않았다. 법원에서는 미국 인디언 보호 구역의 구성 여부의 기준을 법적 정의보다는 실질 관행의 문제로서 판단하였고, the pueblos는 미국 정부에 의해 항상 인디언 보호 구역으로서 여겨져 왔던 것으로 판단하였다. 이런 실용적 접근 Arizona v. California(1963)년 판례에서도 뒷받침되고 있는데, 이 판례에서, 대법원은, 어떤 연방 정부 보호구역이 만들어지는 방식이 그 보호구역에 Winters doctrine이 적용될지 말지 여부에 영향을 주지 말아야 한된다라고 지적하였다. 따라서, Pueblo인디언들은 Pueblos가 인디언 보호 구역이 되었다고 여겨짐에 틀림이 없는 1848년 이래로, 다른 시민들의 물 권리에 비해 우선적인 물권리를 보유하게 되어왔다.

501. 본문에 따르면, Fort Berthold 인디어 보호구역을 확립하였던 조역과 관련하여 다음 중 무엇이 사실인가?

해설:line5~6에서 "상기 조약에서는 물권리를 언급하지는 않았지만,"이라고 서술하였으므로 정답은 "D:그 조약은 인디언 보호구역 거주자들에 의해 행사될 물권리를 언급하지는 않았다"이다.

502. line 10~20에서 논의된 기준들이 인디언 보호구역의 물관리를 확립하기 위한 유일한 기준들이었다면, 다음 중 무엇이 사실일 것이라고 본문은 시사하는가?

해설:line 28~32에 따르면, "Pueblos토지는 공식적으로 연방정부 공유지의 일부를 구성한 적은 결코 없었고, 어떤 경우에도, 조약이나 법령이나 행정명령을 통해 연방 정부 공유지로부터 Puelos토지를 미국 인디언 보호 구역으로서 떼어내어 지정한 적이 없었다"라고 서술하였는 바, 정답은 "C:Rio Grande publos들의 물권리에 대해서는 법적 근거가 없을 것이다"이다.

503. Arizona V. California 판례와 line 10~20에서 논의된 기준들과의 관계를 가장 정확하게 요약한 것은 무엇인가?

해설:line33~42에 따르면, 법원에서는 미국 인디언 보호 구역의 구성 여부의 기준을 line10~20에서 정립된 엄격한 법적 정의보다는 실질 관행의 문제로서 판단하였고, 이런 실용적 접근 Arizona v. California(1963) 판례를 예시하고 있으므로, 정답은 "B: Arizona V. California 는 Winters원칙이 line10~20에서 규정된 상황보다 다양한 상황에서 적용됨을 입증한다"이다.

504. line 37~38에서 언급된 "실용적 접근"은 ~으로서 가장 잘 정의된다.

해설: line33~42에 따르면, 법원에서는 미국 인디언 보호 구역의 구성 여부의 기준을 line10~20에서 정립된 엄격한 법적 정의보다는 실질 관행의 문제로서 판단하였고, 이를 실용적 접근으로 지칭하였으므로, 실용적 접근에서는 인디언 보호 구역의 적용 범위를 line10~20에서 정의된 기준보다 폭넓게 적용하였음을 알 수 있다. 따라서, A가 정답이다.

505. Winters doctrine은 다음 중 무엇을 확립하기 위하여 사용되었음을 추론할 수 있는가?

해설:line10~12에 따르면, "Winters 판례를 인용하면서, 훗날의 법원 결정들은 다음과 같은 조건을 갖출 경우 특정 목적을 위해 물권리를 지정할 수 있는 연방정부의 권리에 대해 유권해석을 내릴 수 있음이 확립되었다" 라고 하였으므로, 정답은 "E:어떤 조건이 갖춰질 경우 명시적으로뿐만 아니라 묵시적으로 물권리를 특정인의 권리로 지정할 수 있는 연방정부 권한"이다.

506. 작가는 Rio Grande pueblos는 공식적인 절차를 밟아서 공유지로부터 탈퇴한적이 없다는 사실을 언급한 주된 목적은 무엇인가?

해설: line14~15에 따르면, Winters doctrine이 적용되기 위한 기준 중 하나가 "공식적인 절차를 밟아서 공유지로부터 탈퇴할 것"으로 기술되어 있으므로, Rio Grande pueblos가 이 절차가 없었다면, Winters doctrine적용 기준에 맞지 않음을 나타낸다. 따라서, 정답은 "A:왜 Winters 원칙이 pueblos lands에는 적용되지 말아야 한다라는 주장이 제기될 수 있는 지 그 이유를 시사하기 위해서"이다.

507. 본문의 주된 목적은 무엇인가?

해설: 본문은 미국 인디언들의 물권리에 대해, 미국 법원에서 실용적인 해석을 통해 그 물권리를 폭넓게 인정해주었음을 주된 내용으로 서술하고 있으므로 정답은 "B:미국 인디언 부족들의 물권리에 대한 법적 근거를 설명하기 위함"이다.

508. 본문이 시사하는 바에 따르면, 미국 인디언 이외의 시민들이 지니는 Rio Grande pueblos로 흘러가는 물의 사용권한은 -----이다.

해설:본문 마지막 문장에서, "Pueblo인디언들은 Pueblos가 인디언 보호 구역이 되었다고 여겨짐에 틀림이 없는 1848년 이래로, 다른 시민들의 물 권리에 비해 우선적인 물권리를 보유하게 되어왔다" 라고 서술하였으므로 정답은 "E:Pueblos 인디언들의 선순위 권리 주장에 의해 제한을 받는다"이다.

Sample Passage #2 : OG2025 p449~p450(Q527~Q531) ▼

본문 해설 :

제조업체들은 규모의 경제를 실현하려면, 커다란 공장을 짓는 이상을 해야만 한다. 물론, 제조 운영 규모가 커질수록, 생산 규모가 생산 단위 원가가 최소에 이르는 "최소효율규모"에 근접해감에 따라 단위 원가가 줄어드는 것은 맞다. 그러나, 꾸준한 "처리효율"이 달성되지 않고서는 최소효율 규모는 충분히 실현될 수 없다. 적절 생산 규모를 유지하는데 필요로 되는 처리효율은 생산 공정 전반에 걸친 물품들의 흐름을 조율할 것을 필요로 할 뿐 아니라, 부품공급 업체로부터의 투입의 흐름을 관리할 것과 생산품이 도매상 및 최종 소비자에게 전달되는 흐름까지 관리할 것을 필요로 한다. 만약 처리효율이 임계점 아래로 내려가면, 단위 원가는 급격하게 치솟고 이익은 사라진다. 원자재 공급차질, 작업현장의 문제 발생, 혹은 비효율적인 판매망 등의 요인으로 인해 생산이 줄어들어도 제조업체의 고정비용이나 매몰비용은 줄어들지 않는다. 결과적으로, 잠재적인 규모의 경제는 생산시설 즉, 유형 자본의 물리적이고 엔지니어링적인 특징들에 의해 좌우되는 반면, 실제 실현되는 규모의 경제는 운영과 조직관리에 밀접한 관계가 있는 바, 지식,기술,경험,팀웍 등의 무형자본에 의해 좌우된다.

무형자본 투자의 중요성은 새로운 자본집약적 제조산업에서 일어나는 현상을 보면 분명해진다. 새로운 자본 집약적 산업에서 지배기업으로 등장하는 기업은, 이론적 최적 규모의 기술적으로 고도화된 공장을 획득한 첫번째 회사가 아니라 그런 공장의 잠재력을 충분히 실현시키는 첫번째 회사가 지배기업으로 등장한다. 일단, 일부 회사들이 이런 잠재력 실현 능력을 얻고 나면, 시장 진입은 극도로 어려워진다. 즉, 후발 주자들은 비슷한 공장을 지어야 하는데, 이미 선도 주자들이 부품 공급업체들 혹은 새로운 생산 공정과 관련된 문제점들을 다 해결한 이후에서야 그렇게 공장을 지어야 하니 경쟁력을 갖추기 어렵다. 또, 후발 주자들은 선도주자들이 연락처와 knowhow를 다 꿰차고 있는 시장에서 새로운 유통망과 마케팅 시스템을 구축해야 하니, 경쟁력을 갖추기 어렵다. 그리고, 이미 기능적, 전략적 활동을 다 습득한 경영팀들과 경쟁을 할 새로운 경영팀을 꾸려야 하는 점도 후발주자들의 경쟁력을 어렵게 만든다.

527. 본문은, "자본집약적인 산업에서 한 제조업체가 비슷한 제품을 만드는 경쟁사들에 비해 결정적 우위를 지니기 위해서 반드시 --------------해야 한다"라고 시사한다.

해설:line27~33에서, "새로운 자본 집약적 산업에서 지배기업으로 등장하는 기업은, 이론적 최적 규모의 기술적으로 정교한 공장을 획득한 첫번째 회사가 아니라 그런 공장의 잠재력을 충분히 실현시키는 첫번째 회사가 지배기업으로 등장한다"라고, 서술하였으므로 정답은 "C:최소효율구모로 공장을 운영하는 첫번째 회사가 되어야만 한다"이다.

528. 본문에서 제조업체의 고정비와 매몰비용에 대해 시사하는 바는 무엇인가?

해설: line16~20에서, "처리효율이 임계점 아래로 내려가더라도, 제조업체의 고정비용이나 매몰비용은 줄어들지 않는다"라고 서술하였으므로, 정답은 "E:고정비와 매몰 비용은 제조공장의 처리효율 변화에 의해 영향을 받지 않는다"이다.

529. 본문 전체 맥락 속에서, 두번째 문단의 주된 기능은 무엇인가?

해설:두번째 문단, 첫문장에서 "무형자본 투자의 중요성은 새로운 자본집약적 제조산업에서 일어나는 현상을 보면 분명해진다"라고 서술하였으므로, 첫번째 문단에서 언급한 무형자본 투자의 중요성을 강화하는 역할을 하고 있음을 알 수 있다. 따라서, 정답은 "A:첫번째 문단에서 제시된 주장을 뒷받침하는 예를 제공한다"이다.

530. 본문에서, 한 제조업체의 처리 효율이 나빠지는 원인으로 지적되지 않은 것은 무엇인가?

해설:line16~17에서, "처리효율이 임계점 이하로 내려가면, 단위원가가 치솟는다" 라고 서술하였으므로, "D:생산 단위당 원가 상승"은 처리효율이 나빠져서 나타나는 결과이지, 원인이 아님을 알 수 있다. 따라서, 정답은 D이다.

531. 본문의 주된 목적은 무엇인가?

해설: 첫 문단에서 "실제 실현되는 규모의 경제는 운영과 조직관리에 밀접한 관계가 있는 바, 지식,기술,경험,팀웍 등의 무형자본에 의해 좌우된다"라고 결론을 내리고, 두 번째 문단은 이 결론을 뒷받침하고 있으므로, 정답은 "A:제조업에 있어서, 규모의 경제를 실현시키기 위한 무형 자본의 중요성을 강조하기 위함"이다.

Sample Passage #3 : OG2025 p481~p482(Q601~Q605) ▼

본문 해설 :

1787년에 쓰여진 미국 헌법의 입안자들은 발명과 관련된 재산권을 보호하는 것이 새로 건설될 국가의 경제 성장을 촉진할 것으로 믿었기 때문에, 의회에게 발명에 대한 특허권을 부여할 위임권을 주었다. 결과적으로 생겨난 특허시스템은 다른 국가들의 특허시스템의 모델역할을 했다. 그러나, 최근에 학자들은 미국의 특허시스템이 헌법 입안자들의 목적 달성에 도움을 주었는지 여부에 대해 의구심을 제기해왔다. 그 학자들은 1797년에서 1830년 무렵까지, 판사들이 특허에 대해 적대적이었고, 자의적인 이유를 들어 특허를 무효화하였기 때문에, 이 기간 동안 미국의 발명자들은 특허권을 제대로 행사할 수 없었다고 주장해왔다. 이러한 주장은 특허권자가 특허권 침해를 주장하며 소송을 제기한 법원 결정들에 대한 분석에 기초하고 있다. 예를 들어 1820년대에 특허권 침해 소송 판결의 75%는 특허권자에게 패소 판결을 내렸다. 1830년대, 특허권자 승소 판결이 늘어나기 시작했는 바, 이를 학자들은 특허권에 대한 판사들의 태도가 이때쯤 바뀌어지기 시작한 것으로 해석했다.

그러나, 19세기 초반 모든 특허 분쟁들이 법정 다툼이 벌어진 게 아니었고, 또 그런 법정 다툼까지 가게 된 경우들은 무작위적인게 아니라, 법정 다툼까지 가게 될만한 이유가 있었던 것으로 보여진다. 따라서, 특허권자 승소 판결의 비율 그 자체만으로는, 판사들의 태도 변화나 특허권 행사 가능성의 변화를 보여준다고 볼 수 없다. 만약, 초창기 판결들이 특허권자들에 대한 편견을 지녔다면, 특허권에 대해 보다 전향적이었던 훗날의 법원들은 이전의 판결들을 판례로서 받아들이지 않았을 것이다. 그러나, 1830년 이전의 판결들이 그 이후의 판결들만큼 빈번하게 판례로서 인용되어져 왔고, 오늘날에도 여전히 인용되고 있다는 사실은 초창기 판결들-많은 초기 판결들도 특허권은 창의력에 대한 정당한 보상이라는 점을 명확히 선언하였음-이 특허법을 지탱하는 지속적 토대를 제공함을 시사해준다. 사실, 1830년대 특허권자 승소 판결 비율이 늘어났던 원인은 재판에 회부되는 특허권 소송 자체의 변화 때문이었다. 이 변화는 1836년 특허시스템 개정으로 인한 것인데, 그 내용은 매 특허 출원에 대해 특허법 준수 여부를 철저하게 조사하는 것이었다. 이런 개정 이전에는 $30의 특허 출원료를 내면 특허는 자동적으로 부여되었다.

두번째 문단 첫 문장의 however를 분기점으로 특허권자 승소 판결 비율이 1830년대 늘어난 실제 이유는 판사들의 태도 변화 때문이 아니라, 특허 절차 개정에 따라 특허권의 특허법 준수가 철저해졌기 때문에, 특허권 분쟁 소송에서 특허권자가 승소하는 비율이 늘어났음을 분석하고 있다.

601. 본문에서는 1830년대 특허권자들의 승소 비율이 늘어난 이유가 무엇이라고 시사하는가?

해설 : 본문 41번째 줄 이하의 문장을 참고하면, "1830년대 특허권자 승소 판결 비율이 늘어났던 원인은 1836년 특허시스템 개정으로 인해 특허 출원에 대해 특허법 준수 여부를 철저하게 조사했기 때문이다"라고 분석하고 있는 바 특허권 분쟁에서 승소할 수 있었던 이유가, 특허권자들의 특허법 준수가 철저해졌기 때문임을 알 수 있다. 따라서, 정답은 "A:1836년 이후 승인된 특허 출원들은 특허법을 준수할 가능성이 커졌다"이다.

602. 본문에서는 8번째 줄에 언급된 학자들이 1830년 이전의 미국 특허 시스템에 대한 다음 중 어떤 비판에 동의할 것이라고 시사하는가?

해설 : 문제에서 지적한 문장에서는 "최근에 학자들은 미국의 특허시스템이 헌법 입안자들의 목적 달성에 도움을 주었는지 여부에 대해 의구심을 제기해왔다"라고 하였는 바, 상기 학자들은 "미국의 특허 시스템이 당초의 목적인 미국 경제 성장의 촉진에 기여하지 못하였다"라고 생각함을 알 수 있다.

603. 본문에 따르면, 1830년 이전의 판결들이 법원 결정에서 인용되어져 왔던 빈도를 증거삼아 내릴 수 있는 결론은 무엇인가?

해설: 본문 Line 30~39까지 두 문장을 요약하면, "초창기 법원의 판결들이 특허권자들에 대한 편견을 지니고 판결을 내린 것이라면, 훗날의 법원들에 의해 판례로서 인용되지 않았을 텐데, 실제로는 초창기 법원의 판결들이 훗날의 법원들에 의해 자주 판례로서인용되었음"을 알 수 있다. 따라서, 1830년 이전에 판사들이 특허권에 대해 부정적인 편견을 가지고 있다가 1830년 이후 편견이 없어지면서 특허권 승소 판결이 늘어난 건 아니라는 것을 추론할 수 있는 바, 정답은 "B:특허권에 대한 판사들의 지지가 1830년 이후 증가하지는 않았다"이다.

604. 본문은 작가와 Line21 에서 언급된 학자들이 1830년 이전에 특허침해소송에서 변호되는 특허와 관련하여 다음 중 어떤 점에 대해 의견이 다른 것임을 나타내는가?

해설: Line 21문장에 따르면, 학자들의 견해는 "1830년대 특허권 승소 비율이 늘어난 이유가 특허권에 대한 판사들의 태도가 변했기 때문이다"라고 분석한다. 반면, 두번째 문단 Line30~Line44에 따르면, 작가는 "특허권 승소 비율 증가의 원인을 판사들의 태도 변화 때문이 아니라, 특허심사절차의 변동에 따라 특허권들이 특허법을 철저하게 준수하기 때문에 특허 침해 소송에서 특허권자들의 승소 비율이 늘어난 것"으로 분석하고 있다. 따라서, 1830년 이전 특허침해소송에서 변호되는 특허와 관련하여 작가와 학자들의 의견이 불일치하는 점은 정답 "D:특허들이 자의적인 이유 때문에 종종 무효화되었는가"임을 알 수 있다.

605. 본문의 주된 목적은 무엇인가?

해설: 첫 문단에서 "실제 실현되는 규모의 경제는 운영과 조직관리에 밀접한 관계가 있는 바, 지식,기술,경험,팀웍 등의 무형자본에 의해 좌우된다"라고 결론을 내리고, 두 번째 문단은 이 결론을 뒷받침하고 있으므로, 정답은 "A:제조업에 있어서, 규모의 경제를 실현시키기 위한 무형 자본의 중요성을 강조하기 위함"이다.

PART V
Voca from official Guide

1 DAY

empirical = observational(opp) theoretical
This is the empirical evidence showing that the "rods" themselves can be captured, and that they do indeed prove to be ordinary animals.

recoup = recover
It may even pay more for products with better packaging, as long as it would recoup the money through recycling revenues or lowered disposal costs.

initially = at the beginning = originally
When he initially began the school, business was poor because his students typically stayed for only a couple of months before leaving.

desperation = despair
This trend also contributed to the creation of a" Win At All Costs"culture, which results in professional frustration and desperation among many litigators.

manipulate = steer = manoeuvre
Its ability to manipulate time and its barrage of homing missiles is devastating against large numbers of enemies, and great against larger enemies with more health.

dominate = prevail
Given stable political conditions, the United Kingdom could dominate overseas markets for industrial goods through free trade alone

without having to resort to formal rule.

obscure
1) blur = confuse
   We mustn't let these minor details obscure the main issue.
2) incomprehensible = unclear
   It is easier than most Putnam Competition problems, but the competition often features seemingly obscure problems that turn out to refer to something very familiar.

refute = rebut = disprove
The growth of Cultural Resources Management, wherein archaeology is used to guide political decisions, does little to refute these ideas.

artificial = synthetic
It is important to remember that in evening settings, you will be surrounded by artificial lighting, which can often make your skin look pale and lifeless.

decipher = decode
This enabled operators to read the tape without having to decipher the holes, which would facilitate relaying the message on to another station in the network.

verify = confirm = corroborate = bear out
We have no way of verifying the safety of beef imported from US.

grassroots = ordinary people rather than leaders

Some argued that the financing restrictions diminished the chances that surprise candidates could emerge from the grassroots and be propelled to national prominence by well-placed benefactors.

franchise = suffrage

distance set up here between James' feelings of failure and inadequacy and what we now know about his final reputation.

pit A against B = to set against in a competition

Analysts said the service would pit Apple against the main British broadcasters, which started on-demand download services of their own in the past year.

given = considering

The government and the Uri Party have decided to revise the initial plan for second-phase bancassurance considerably given banks' unfair sales practices during the first-phase bancassurance and over concerns that implementation of the initial plan may greatly weaken the base of traditional sales agents, they said in a statement.

precarious = insecure

These proposals failed to gain any significant response from the Greek government, mostly because of the precarious state of Yugoslavia at the time.

stringent = demanding

Safety requirements are now being applied to the system as a whole and even master station software must meet stringent safety standards for some markets.

disaster = catastrophe

In these novels everyday characters are placed into a setting in which they experience a major disaster which has severe implications for society and the world

strenuous = arduous = effortful

Performance of the program is reviewed regularly and strenuous efforts are made to maintain a system that catches every infant with these diagnoses.

circumvent = avoid = evade

Protesters believed the planned separate east and west entrances amounted to an attempt to circumvent recent federal law that banned racially segregated facilities.

dispute = challenge

Arguing about whether a person who is hanged dies of strangulation or a broken neck, they decide to settle the dispute by hanging a cat

exploit

1) use – The mobilization of the capital necessary to exploit these new systems required a larger number of workers and managers, and larger physical plants than ever before.

2) abuse – What is being done to stop employers from exploiting young people?

alienate = estrange

If he had not stopped the revolts, India would probably have descended into an anarchy-style rebellion which would alienate common Indians and impress only violent revolutionaries.

2 DAY

laudable = commendable

Despite its laudable attributes to guard against luck it still can be regarded as rewarding a racer that happened to be hot that one day.

discard = get rid of

The most efficient caching algorithm would be to always discard the information that will not be needed for the longest time in the future.

sustain = maintain = uphold

The government was providing too many men to search for spies within the country and not enough to perform the productive work to sustain the economy.

exclusively = only

They live almost exclusively on land, and some have been found up to 6km from the ocean.

compelling = persuasive = convincing

National associations must now enforce immediate suspensions of all players sent off during a game, even if television replays offer compelling evidence of a player's innocence.

distract = divert

Focusing on the lighter subject material in the book, even for a little while, will help distract your thoughts from those that have been scaring you.

foster = encourage = promote

Political power resided in the Council of the Revolution, a predominantly military body intended to foster cooperation among various factions in the army and the party.

fracture = crack

The diamond material removed during the drilling process is destroyed, and is often replaced with glass infilling, using the fracture filling techniques described below.

preserve = conserve

The confidentiality of the person, and the priest's absolute obligation to preserve the secrecy of the Sacrament of Penance, are still in force in such cases.

dismiss = reject = ignore

Constitutional amendments were rushed through Parliament in February strengthening the powers of the President to dismiss Parliament and creating the post of Prime Minister.

demography
The changing number of births, deaths, diseases, etc. in a community over a period of time Finally, he believed the basis for good social relationships between humans was good relationship between men and women, thus arguing demography control relied on women emancipation.

bias = prejudice
One of the most controversial issues in modern reporting is media bias, especially on political issues, but also with regard to cultural and other issues.

abrasion = attrition
Thin coatings cannot remain intact indefinitely when subject to surface abrasion, and the galvanic protection offered by zinc can be sharply contrasted to more noble metals.

rule out = exclude
The investigation also did not rule out embers of cigarettes as a possible cause, which were present in several trashcans.

plausible = reasonable
Such an interactive account of publics and institutions gives a plausible practical meaning to the extending of the project of democracy to the global level.

intense = fierce
It begins with clouds building up from the south in the early afternoon followed by intense thunderstorms and rainfall, which can cause flash floods.

paltry = meager
Despite the Pentagon crack down, civilian contractors still report problems of poor working conditions and paltry working conditions.

priceless = valuable
Most of the houses along the avenue, including priceless examples of art nouveau and modernist architecture, were destroyed in the aftermath of the Warsaw Uprising.

outrageous = shocking
The detachment of Progenitor scientists often goes so far that they will consider the most outrageous experiments as justifiable in the name of science.

substantial = considerable
The plague did more than just devastate the medieval population; it caused a substantial change in economy and society in all areas of the world.

part company = to end a relationship
I'm afraid I have to part company with you on the question of nuclear energy.

duplicate = copy
This practice had downsides, notably that outside contributors had no way to closely follow a project's development and contributed work would often duplicate already completed efforts.

precious = valuable
Gold prices had their steepest fall since June and silver prices also dropped as plunging equity markets prompted investors to sell precious metals to raise cash.

clandestine = covert
During the Second World War, he joined the Resistance and organized clandestine trade union committees.

curb = check
The agreements have ultimately been an effective way to curb inflation, particularly in the recent times where globalization puts pressure on both the employer and employee.

3 DAY

traditionally = conventionally
The organization's name has changed several times, and due to the autonomous status of the individual branches, some have traditionally preferred alternative names.

unique = distinctive
The unusual upbringing of the Glass children, with radio appearances as child geniuses and philosophy around the dinner table, has created a unique bond among them.

adapt = adjust
Research is still necessary, however, particularly as insects and diseases continue to adapt to pesticides and as soil fertility and water quality continue to need improvement.

integrate = combine
The school is designed to integrate academic and technological education in career clusters that require students to have a strong background in mathematics and science.

alliance = coalition
The Provisional government was an alliance between liberals and socialists who wanted to instigate political reform, creating a democratically-elected executive and constituent assembly.

reluctant = grudging = unwilling
Cheating is considered immoral by most, and may face stiff punishment if discovered, although some faculty indicate they are reluctant to take action against suspected cheaters.

substantial = considerable
It is much more common for employee ownership companies to provide for substantial employee involvement in work-level decisions, often through various kinds of teams.

head start : an advantage that sb already has before they start doing sth
Dual enrollment in both secondary school and college is advantageous to students because it allows them to get a head start on their college careers.

dominant = overriding
Sometimes the dominant party maintains power through election fraud, while other times the elections themselves are fair, but the electoral campaigns preceding them are not.

reinforce = buttress = support
Trends indicated that viewers appear to prefer to get their news from sources that reinforce their opinions rather than seek out information that challenges these opinions.

advance = suggest
The article advances a new theory to explain changes in the climate.

terrestrial
1) earthly
   There are distinct chemical differences between meteorites and terrestrial rocks, but these usually require fairly sophisticated testing to determine.
2) onshore = on the land
   The legs were strong and indicate a terrestrial animal, and the tail was short.

critical :
1) crucial - Your decision is critical to our future.
2) condemnatory - Tom's parents were highly critical of the school.

gradient = slope
Flow separation occurs when the boundary layer travels far enough against an adverse pressure gradient that the speed of the boundary layer falls almost to zero.

tilt = tip
The result is similar to that of steroscopic viewing using linearly polarized glasses; except the viewer can tilt his head and still maintain left/right separation.

entail = involve
Producing the musical would entail having the interior of the Broadway Theatre scooped out and turned into a freewheeling environmental theatre representing heaven and hell.

arboreal = branchy = living in trees
The term terrestrial is also frequently used for species that live primarily on the ground, in contrast to arboreal species, which live primarily in trees.

wiggle = wriggle
This can be done by simultaneously escaping the back door, or by standing up in an attempt to wiggle the opponent off

contraction = shrinkage
The horizon arises naturally from length contraction seen in special relativity which is a consequence of the speed of light upper bound for physical objects.

acute = sharp
The term usually refers to a condition following acute brain damage, but recent evidence suggests that a congenital form of the disorder may exist.

unfortunately : 아쉽게도
Its goal is to unite all humanity under its sovereign control, and unfortunately the means to do so have been decidedly less than moral.

implement = carry out
This technique has been criticized by some for its unnecessary complexity and being difficult to implement efficiently, though some projects have certainly benefited from its use.

lure = entice
Nature can also be elusive and lure you away from your beaten path, and getting lost in the wilderness can be a scary and frightful event.

moorings : 정박지, 정신적으로 의지할 바
These moorings are used instead of temporary anchors because they have considerably more holding power, cause less damage to the marine environment, and are convenient.

slick = artful = slippery
The album departed greatly from all of their previous efforts and included several mainstream sounding rock songs with slick production values.

shortcoming = defect
The major shortcoming of these heavy field guns was mobility, as they required eight-horse teams as opposed to the six-horse teams of the lighter guns.

fraction = part = portion
This allows them to consider all sectors and include companies that earn a small fraction of their profit from business opportunities related to climate change.

increasingly : 점점더
The game moves at a rather slow pace and levels are often huge, so the bubble is an increasingly more common occurrence as the game progresses.

indigenous = native
This was the last act of resistance by the indigenous people to occur within the limits of the town.

ubiquitous = present
The improvement in heat pump efficiency saves so much energy that cooling towers have become ubiquitous on the rooftops and mechanical floors of skyscrapers.

entice = persuade = lure
A pioneer in the development of luxury hoteliering, he knew how to entice wealthy customers and quickly gained a reputation for good taste and elegance.

foster = encourage = promote
The agreement offers new opportunities for both countries to foster cooperation in air transport bringing valuable inbound tourism industry and commerce between the two countries.

4 DAY

intangible = immaterial = unidentifiable
Many companies now seek to develop ways to measure intangible assets such as intellectual capital.

sustain = maintain = uphold
Additionally, many lightkeepers also maintained a garden on the property which would sustain them with enough fresh vegetables when tenders would not come.

ambiguous = equivocal
There is also ambiguous evidence whether the level of violence among tribal societies is greater or lesser than the levels of violence among civilized societies.

arbitrary = discretional = impulsive
Liberty is generally considered a concept of political philosophy and identifies the condition in which an individual has immunity from the arbitrary exercise of authority

reflect = show
This may reflect cultural differences among the provinces, perhaps including the physical distance between various areas of Canada and major American population centres.

fail to V = not V
The moment things slow down, the burden of guarantees extended to works that will fail to sell because of wild estimates will become unbearable.

explore = analyze
Panic offered him a chance to explore these styles further by experimenting with cinematography and casting real people.

pragmatic = practical
The only possible reason to prefer one political system over another, he believed, depends not on eternal truths but on purely pragmatic grounds.

flaw = defect = fault
The changes, which would have introduced a security flaw to the kernel, never became a part of the Linux code.

encourage = promote = foster
Special prizes are offered to encourage young artists and established practitioners, and some grants are given each year to enable them to train abroad.

validate = corroborate
This partial implementation of the system serves to validate the architecture and act as a foundation for remaining development

furnish = provide
In redox reactions, gram equivalents denote the mass of oxidizing or reducing agent that can accept or furnish a given molarity of electrons.

cautious = chary = guarded
When the Visitors arrived on Earth, Randy remained cautious about their true intentions,

but nonetheless continued to serve the force he had dedicated his life to.

disinterested = unbiased = impartial
The pub landlords, now civil servants, were instructed to follow a disinterested management policy and not allow people to get drunk in the pubs

rhetoric = oratory
It may be great political theater and political rhetoric, but it's not the truth.

pivotal = important = crucial = vital
Royalties for Internet streaming were a pivotal issue in the writers' strike that halted television production last winter.

unwittingly = unknowingly
This can be used to send people unwittingly to sites that offend their sensibilities, or crash or compromise their computer using browser vulnerabilities.

drawback = disadvantage = snag
These weapons have a noticeable drawback in that they have low accuracy and thus, rounds are likely to miss instead of hit the target.

refrain from = abstain from
These notifications are meant to encourage tourists and residents to refrain from visiting the beach in the evening hours during these time periods.

dilemma = predicament
The interesting dilemma is that both advocates and opponents must cite the Gospels in order to admit or omit their contents.

wade through = plough through : to spend a lot of time and effort reading sth or dealing with sth
I had to wade through pages and pages of statistics
Many remained in their homes had to swim for their lives, wade through deep water, or remain trapped in their attics or on their rooftops.

challenging = difficult
This makes computer security particularly challenging because we find it hard enough just to make computer programs just do everything they are designed to do correctly.

preponderance = predominance
A successful naval defense, however, usually requires a preponderance of naval power and the ability to sustain and service that defense force.

5 DAY

segregation = separation
This article has been discussed at The Center on Juvenile and Criminal Justice and by several school boards attempting to address the issue of continued segregation.

eligible = entitled
This means that they each have a community council chosen by the eligible voters at each municipal election, and each one with a chairman or chairwoman.

interrupt = disturb
The phenomenon where the overall system performance is severely hindered by excessive amounts of processing time spent handling interrupts is called an interrupt storm.

posit = postulate
It seeks to describe or posit the basic categories and relationships of being or existence to define entities and types of entities within its framework.

carry out = perform
Many businesses can now be involved in business-tobusiness commercial activity and will create a specific area within a virtual world to carry out their business.

stem from = result from
Their use gives rise to the 80-20 rule that 80 percent of the problems stem from 20 percent of the causes.

articulate : to express or explain your thoughts or feelings clearly in words
People with severe communication difficulties find it difficult to articulate their health needs, and without adequate support and education might not recognise ill health.

substantiate : to provide information or evidence to prove that sth is true
The evidence used to substantiate these hypotheses remain largely circumstantial and are not supported by anything released so far under the Freedom of Information Act.

temporary = short-lived (opp) permanent
A wide range of temporary exhibitions are displayed in the art gallery throughout the season and events are organized throughout the year.

account for = explain
These exceptional groups account for many special examples and configurations in other branches of mathematics, as well as contemporary theoretical physics.

adapt to = adjust to
Societies adapt to their surrounding environments, but they interact with other societies which further contributes to their progress and development.

bargaining power : the amount of control a person or group has when trying to reach an agreement with another group in a business or political situation

The new rule would shift the bargaining power over cable and broadband services to apartment residents from landlords and tenant associations.

explicit = literal = overt
The film attracted widespread publicity due to its explicit nature, but generally poor reviews and was only a moderate commercial success.

facilitate = help = assist
These laws provide tools which facilitate computation, as well as describe the fundamental nature of numbers, their operations and relations.

adjacent = close
Yards may have multiple industries adjacent to them where railroad cars are loaded or unloaded and then stored before they move on to their new destination.

in question : 대상이 되는
Once someone announced under oath that he intended to bring such a suit, the legislation or decree in question was suspended until the matter was resolved.

enclave = territory
The formal use of enclave implies a community or population that is essentially trapped within walls and completely surrounded by an unfriendly population or government.

diversion = distraction
The authorities had been draining the Tangjiashan lake since early Saturday, using a hastily dug diversion channel to relieve pressure on dam.

sovereignty = reign
The Union shall at all times remain an autonomous body with ultimate sovereignty vested in the members in General Meeting.

rescind = repeal
Numerous efforts from both the Australian government, Queen's Counsels and petitions from organizations such as Amnesty International failed to persuade Singapore to rescind its decision.

6 DAY

unfortunately : 아쉽게도
Many believed Hug was a heavy favorite to win it all considering he already beat Cikatic a few months earlier but unfortunately that wasn't to be

allege = assert
They disagree with the plural constitution of the merged church which they allege contains partly contradicting Reformed and Lutheran confessions.

intricate = complex
Organizations of scalpers have emerged, and the scalpers inside the sometimes intricate network work collectively to make the most gain out of the tickets.

brazen = shameless
Regulators here have enforced midday sun breaks, improved health benefits, upgraded living conditions and cracked down on employers brazen enough to stop paying workers.

bizarre = grotesque = weird
The game is considered to be extremely bizarre, as the playing character is a giant floating zombie head who shoots eyeballs and vomit as a weapon.

chronology : the order in which a series of events happened; a list of these events in order
The most intriguing example is perhaps A History of Bombing, which is made up of short chapters dispersed with no obvious chronology throughout the book.

deduce = infer
Pronunciation spellings may be used informally to indicate the pronunciation of foreign words or those whose spelling is irregular or not sufficient to deduce the pronunciation.

incorporate = integrate
At the same time, these programs incorporate computational formulations of scientific knowledge that can form the foundations of better ways to teach science and engineering.

evaporate = vaporize = disappear
This occurs because the cornea is normally thicker in the morning; it retains fluids during sleep that evaporate in the tear film while we are awake.

sediment : the solid material that settles at the bottom of a liquid
It was decided to lower the dam instead of completely removing it because of the large amount of sediment that had accumulated behind the dam.

configuration = form or shape
It allows a central administration model for all slave nodes and includes the tools needed to build configuration files, monitor, and control the nodes.

initiate = set in motion
The infant gradually realises that gratification is not immediate and that it has to produce certain behaviours to initiate actions that lead to gratification.

plausible = reasonable
A more plausible theory is that tektites are produced by the impact of meteorites on the Moon.

assess = evaluate

The apparatus summarizes all of the textual evidence, allowing readers to assess for themselves whether the editor has made the best choice.

refine = improve

This category includes music by groups led by music professionals who take authentic music, refine it, and perform it in a manner suitable for Western audiences.

autonomy = independence

The pendulum would swing back toward the medieval model where students could enjoy significant autonomy in their choice of residence and habits.

frame of reference : 준거체계

The values of the representing array are given relative to some frame of reference, and undergo a linear transformation when the frame is changed.

foster = encourage = promote

Political power resided in the Council of the Revolution, a predominantly military body intended to foster cooperation among various factions in the army and the party.

7 DAY

metabolism : 신진대사

This allows coordination of root development with leaf development, enabling a balance between carbon and nitrogen metabolism to be established.

injection = insertion

This places stringent requirements on the pressure and temperature of the flow, and requires that the fuel injection and mixing be extremely efficient.

immediate = instant = prompt

Beyond its immediate neighbors, Japan has pursued a more active foreign policy in recent years, recognizing the responsibility which accompanies its economic strength.

elicit = evoke

It is an adaptation of the consequences type of test designed to elicit a higher degree of spontaneity and to be more effective with children.

secrete = release

The forms associated with degenerative diseases or cancer reportedly secrete growth hormones and toxic substances that disrupt normal cellular metabolism and damage the immune system.

subsequent = later
Fetting reported that the angel visited him on numerous subsequent occasions, delivering messages each time, and these messages began to be collected into a book form.

depress = deject
There is widespread concern that falling property prices could depress consumption and that the turmoil in the financial markets could dampen business investment.

exclusively = only
They live almost exclusively on land, and some have been found up to 6 from the ocean.

durable = imperishable
The opinion supports arguments by some dentists and governments, who have said the material is safer and more durable than alternatives.

hamper = hinder
Government television and radio remained off the air, and mobile telephone networks that were taken offline to hamper rebel communication were still off Tuesday.

ramification = complication = implication
The subject of the probe that led to the search remains unclear, leaving investors uncertain about the ultimate ramifications for the company.

foreshadow = foretell
This produced profound changes that, in many ways, would foreshadow the character of the coming Middle Ages.

enduring = lasting
The committee is charged with evaluating subjects to ensure they will be of an enduring interest to large segments of the American population.

bias = prejudice
One of the most controversial issues in modern reporting is media bias, especially on political issues, but also with regard to cultural and other issues.

rational = reasonable
It is not enough under the rational basis test, however, for the government to simply announce some theoretical and noble purpose behind the statute.

formulate : to create or prepare sth carefully, giving particular attention to the details
The Inquiry courses are dedicated to helping students formulate the questions they want to examine in their individual research.

tactical = strategic
The larger boards have more strategic combinations available than the smaller boards, and the four player game offers more tactical intrigue than the two player game.

intuition = hunch : the ability to know sth by using your feelings rather than considering the facts
Geometric intuition clearly played a strong role in the first two and, accordingly, theories of

relativity were formulated entirely in terms of geometric concepts.

ambiguous = equivocal
The green and red colors that make up the background field hold a much more ambiguous and mysterious meaning than the most common explanations

novel = new
There have also been graphic novel collections in both color and black and white, as well as novelizations and original anthologies based on the series.

grasp = grip
Research some background information on the painting itself to fully grasp the religious history and the artistic techniques behind the paintings.

capricious = unpredictable = changeable = arbitrary
Republicans working in the government who were not political appointees are protected by law from capricious termination.

rather = more exactly
She worked as a secretary, or rather, a personal assistant.

arbitrary = discretional
The remedy is usually to have an executor act in an arbitrary fashion and have no financial interest in how the estate will be divided up.

leery = wary
The lingering thought of violence makes some legislators,& liquor board members leery of opposing these companies.

engender = to make a feeling or situation exist
These species are chosen for their vulnerability, attractiveness or distinctiveness in order to best engender support and acknowledgement from the public at large.

inextricable = unresolvable
Baden spends most of his time in his studio although he regards conscientious networking as a crucial and inextricable part of being an artist today.

instigate = bring about = incite
The Provisional government was an alliance between liberals and socialists who wanted to instigate political reform, creating a democratically-elected executive and constituent assembly.

stipulate = specify
Particularly interested in the transit system, she stipulates that a better transit system would reduce pollution and increase quality of life for everyone involved.

8 DAY

strict = stringent = rigid
That has created a tremendous demand for donor organs, and over the years the medical community has established strict protocols to govern organ harvesting.

substantial = considerable
It could be that one or more substantial calendar shift shave occurred, or the years counted might in certain periods have differed from astronomical years.

overlook = neglect
He seems to have overlooked one important fact.

ailment = disease
Even if Obecalp proved helpful, some doctors worry that giving children " medicine"for every ache and pain teaches that every ailment has a cure in a bottle.

ideal = unreal
In an ideal world there would be no poverty and disease.

affect = influence
These angles are measured from the horizontal, and drastically affect the rider position and performance characteristics of the bicycle.

substantiate = validate
A good project design should be able to substantiate its assumptions, especially those with a high potential to have a negative impact.

expend = use up
Competent intermediaries can expend the same amount of time and effort on larger transactions and for a smaller percentage of its value earn more.

compromise = peril
Defeat at this stage would compromise their chances (=reduce their chances) of reaching the finals of the competition.

fluid
1) noun : liquid
   The distribution of heat transfer fluid is also far from ideal and the heating or cooling tends to vary between the side walls and bottom dish.
2) adjective : changeable
   Our ideas on the subject are still fluid.

deposit = sediment
The rain left a deposit of mud on the windows.

trail = track
The mountain bike trail is probably one of the most challenging trails in the Twin Cities due to its long climbs and rapid descents.

occasional = intermittent = sporadic

The interior scenes are based on earlier understanding of perspective, but occasional errors suggest that the artists did not fully understand the models used.

unravel = separate = divide

Archaeologists have yet to unravel the mystery, and some modern Pohnpeians believe the stones were flown to the island by use of black magic.

subtle = impalpable

The difference between an event being almost sure and sure is the same as the subtle difference between something happening with probability 1 and happening always.

theoretical = conjectural (opp) empirical

It has been assumed that those who are able to understand the theoretical analysis ought to be able to demonstrate the stated behaviour from first principles.

empirical = experimental = observational

Supernatural healing is an umbrella term for a family of treatment methods which use claimed revelations rather than empirical evidence as their foundation.

critical :

1) crucial

Your decision is critical to our future.

2) condemnatory

Tom's parents were highly critical of the school.

enumerate = list

It is straightforward to enumerate all sixteen configurations and map them to vertex index lists defining the appropriate triangle strips.

furnish = supply = provide

Railroads were not able to furnish transportation for the great crowds; the lack of adequate housing meant that not even sanitary conditions prevailed.

expand = enlarge

This might be associated with paying a job agency to expand their search beyond the urban residential area or locating an agency in the suburbs.

indefinite = unfixed

The present definite is used to mark naturally occurring phenomena, while the present indefinite indicates the habits of animals.

constituent = element

The chancellor is the notional head of the university, and constituent universities and recognised colleges will have their own heads which exercise most power.

luminous = bright

The most common modern application of oil paint is domestic, where its hard-wearing properties and luminous colors make it desirable for both interior and exterior use.

intense = fiery = passionate
These hair extensions do not require any heating elements, as the intense heat used to apply traditional hair extensions may damage them.

converge = approach
Measuring the proper motions of cluster members and plotting their apparent motions across the sky will reveal that they converge on a vanishing point.

9 DAY

solid = firm
As yet, they have no solid evidence.

encompass = cover
The ability of the players to encompass all these areas, often within one composition, removed any sameness or sterility from the quartet format.

construe = interpret
This agreement included preventing an expatriate or a refugee from publishing a statement which his/her government could construe as a contribution to unrest within its territory.

refute = rebut = disprove
The growth of Cultural Resources Management, wherein archaeology is used to guide political decisions, does little to refute these ideas.

theoretical = conjectural (opp) empirical
It has been assumed that those who are able to understand the theoretical analysis ought to be able to demonstrate the stated behaviour from first principles.

concrete = specific
It is easier to think in concrete terms rather than in the abstract.

consent = agreement
There was also discontent caused by the attempt of the last Company-appointed governor to rule without the consent of the colonial parliament.

accomplish = fulfill
Characters may finally accomplish things they have never done, running gags are brought to an end, and unseen characters are revealed.

identify = discern
This article will help you to identify the phases of culture shock and ways that you can cope and handle culture shock.

artificial = synthetic
The monkey and banana problem is a famous toy problem in artificial intelligence, particularly in logic programming and planning.

lateral = side
Spacing of the source and drain with respect to the gate, and the lateral extent of the gate are important though somewhat less critical design parameters.

analogous = similar
This is somewhat analogous to the boundaries that form between crystal grains in solidifying liquids, or the cracks that form when water freezes into ice.

inhibit = suppress
Some economists claim that true predatory pricing is rare because it is an irrational practice and that laws designed to stem the practice only inhibit competition.

hierarchy : 위계질서 = pecking order
In theoretical computer science, the time hierarchy is a classification of decision problems according to the amount of time required to solve them.

duplicate = copy
In some implementations, duplicate sections simply merge their parameters together, as if they occurred contiguously.

preponderance = predominance
The standard of proof in the United States is typically preponderance of the evidence as opposed to clear and convincing or beyond a reasonable doubt.

migrate = move
It is largely a resident species, but may migrate short distances from northern areas where the water surfaces freeze.

rural = countrified (opp) urban
The level of violence associated with these reforms in some rural areas made the position of the wider white community uncomfortable.

concurrent = synchronous
The fair also involves several concurrent cultural events, usually featuring aspects of the culture of the guest country.

actual = real
The speed of retrieving a correct form or the actual production of an incorrect form is not indicative of loss but may be retrieval failure instead.

rigorous = strict
To obtain the intended benefits from unit testing, a rigorous sense of discipline is needed throughout the software development process.

exodus : a situation in which many people leave a place at the same time
There has been a mass exodus of its professionals and managers, civil servants and entrepreneurs, a haemorrhage of its future.

entice = persuade
Negative news, such as litigation against a company will also entice professional traders to sell the stock short.

obsolescent = non-current
The vacuum brake system is now obsolescent ; it is not in large-scale use anywhere in the world, supplanted in the main by air brakes.

10 DAY

solely = only
The airport is however not open to the public, and is solely used by the navy and by important government dignitaries visiting the city.

intrinsic = inherent
The intention is to search for universal, practical spiritual principles that have intrinsic value, and do not depend on ecclesiastical authority.

cohesive = adhesive
This means that the next cohesive group that conquers the diminished civilization is, by comparison, a group of barbarians.

erosion = wear away = corrosion
The valley was originally not only made through glacial erosion but by the high pressure melting water which pushed its way beneath the ice.

shortcoming = defect
The attorney general also is examining if Wall Street firms concealed information about shortcomings from rating agencies, the people familiar with the matter told the Journal.

refute = rebut = disprove
Experiments which disagree significantly with the predictions of the theory refute it; those that agree with its predictions validate it.

be conducive to ~ing = be helpful in ~ing
Athletes learn through personal experience what types of foods are best conducive to training and performance.

conflate = mix
Social science research has rendered dubious any claim that race can simply be conflated with color, or gender with genitalia, or even class with paychecks.

fragile = delicate = brittle
The violence underscored the fragile nature of the security improvements that have been partly credited to the American troop increase that began last year.

diverse = varied = heterogeneous
The movement linked representatives from diverse political backgrounds under the common cause of direct elections for president.

fascinating = interesting
This powerful and strikingly original picture book provides a fascinating glimpse into the

prehistoric world as it imagines who the first painter might have been.

prolific = productive
Occasionally collections of outtakes become recognized as part of an artist's major creative output, especially in cases where an artist is unusually prolific or dies young.

metabolism : the chemical processes in living things that change food, etc. into energy and materials for growth
The amount of heat produced by the high rate of metabolism and the heat gained from its surrounding environment will give a high risk of overheating.

sparse : only present in small amounts or numbers and often spread over a large area
The survey found aquatic vegetation to be relatively sparse, with only localized growths of emergent and submergent species along the shorelines and shallows of the lake.

unfortunately : 아쉽게도
The video feed I was watching unfortunately didn't show the president's reaction, but I can only imagine he wasn't happy.

shallow
1) ankle-deep
   This requirement may be fulfilled simply by making the bowl or container part shallow enough to allow birds to perch in the water.
2) superficial
   His shallow arguments are not convincing.

subtle = impalpable
The complex nature of the human nose, its ability to detect even the most subtle of scents, is at the present moment difficult to replicate.

mutation : a process in which the genetic material of a person, a plant or an animal changes in structure when it is passed on to children, etc., causing different physical characteristics to develop; a change of this kind
The effect of a low mutation rate on a population is that few variations are available to respond to sudden environmental change.

epidemic = pandemic
The application of memory bound functions could prove to be valuable in preventing spam, which has become a problem of epidemic proportions on the Internet.

sanitation = hygiene
Provisions for food and water were just barely adequate; sanitation, medical, and crowd control did not achieve that level.

foster = encourage = promote
The club organizes activities such as awareness programs for academic majors, as well as other activities to foster greater unity between members of the school.

sporadic = intermittent = occasional
The group called themselves Guardians of the White Horse Stone and looked after the area around the stone but activities were sporadic and unorganised.

prevalent = widespread = common
This feature interaction is a specific example of a general and common problem that has become prevalent due to increasing system complexity.

inadvertent = unintended
The demarcation would also prevent the inadvertent crossing over of fishermen of both nations into each others' territories.

suburb = an area where people live that is outside the centre of a city
Originally a working class suburb of the city with a rather bad reputation, it was gradually transformed into a popular visiting place for tourists and Gothenburgers.

disseminate = spread
The University of the World has been designed to use electronic telecommunications to disseminate educational resources to students and faculty in all countries.

proliferate = multiply
The economy remains agriculturally centered, although the milk farms which proliferated only twenty years ago are in considerable decline.

11 DAY

distinct = different
Local community police forces will be established by municipal governments as operations distinct from the state-run police forces and will provide services tailored to meet the demands of regional policing for matters such as neighborhood security, traffic control, food safety and minor criminal offenses.

supplement = complement
The Educational Broadcasting Service said yesterday that it will provide television and online lectures to supplement high school classes.

from without = from the outside
New Crobuzon is being ripped apart from without and within.

preserve = save
The Constitutional and Supreme Courts had said in recent weeks that the National Security Law was constitutional and must be preserved.

posterity : all the people who will live in the future
It is the view of the Institute that historic swimming pools that are good examples of these early swimming pools should be preserved for posterity.

pervert = corrupt
The ethics committee was told by the ministry to find and block sites that contain yeopgi, a Korean word for perverted and gruesome content.

tinge = to add a small amount of color
The sky is tinged with red from the neon lights.

inevitable = unavoidable
To revive the ailing economy, economic policymakers such as Finance Minister Lee Hun-jai believe a further interest rate cut is inevitable coupled with an aggressive fiscal policy.

distort = fiddle = misrepresent
The most important thing at the moment is to quell the exaggerated theory of economic crisis that distorts the market and can bring a real crisis, he noted.

speculation = conjecture
The government's latest move to crack down on property speculation has had little impact on the profits of builders slowly recovering from a lengthy-doldrums but has dampened their sentiments, analysts say.

valid = reasoned
In view of the above court rulings, there remains no unequivocal answer to the question of whether such an elective arbitration clause will be upheld as valid and binding on the parties.

invoke = appeal to
In the event of an extreme crisis, a nation can invoke a compulsory license which would ignore the rights of patent holders.

unconditional = unqualified
He will need your unconditional love and support to strengthen his self-worth, and tactics for ignoring unwarranted insults.

fail to V = not V
The moment things slow down, the burden of guarantees extended to works that will fail to sell because of wild estimates will become unbearable.

cautious = guarded
Industry analysts regard the latest move as the beginning of the globalization of domestic financial institutions but say a more cautious approach is needed to avoid a repeat of earlier missteps.

grave = serious
The leakage of some examination papers led to a grave complication.

hinder = hamper
Entrepreneurs contest that the rule hinders their investment activity, exposing them to hostile takeover bids by foreign hedge funds.

sophisticated = experienced = urbane = suave
To make Korea a more attractive investment destination, Korea would need sophisticated strategies by setting target industries, he added.

mislead = deceive = delude

In the past, the Japanese government has often deflected criticism from the Korean people and government against misleading textbooks, claiming private publications were beyond government control.

outstanding = conspicuous = prominent

The military division recognizes individuals for outstanding professionalism and for bringing honor to the Canadian Forces and to Canada.

commensurate = proportionate

Your co-worker's technique makes me wonder if her acknowledgement is given on a sliding scale, commensurate with the tip.

gimmick = trick

It is all a huge marketing gimmick.

account for = explain

Deposit these rolls straight into your savings account for a little boost every couple months that can really add up.

proclaim = declare

Though an intelligent person could declare this as unreasonable, men who proclaim racial superiority are generally without reason.

solidarity = support by one person or group of people for another because they share feelings, opinions, aims, etc.

As they endure ever-increasing hardship and oppression, we must continue to reaffirm our solidarity with them until they gain their liberation and dignity.

tactic = ploy = manoeuvre

Appeared to misjudge his tactics, with Arsenal reduced to a defensive shambles once they went ahead, and Adebayor unusually subdued.

continuum = cline

In proving the simple theory of everything we are likely to unearth one of the gravitational particles that anchors us into the space/time continuum.

reflect = show

Tensions clearly exist at Northern Ireland Policing Board and Community Safety Unit level; these tensions are reflected down to both partnerships.

pragmatic = practical

The most pragmatic solution is simply to stop recording previously undiscovered BOATs that have not been claimed before the deadline.

divulge = reveal

You can never be forced to divulge anything a client tells you.

12 DAY

tangible = palpable = perceptible

The Government therefore looks forward to seeing tangible proof of stakeholder input and strengthening the evidencebase of proposals from now on.

superior = surpassing (opp) inferior

The Lords had primacy for centuries because the landed aristocracy were perceived to be superior to the lower social orders.

inertia : a property (= characteristic) of matter (= a substance)

by which it stays still or, if moving, continues moving in a straight line unless it is acted on by a force outside itself

The combination of morally hazardous risk origination during booming economic environments and relative inertia during market downturns has pro-cyclical economic consequences.

sustain = maintain = uphold

Next month, we're going to be training the farmers to grow maize, enabling them to sustain their incomes beyond the barley season

per se = by itself

Through our bilateral programme, we do not support accession per se but we support projects, including environmental ones, which help those states graduate towards accession.

predominant = dominant = frequent

The Committee's predominant concern is pornographic photographs, prints, drawings and other images.

explore = analyze

In both cases, local inspectors are meeting with the providers to discuss the key concerns and explore ways forward.

accretion = increase

In science, accretion is a process in which the size of something gradually increases by steady addition of smaller parts.

interrupt = disturb

The students were encouraged to interrupt their teacher by raising their hands if they failed to understand what she was explaining.

thrive = flourish

A new report by the United Nations says contrary to general assumptions, urban populations are not healthier, more literate or more thriving than rural populations.

refute = rebut = disprove

That board had the power to refute contracts, lay people off, cancel capital projects.

13 DAY

initiate = set in motion

Every male citizen is required to initiate military service within two years of graduation from high school, excluding arrangements are made for a deferment.

consummate = fulfill

Fennell the jeweller is a consummate professional, uncompromising about the integrity of his designs.

prospective = potential

Some companies have developed computer blacklists that help alert landlords and physicians to prospective tenants and patients who have a history of filing lawsuits.

desirable = preferable

If homes near business districts become more desirable because of high gas prices, their prices will go up too.

derive from = evolve from

She was named after an Aunt Willela who had died; however, she chose to believe that her name was derived from her grandparent's names

detrimental = harmful

So for years, scientists have been searching for substitutes to satisfy our craving for things sweet, without the detrimental effects.

inhibit = suppress

We know that the frontal lobes are regions of the brain that are responsible for things like planning, organization, inhibiting inappropriate responses, controlling emotion.

receptor : 수용체

They found that young alcoholics had slightly higher receptor activity than the healthy control group, but older alcoholics had a markedly lower density of receptor sites, as compared to the control group.

membrane : 막

The only thing that remains is the delicate membrane of the egg!

readily = easily

In the event your Pulsar is damaged, all of its parts are readily available through watch retailers and jewelers everywhere.

prolong = extend=protract

Many doctors suggest prolonged exercise at the gym or outside before work, in order to reduce stress and strengthen your heart.

buttress = support = reinforce

The sharp increase in crime seems to buttress the argument for more police officers on the street.

dislodge : to force or knock sth out of its position

The wind dislodged one or two tiles from the roof.

apparent

1) evident = obvious
   Then, for no apparent reason, the train suddenly stopped.
2) seeming = ostensible
   The way the information gets out seems to be that a true
   event horizon never forms, just an apparent horizon.

Unfortunately : 아쉽게도

I appreciate the good quality of these clothes, but unfortunately your prices appear to be on the high side even for clothes of this quality.

profound = intense = significant
Opera uses the profound power of music to communicate feelings and to express emotions.

prevailing = predominant
Malicious exposing of secrets and slander are prevailing as the election draws close.

make much of = treat ~ as important
The opposition would make much of the problematic benefit–cost issue throughout the 1970s.

hoary = very old
According to hoary Freudian psychoanalysis, the unconscious mind is a part of the mind which stores repressed memories.

purview = horizon
Some of the bank's lending operations come under the purview of the deputy manager, and some are handled directly by the manager

readily = easily
In the event your Pulsar is damaged, all of its parts are readily available through watch retailers and jewelers everywhere.

commensurate = proportionate
Your co-worker's technique makes me wonder if her acknowledgement is given on a sliding scale, commensurate with the tip.

emancipate = set free
Reconstruction after the civil war, the votes of newly emancipated black southerners put the Republicans in power throughout the states.

14 DAY

posit = postulate
Hollow Earth theories posit that the planet Earth has a hollow interior and, possibly, a habitable inner surface.

autonomy = independence
His argument is to retain one's moral autonomy; one must always reserve the right to decide for oneself on any moral issue.

dominant = overriding
Specialist cereal holdings are therefore characterized by cereals production being the dominant activity.

strain
Two old friends were happy to meet again after such a long separation; however, the meeting was a strain for both of them.

including = such as
These bacteria are hitchhikers, passed on from mother to daughters because they live within cells, including the egg cell.

pitfall = trap
Career coaches say that making effective use of online resources requires sophisticated strategies and an awareness of potential pitfalls.

appropriate
1) proper
  Now that the problem has been identified, appropriate action can be taken.
2) arrogate = purloin
  He was accused of appropriating club funds.

primordial = primeval
The planet Jupiter contains large amounts of the primordial gas and dust out of which the solar system was formed.

luminosity = brightness
The low mass and luminosity means any changes to the star due to an Earth-mass planet are much more likely to be detected.

substantial = considerable
And over generations, slowly, despite facing substantial discrimination, slowly integrated themselves into the community, and sort of found their peace with the whites there.

rescue = save
The hikers were stranded in the national forest for several days before the rescue team found them.

disaster = catastrophe
All buildings should be firm enough to withstand the bare weight and the overall weight in use, earthquake, wind and other natural disaster forces.

enthusiastic = glowing
She was even less enthusiastic about going to Spain.

eligible = entitled
There is then fine print describing the prizes, how to enter, and how to determine if you are eligible for the prizes.

inevitable = unavoidable
It was an inevitable consequence of the decision.

inappropriate = improper
It would be inappropriate for me to comment.

conform = comply
He refused to conform to the local customs.

implement = carry out
They also work with several schools around the country, to help teachers implement the lesson plans.

inappropriate = improper
It would be inappropriate for me to comment.

conform = comply
He refused to conform to the local customs.

implement = carry out
They also work with several schools around the country, to help teachers implement the lesson plans.

국병철/이병호 GMAT Focus Program

초판발행 2025년3월10일

지은이 국병철, 이병호
발행인 국병철 | 발행처 ㈜에듀켄연구소 | 등록 제2007-07호

주소 경기 고양시 일산서구 강성로 271, 205-18호
전화 010-7109-6847 | 팩스 031-629-6130
홈페이지 www.eduken.kr | 이메일 eduken@daum.net

ISBN 979-11-991657-0-0
©국병철, 저작권자와 맺은 특약에 따라 검인은 생략합니다.
GMAT® is a registered trademarks of the Graduate Management
Admission Test.

이 책은 저작권법에 따라 보호되는 저작물이므로
무단전재와 무단복제를 금지하며, 이 책의 전부 또는 일부를
이용하려면 반드시 저작권자와 (주)에듀켄연구소의
서면동의를 받아야 합니다.

책값은 뒷표지에 있습니다.
잘못 만들어진 책은 바꾸어 드립니다.